THE FANTASY SPORTS BOSS 2015 FANTASY BASEBALL DRAFT GUIDE: EARLY OFFSEASON EDITION

BY MICHAEL E. KENESKI

TABLE OF CONTENTS

Editor's Note

To Our Readers:

Before we delve into the usual fantasy baseball draft guide trimmings such as sleepers, busts, rookie reports, rankings, and player analysis; please allow yours truly to take a moment to thank all of our faithful readers for your unending devotion to everything we do here. After all, without your support, we would not be starting our SECOND decade in the fantasy sports business where our website and annual draft guides continue to separate us from the rest of the industry. When I first started our website all those years ago, 10 daily hits was considered a bunch. Today that number has jumped to the thousands as our website continues to gain followers through our daily news breakers, analysis, and player profiles. Our annual draft guides (fantasy football, fantasy baseball, NFL Draft) are also becoming a staple of the community as well; in particular through our player analysis that goes a full paragraph deep or more while the other publications only supply you with a few sentences. In the end, our only goal is to present our readers with all the tools they need to succeed in their leagues and we are confident this year's draft guide hits the mark on all cylinders. At over 200 pages, we literally left no stone unturned in identifying those players who stand the best chance of helping you; while at the same time placing a lens on those who are prone to going bust for your teams. While some knock the book-like version of the guide due to the lack of pictures and charts, we and the majority of the readers are only concerned about the analysis which is why our publications are annually the largest in the industry. With all that said, the work is really only just beginning as the draft is the first step toward a six-month-plus odyssey that will test all of our patience/dedication at one point or another. As long as you stay the course and continue following our daily recommendations, we are confident good things will happen for you in your league. So as always, allow me to wish you all good luck and we will see each other at the finish line with some league titles under our belt.

Sincerely,

Michael E. Keneski

The Fantasy Sports Boss

2019 FANTASY BASEBALL TEN BURNING QUESTIONS

As sure as the sun coming up in the morning, the arrival of the fantasy baseball draft season brings with it a slew of questions, debates, and hot topics that need to be worked out before the first picks are made. While we could write a whole separate book addressing all of these topics by themselves, in this space the focus shifts mainly to the story-lines that are on the minds of the majority of those in the fantasy baseball community. So as we do every season in this feature, below are 10 questions and their subsequent answers centering on the more pressing subjects that figure to shape upcoming fantasy baseball drafts. So without further delay, let's get right to it.

1. Q: And the number 1 overall pick is?
A: The knee-jerk answer over the last few seasons has deservedly been Los Angeles Angels outfielder Mike Trout but for the second time in three years, his Boston Red Sox counterpart Mookie Betts deserves strong consideration. On the 2018 numbers alone, Betts has a great argument to be the top guy as he bested Trout in four out of the five standard ROTO categories (all but home runs) and he also has been slightly more durable. Trout wins on ultimate consistency though and for that reason, we give him the slight nod yet again. However, we would not argue against anyone bucking the Trout trend with Betts by any means this season as the numbers suggest the latter is fully deserving of being the top name off the 2019 draft board.

2. Q: With Trout and Betts locked-in as top two picks, who makes up the other 10 first-rounders in standard ROTO leagues this spring?
A: Joining Trout and Betts in such a lofty group this spring include the following in our opinion and in no particular order: Jose Ramirez, Francisco Lindor, Nolan Arenado, Jose Altuve, J.D. Martinez. Manny Machado, Alex Bregman, Max Scherzer, Bryce Harper, and Christian Yelich.

3. Q: Is Clayton Kershaw even a worthy of being a top-24 anymore?
A: This is the wrong publication to ask such a question as we have sounded the alarms on Kershaw going back to 2017 and that has only intensified since. The injuries are really becoming a problem here as Kershaw once again spent a lengthy stint on the DL in 2018 and we also now have vastly declining velocity which has made the multiple CY Young winner more hittable than ever. On reputation alone, Kershaw still rates as a top-tier guy

but the ill health and actual recent production suggest this shouldn't be the case any longer.

4. Q: Where does Ronald Acuna Jr. go from here?

A: How about right into the first round for 2020 fantasy baseball drafts? You absolutely get the sense this is where we are heading with the five-tool dynamo as Acuna Jr. became the rare uber-hyped rookie to come through with spectacular numbers on a per game basis once he was finally summoned to the majors by the Atlanta Braves last spring. The .293 average with 26 home runs and 16 stolen bases in just 433 at-bats last season represent the floor for Acuna Jr. in 2019 and a run at 30/20/.300 seem well within reach. Sometimes a guy is just destined to be a star and that is what we are getting out of Acuna Jr. both now and well into the future.

5. Q: Besides Ronald Acuna Jr., who else is set to make a strong push towards possible first-round status moving forward?

A: Overshadowed to a great extent by teammates Mookie Betts and J.D. Martinez, Boston Red Sox outfielder Andrew Benintendi is easy to overlook on a team filled with such high-end nuclear bats. Don't think for a second though that Benintendi is not on the verge of superstardom as he comes off a 2018 campaign which saw him post an 18/21 mark in homers/steals and also bat .290 for the World Series champions. Still just 24, Benintendi is growing into his power and with a superb batting approach that will continue to churn out .300 averages and speed to remain a key stolen base asset, the numbers could become Christian Yelich-like in 2019.

6. Q: Was everyone guilty of collectively overrating Trea Turner last spring?

A: Yes we all fell prey to the allure Turner brought forth last spring but it was very hard not to do so as visions of 60 steals to go with growing power and the anticipation of 100-plus runs fronting a powerful Washington Nationals lineup danced in all of our heads. While Turner still had a terrific year overall, he batted just .271 and his 19 homers in 664 at-bats were not very impressive. Also, while the 43 steals were a very potent number, Turner didn't go near the 60 plateau we all thought was in the cards. The bottom line here is that while Turner is still a potentially monstrous fantasy baseball offensive juggernaut; he should be picked in Round 2 this time around as opposed to being among the initial 12 names going off the draft board this spring.

7. Q: Can Cleveland Indians third baseman Jose Ramirez go 40/40 in 2019?

A: It sure seemed like Ramirez realized he had a shot at the hallowed ratio during the second half of 2018 as he really picked up his running in an effort to catch up his steal totals with the absolutely monstrous power he put forth. While Ramirez fell short of the goal, his 39 homers and 34 steals were tantalizingly close to joining such a lofty club. Now in terms of his chances of getting there in 2019, you always go into such a rare scenario ignoring the possibility with regards to projecting prospective numbers. First of all, the 34 steals were of the outlier variety when it comes to Ramirez' past rates in that category and you also need to consider the notion that opposing pitchers will be much more careful approaching the guy this season which could slightly lessen the home run output as well. So while Ramirez has the skill set to make another run at the mark, the smart money says it won't happen.

8. Q: Since you have Max Scherzer down as the top pitcher for 2019 fantasy baseball, who should go behind him at the position among Chris Sale, Corey Kluber. and Jacob DeGrom and in what order?
A: We have it Sale, DeGrom, Kluber in order of preference and are in particular leery of the latter. While Sale has had some issues with wearing down late in the season the last two years, his raw stuff is right there with Scherzer as the best in all of baseball. DeGrom comes off a truly phenomenal 2019 campaign that rightly netted his first Cy Young award but we have him behind Sale due to the fact the Red Sox ace has a longer track record achieving such superstar production. Finally, we have Kluber last in the bunch due to the fact he has been leaking velocity for four years now and five straight seasons of 200-plus innings is a red flag issue that could result in some declining numbers going forward.

9. Q: What can Blake Snell do for an encore?
A: Boy was that impressive. A freshly minted member of the fantasy baseball ace club, Tampa Bay Rays starter Blake Snell really has no direction to go but down after putting forth a breakout season for the ages in 2018. Recording 21 wins, 1.89 ERA, 0.97 WHIP, and 221 K's in 180.2 innings while operating in the AL East was visually stunning work from Snell and honestly, it would be almost impossible to expect another similar haul of numbers given how high the bar was set. With that said, Snell will absolutely be in line for more ace-like numbers in 2019 and so he should be grouped right in with the other top arms for the upcoming fantasy baseball season. So while a .241 BABIP was well into the lucky range, Snell's excellent control, potent strikeout ability, and skill in keeping the ball in the park could have him in range of another Cy Young run.

10. Q: Continue panning for late-round gold at catcher?

A: It was ugly yet again among the catching fraternity in 2018 fantasy baseball as top dogs Buster Posey and Gary Sanchez both horrific seasons, while affordable spring options Yan Gomes, Wilson Ramos, Yadier Molina, and Jorge Alfaro all had nice years. We sound like a broken clock in our firm belief that drafting catchers with an early round pick is a colossal mistake and that holds true yet again for 2019 given how sketchy some of the top names now appear. The volatility is off-the-charts here given the high incidence of injury and the tendency for offensive numbers to swing wildly from one season to the next. Instead, look for value in the middle-to-late rounds which is where some true gems can be found. Such 2019 options that may fit this latter profile include the Los Angeles Dodgers' Austin Barnes. the Baltimore Orioles' Chance Sisco and the Colorado Rockies' Tom Murphy.

2019 FANTASY BASEBALL ROOKIE REPORT

Unlike in fantasy football where rookie quarterbacks, running backs, wide receivers, and tight ends instantly become major overnight persons of interest, the rookies that arrive each season in fantasy baseball have a much more wide-range of outcomes and volatility. While the rookies in fantasy football start contributing right from the start in Week 1, often it takes months for the top first-year MLB hitters and pitchers to make their way to their respective major league clubs. Be that as it may, this trend still doesn't prevent many draft participants from reaching a bit higher than they should to secure those on the verge of making the "Big Show" and often this increases the likelihood of those players going bust. With that said, the talents of those who make up the list below are too obvious to ignore and fantasy baseball community should get as familiar as they can with their potential impacts and ETA's (Expected Time of Arrival).

Vladimir Guerrero Jr.: Wow is this kid a sick talent. Already possessing genes from one of the greatest hitters the game has ever seen in Hall of Famer Vladimir Guerrero, junior looked just like his father as the Toronto Blue Jays third base prospect put up true video game numbers in the minors last season. First, there was the ridiculous .402 average, 14 home runs, and 60 RBI at Double-A and then just as insane respective slashes of .336/6 HR/16 RBI) once moved to Triple-A to complete the year. It is truly amazing to see someone at 19 put up K/9 rates under 11.0 like Guerrero Jr. did at Double and Triple-A last season and it just speaks to the off-the-charts ability the kid has with a bat in his hands. About the only knock you can place on Guerrero Jr. is the fact he doesn't steal bases but my goodness this is going to be fun to watch when the Blue Jays finally make the call early in the 2019 season.
ETA: May 2019

Fernando Tatis Jr.: Things didn't go according to plan for arguably the top hitting prospect in all of baseball in 2018 as San Diego Padres third base property Fernando Tatis Jr. failed to log a single at-bat in the majors before having his season end in mid-July due to the need for surgery to repair a fractured left thumb. Prior to the injury, Tatis Jr. looked like a future first-round fantasy baseball monster as he smacked 16 home runs, stole 16 bases, and batted .286 in 394 at-bats at the age of only 19 and so he clearly has nothing left to prove in the minor leagues. So other than maybe waiting out the first two weeks or so for his arbitration clock to scale back another year at the start of the season, there is no reason the Blue Jays shouldn't unleash Tatis Jr. to the majors before calendar flips to May.
ETA: April 2019

Forrest Whitley: A PED bust that netted a 50-game suspension last February likely cost Houston Astros top pitching prospect Forrest Whitley a chance at a possible mid-season promotion but the 2015 first-round pick seems ready to finally make such an ascension on the strength of some of the most eye-popping strikeout ability we have seen come up the minor league ladder. Think Tim Lincecum or Stephen Strasburg in terms of Whitley's ability to collect K's by the bunches and this alone makes him the pitching version of Fernando Tatis Jr. While it is currently unknown what the Astros have planned in terms of a promotion timeline, the free agency status of Dallas Keuchel and the retirement rumors of Charlie Morton will likely add clarity there.
ETA: May 2019

Eloy Jimenez: It was the crime of the fantasy baseball century that the rebuilding Chicago White Sox failed to give top hitting farmhand Eloy Jimenez even a cup of coffee look with the big club last season but this still doesn't change the fact the kid is right there with Vladimir Guerrero Jr. in heading any prospect list entering into 2019. The righthanded slugger took no prisoners last season as Jimenez swatted a collective 22 home runs, drove in 75 batters, and hit well over .300 both at Double-A (.317) and Triple-A (.355) which made the White Sox' decision not to call him up during the summer that much more ridiculous. Having turned just 22 this past November, Jimenez should take the Kris Bryant route to the majors next April (i.e. waiting about two weeks in the minors for service time reasons) and then quickly get acclimated to destroying top-level pitching. 30 home runs out of the gate are certainly not out of the question here and that could go along with a .300 average as well.
ETA: April 2019

Kyle Tucker: Already swelling with top-end prospects that have made the jump to the majors with tremendous success, the Houston Astros will welcome in future star third baseman Kyle Tucker to hold down the hot corner for 2019. Still, just 22 when the new season gets underway, Tucker actually got a 28-game trial look with the team a year ago but the kid was clearly not yet ready (.141, zero home runs in 72 at-bats). Don't let that cup of coffee stint fool you though as Tucker profiles as a future superstar five-category monster who hit 24 homers, stole 24 bases, and batted a scorching .332 at Triple-A last season. Already possessing impressive strikeout and walk rates to go with the power/speed game, Tucker is going to be something special.
ETA: May 2019

Victor Robles: While he was passed by 19-year-old wunderkind Juan Soto as the top hitting prospect in the team's system early in 2018, Washington Nationals outfield property Victor Robles still retains well above-average ability with the bat to keep him in the conversation for an early promotion this season. Injuries opened the door for Soto to jump ahead of Robles in the Nats' prospect pecking order and we all know how the former went nuts as a rookie almost from the minute of his promotion. Be that as it may, Robles acquitted himself nicely in his 21 late-season games with the team last summer (.288, 3 homers, 3 steals in 66 at-bats) and with terrific BB/9 and K/9 rates throughout his minor league career, the upside is massive. We are talking about power that is not too far below Soto's standard and with much better speed; Robles can have his own tremendous 2019 breakout if the promotion comes early enough.
ETA: May 2019

Peter Alonso: Another top hitting prospect who should have gotten a call to the majors sometime last summer but didn't was undoubtedly New York Mets slugging first baseman Peter Alonso. The team's 2016 second-round pick put on a power-hitting show all throughout last season as a 15-homer/.314 start at Double-A earned Alonso a promotion to Triple-A where he slugged another 21 bombs with a .260 average. While there are some genuine concerns about Alonso's defense and strikeout-prone ways (25.9 K/9 at Triple-A last season) putting a hurt on his average, the power is immense and will likely be the kid's calling card for a while before the rest of his hitting approach develops. The Mets also have a history of proceeding cautiously with their prospects and so with Jay Bruce expected to be the team's everyday first baseman in 2019, a promotion may not happen until the summer which lessens the need to target Alonso heavily during the draft. At the very least though, Alonso needs to be on everybody's "watch" lists this spring.
ETA: June 2019

Willie Calhoun: Having not accrued enough at-bats in 2018, Texas Rangers top outfield prospect Willie Calhoun retains rookie status for the upcoming season. Last spring at this time Calhoun was widely considered an overall top-five hitting prospect and a solid spring training performance only added to the hype. Unfortunately, the Rangers sent Calhoun back to the minors to begin the year and unbelievably gave the slugger just a 35-game look during the summer which came out to 2 home runs, 11 RBI, and a .222 average in 108 at-bats. Since it was such a small sample size, don't think for a second that Calhoun doesn't remain one of the very best prospects for 2019 and this time he should break camp with a starting spot. Capable of hitting .300 in his sleep with potential 25-home run power right out of the gate, Calhoun's slightly diminished price tag this spring makes him even a better buy.

ETA: April 2019

Bo Bichette: Already having the pedigree down pat as the son of former Colorado Rockies All-Star slugger Dante, Toronto Blue Jays shortstop prospect Bo Bichette looks like one of the next prime five-category fantasy baseball commodities as he comes off a 2018 campaign at Double-A that included 11 home runs, 32 steals, and a .323 average. Turning only 21 in March, Bichette gets a bit overshadowed by consensus number 1 overall prospect Vladimir Guerrero Jr. being in the same system but in no way should this diminish the high-level talent we are talking about here. With uncanny contact ability (14.3 K/9) for such a young hitter, you can be sure Bichette will be a batting average asset to go along with moderate power and top-end stolen base skills.

ETA: June 2019

Brent Honeywell: Just when the excitement surrounding top Tampa Bay Rays pitching prospect Brent Honeywell began to reach a new height for the fantasy baseball community at the start of 2018 spring training, an early bout of elbow trouble predictably resulted in Tommy John surgery being performed on the talented righty. With the surgery having wiped out his entire season, Honeywell gets a complete re-set for 2019 as he will be almost a full year removed from the procedure when spring training gets underway. While the Rays will tread very carefully with Honeywell in likely having him begin the season in the minors, the high-end skills are obvious here and we all know the Rays churn out power pitching prospects like no one else in baseball. What really stands out about Honeywell is the fact that not only does he get the fastball into the upper 90's which elicit a ton of strikeouts (K/9 of 11.06 in Triple-A in 2017) but the kid also has uncanny control for a young power pitcher. Since the hype will undoubtedly be faded on Honeywell this spring coming off the surgery, he makes for an excellent pitching stash for a possible summer promotion.

ETA: August 2019

Brendan Rodgers: With former All-Star stud shortstop Troy Tulowitzki having left town years ago, now is the time for the Colorado Rockies to unleash power/speed prospect Brendan Rodgers at some point in 2019. 17 home, 12 steals, and a .275 average highlighted the Rodgers offensive haul last season at Triple-A and so there is not much more for the 22-year-old lefty to prove at the minor league level.

ETA: July 2018

Nick Senzel: If it weren't for suffering a torn finger tendon that required season-ending surgery last June, it is very likely that top Cincinnati Reds third base prospect Nick Senzel would have been promoted to the big league club sometime last summer. Be that as it may, the surgery doesn't change the fact one bit that Senzel remains a supreme talent who possesses true five-tool ability. Comparisons to Kris Bryant seem reasonable as Senzel has hit for power and above .300 at every minor league level so far and he even has added some stolen bases as well to further reinforce the tremendous skills at play here. With the Reds already in the midst of a massive rebuild, Senzel should be up by May 1 at the latest.

Austin Riley: It was a rapid development season for Atlanta Braves third base prospect Austin Riley as he spent time at Single, Double, and Triple-A where he hit a combined 19 home runs and went over a .300 average in two of those stops. Unlike some of the other prime hitting prospects on this list, Riley is no guarantee to make it up to the Braves this season as there are some strikeout issues which need some work.
ETA: May 2020

Jesus Luzardo: The strikeouts are already immense for Oakland A's power pitching prospect Jesus Luzardo and it is that skill which will get the kid on the fast track to the majors. Another rapidly rising prospect that made stops at Single, Double, and Triple-A in 2018, Luzardo's 2.06 BB/9 in 78.2 during the middle stop on that journey shows nice control to go with all the K's. With the A's looking to stay in playoff contention by supplementing all their team power with affordable pitching, Luzardo may get the call sooner than one may think.
ETA: June 2019

Justus Sheffield: Promoted to the New York Yankees at the end of the 2018 season with the aim to help in the team's bullpen for the playoffs, lefty starter Justis Sheffield has a very realistic shot to be a member of the rotation this season at some point. While the Yanks will likely have Sheffield begin 2019 in the minors in order to preserve another year of team control, the kid is more than ready to make the jump as he logged ERA of 2.25 (Double-A) and 2.56 (Triple-A) while keeping the ball in the park. Despite Sheffield's strikeout having run hot-and-cold while coming up the minor league ladder and the control still being a work in progress, the overall upside is vast.
ETA: June 2019

Logan Allen: ERA's of 2.75 (Double-A) and 1.63 (Triple-A) bore out the high skill level of San Diego Padres lefty pitching prospect Logan Allen and a summer promotion are certainly looking within reach. A stark groundball pitcher who doesn't give up home runs, Allen's deceptive pitch movement elicits a solid number of swings-and-misses despite the kid not being a pure power arm.

ETA: September 2019

2019 FANTASY BASEBALL DRAFT ALL-VALUE TEAM

While many in the fantasy baseball community become obsessed with getting their hands on the top rookie hitters and pitchers that arrive into the "Show" each season, a subset group exists that can potentially provide even more value/upside but for a much cheaper draft cost. It is this collection of players that make up our annual "All-Value Team" and it is here that some major value plays can be mined if you know where to look. Whether it is the veteran player who provides solid numbers year after year without anyone paying much attention or whether it is a guy whose previous prospect star has dimmed a bit but who still carries the skills that made him such a hot commodity in the first place our All-Value Team is a roster of players who could really pay off handsomely this season if all breaks right. The best part in all of this is that the draft cost is not prohibitive with any of the names listed below and so the risk is so much lower than it would be when chasing rookies that everyone wants. As a result, do yourself a favor and place these names in bold on your cheat sheets and get set for some major bragging rights if things turn out nicely here like we expect them to.

Catchers: Francisco Mejia, Wilson Ramos, Yan Gomes

First Baseman: Ian Desmond, Matt Olson, Ryon Healy

Second Baseman: Rougned Odor, Scooter Gennett, Jeff McNeil, Jonathan Villar

Shortstops: Jose Peraza, Jurickson Profar, Tim Anderson, Orlando Arcia

Third Baseman: Nick Castellanos, Travis Shaw, Matt Chapman, Mike Moustakas

Outfields: Eddie Rosario, Adam Eaton, David Dahl, Ian Happ, Austin Meadows, Odubel Herrera, Yasiel Puig, Michael Brantley, Ender Inciarte, Mallex Smith, Stephen Piscotty

Starting Pitchers: German Marquez, Jose Berrios, Mike Clevinger, Jameson Taillon, Jack Flaherty, Eduardo Rodriguez, Joey Lucchessi, Mike Soroka, Freddy Peralta, Tyler Glasnow, Caleb Smith

Closers: Jose Alvarado, Taylor Rogers, Jose LeClerc, Seranthony Dominguez, Will Smith, Archie Bradley, Yoshihisa Hirano, Jordan Hicks

★ Lorenzo Cain OF MIL

Ryon Healy 1B SEA

~~Ian Desmond 1B/OF COL~~

Jake Bauers 1B CLE

Jon Villa 2B/OF BAL

★ Miguel Andujar 3B NYY

★ David Dahl OF COL

$2 Brinson

~~NO BUXTON~~

$2 Franmil Reyes OF SD

$2 Franchi Cordero OF SD

★ Enrique Hernandez

Blake Treinen

Pedro Strop

$2 Travis Jankowski

$1 Williams Astodilla CA

2019 FANTASY BASEBALL DRAFT BUSTS

Let's take a trip to the dark side, shall we? The dark side being the fantasy baseball draft bust which is a topic that will make all of us cringe. No matter how much you prepare in spending endless hours poring over scouting reports, avoiding annual fantasy baseball draft busts is almost an impossible endeavor. Whether it was serious injury taking a player out for a large chunk or even all of the season or whether it was simply due to unexpectedly poor performance, the fantasy baseball draft bust is the scourge of all of our existence when it comes to selecting players each spring. While we always state in this space each season that we can't ever predict with 100 percent certainty who will ultimately let us down, what we can feel confident in is identifying those who carry some red flags/risk indicators that hint at the trouble that could be on the way. It is under this premise that we present to you our "2018 Fantasy Baseball Draft Busts" and so as a result, all of these pitchers and hitters listed below should be treated with extra caution when weighing a possible investment this spring.

Buster Posey: Appearing on this section in these pages exactly a year ago, nothing has changed for the better with regards to the offensive outlook on San Francisco Giants catcher Buster Posey. We said last spring that Posey was going right down the Joe Mauer path in terms of losing his power and ability to stay healthy as he moved closer to 30 and 2018 bore this out as the former All-Star batted .284 with just 5 home runs while battling injuries. Turning 32 in April, Posey is barely holding onto mixed league value at catcher which is quite telling given the utter lack of depth here. Making matters worse, Posey no longer carries first base eligibility in the majority of leagues anymore either.

Jorge Alfaro: While many will look at the 10 home runs and solid .262 average in 377 at-bats a year ago from Philadelphia Phillies 25-year-old backstop Jorge Alfaro and think he is only getting started on an offensive upward trajectory, the reality is that the advanced metrics suggest something else entirely. An insane 36.6 K/9 and beyond lucky .406 BABIP last season showed that Alfaro will be lucky to even bat .230 this season since that type of ridiculous luck will not be repeated. Throw in the minuscule 4.8 BB/9 and Alfaro is more likely to get benched given the expected troubled ahead instead of even repeating 2018's haul.

Francisco Cervelli: In a very quiet manner, Pittsburgh Pirates catcher Francisco Cervelli has done a nice job with the bat the last few seasons and he comes off a 2018 where he smacked 12 homers. With that said, Cervelli is turning 33 in March and he is getting pushed heavily by backup Elias

Diaz. Cervelli has also had a pronounced injury problem throughout his career and so the chances of him posting another season worthy of fantasy baseball consideration seem unlikely.

Edwin Encarnacion: On the surface, it certainly looked like Cleveland Indians first baseman Edwin Encarnacion is still at the top of his game as he comes off a 2018 campaign where he hit 32 home runs and drove in 107. Underneath the surface revealed red flags though as Encarnacion's 22.8 K/9 was a career-worst and turning 36 in March, it shows that the holes in the veteran's swing are growing. With Encarnacion's speed declining as well (just 74 runs scored), he is holding just two categories of above-average numbers heading into 2019.

Max Muncy: There is no debating the fact that Los Angeles Dodgers first baseman Max Muncy was a major revelation in 2018 as he came out of the blue to smack 35 homers and drive in 79 batters in just 481 at-bats. Muncy likely caught opposing pitchers off guard early on in the season though since most didn't have much background information on how to attack his swing weaknesses but soon things would even out in the second half. The trends were clear on that front as Muncy's .271/22-homer first half descended into .255/13 in the second and when you add in the ugly overall 27.2 K/9, there is a chance this could be a one-season wonder scenario.

Luke Voit: It is likely many winning fantasy baseball teams last season were put over the top by the addition of New York Yankees first base slugger Luke Voit during the final two months of the year when he seemed to homer every other game and put forth a composite .322 average with 15 bombs in only 161 at-bats. Crazy numbers for sure but we have seen this story before on the Yankees when Shane Spencer achieved such a magical run during back to the 90's and then the very next season was exposed to the point he soon fell into journeyman status. While Voit may prove to be different, the fact the St. Louis Cardinals virtually gave him away to the Yankees last summer is telling and you can also count on opposing pitchers having a better plan of action going against him this time around as well. Given the hype that always attaches itself to big-city sluggers like Voit, it is imperative you tread carefully here.

Jed Lowrie: Sometimes you can see problems a mile away and that is the feeling you get when looking at veteran infielder Jed Lowrie and his 2019 outlook. Turning 35 in April and already with a very long history of injuries, there is almost no way you can count on a full season of production from Lowrie. In addition, the 23 home runs and 99 RBI he accumulated last season belong in the outlier bin as Lowrie has never approached such numbers before.

Adalberto Mondesi: All right here us out on this. First off, there is no arguing how absolutely terrific Mondesi was the last two month of the 2018 season as he absolutely ran wild on the bases, hit home runs at a very high rate, and finally put forth a useful batting average after some major trouble in the latter area previously. With all that said, the hype train is completely out of control here as Mondesi's per game rates during his 75-game stint with the Kansas City Royals last season were completely unsustainable and with remaining ugly advanced rates in walks (3.8 BB/9) and strikeouts (26.5 K/9), this is still a kid who presents some major batting average risk. Since everyone will be out to get Mondesi this spring, the draft cost is going to go beyond where it should be. Under such a scenario, the end results don't usually come out on the positive side.

Justin Turner: Despite this publication always having a soft spot for Los Angeles Dodgers third baseman Justin Turner, even we can't overlook the unending injuries that continue to derail the veteran on a yearly basis. While all the offensive rates and production remain very good, the fact Turner will be 34 when the 2019 season gets underway will only exacerbate the injury issue.

David Peralta: The outlier police are circling around Arizona Diamondbacks outfielder David Peralta after a 31-home run 2018 campaign that was head-and-shoulders above a previous high of 17. Such giant statistical jumps are always a bit suspicious and so it is important to grade Peralta as more of a 20-homer guy than anywhere near what his 2018 numbers would suggest.

Carlos Gonzalez: Heading into free agency this winter at the age of 33, it is expected that veteran outfielder Carlos Gonzalez will be finding a new home as the Colorado Rockies are ready to move on. By now it is common knowledge that Gonzalez has put forth drastic swings in production throughout his career in gaining a Coors Field-fueled edge (.323/142 HR/497 RBI at home and .251/89 HR/278 RBI on the road) and since he will likely be with a new team for 2019, the numbers may look quite ordinary in moving away from the thin air of his old digs. With the speed having also left the station years ago and Gonzalez never serving as a bastion of health, there are way too many red flags to ignore here.

Clayton Kershaw: For the second season in a row Los Angeles Dodgers ace Clayton Kershaw appears in this section and it is well-deserved. It is absolutely startling how scary Kershaw looks under his surface 2.73 ERA from last season and we can start with the vastly declining health which included missing almost two months with additional back trouble that first flared a number of years ago. Then you have the sizable drop in velocity we have seen from Kershaw as the multiple-Cy Young winner has gone from an average fastball of 94.3 in 2015 all the way down to just 91.4 last season. This decline has directly caused Kershaw's home run rate to spike and any further velocity dip will make the former issue more pronounced. With the name brand remaining very high, Kershaw is simply not worth the pricey draft cost given his current condition.

Corey Kluber: Hear us out 2.0. It was certainly another dominant season from Cleveland Indians ace Corey Kluber in 2018 as the hard-throwing veteran posted a 2.89 ERA and punched out 222 batters in 215 innings and that performance put in the conversation for yet another Cy Young Award. With that said, the advanced metrics are starting to suggest decline is already setting in as Kluber gets set to turn 33 in April. Most concerning is Kluber's average fastball velocity of 92.4 which was the FOURTH straight season of decline there. Obviously, it stands to reason that a leaking fastball will be much more hittable and at this rate, Kluber may be slipping towards the 90 range in 2019. Then when you also consider the insane workloads Kluber has undertaken since 2014 (200-plus innings in each campaign), the threat of further erosion and injury increases. Since the draft price remains exceptionally high, it may be a good idea to look for a younger ace to anchor your staff this season.

Kyle Freeland: Never pay for a career year and so on that aspect alone Colorado Rockies pitcher Kyle Freeland should be treated carefully this spring in drafts. Surface numbers of 17 wins and a 2.85 ERA were no doubt tremendous numbers for anyone who picked up Freeland off waivers early in 2018 but the advanced indicators suggest there was a lot of luck involved here. For starters, a lucky .285 BABIP helped knock the ERA below where it should have gone (3.67 FIP, 4.22 XFIP) and a mediocre 7.70 K/9 will not be able to help overcome when the batted ball luck fixes itself this season as anticipated. Given the annual offensive fireworks that emanate from Coors Field, Freeland looks like a major "avoid" candidate this spring.

Trevor Williams: A 3.11 ERA, 1.18 WHIP, and 14 wins were a tremendous haul of statistics supplied from Pittsburgh Pirates starter Trevor Williams last season but the guy doesn't pass the smell test when factoring in all the numbers. For a guy who already doesn't throw hard, Williams needed a lucky .261 BABIP to help him achieve the 3.11 ERA. When you add in the brutal 6.64 K/9, Williams should see his ERA rise by a decent margin if the BABIP luck moves back towards or above the mean as we think it will.

Craig Kimbrel: While a free agent as of this writing, perennial All-Star closer Craig Kimbrel comes off a shaky 2018 that perhaps indicates some major trouble ahead. Not only did Kimbrel struggle throughout the postseason for the Boston Red Sox but his advanced metrics were also downright scary. A 4.48 BB/9 is virtually unheard of for a closer and Kimbrel also gave up home runs at a career-worst 1.01 HR/9 rate last season. So while the surface 2.74 ERA, 0.99 WHIP, and 13.86 K/9 were all tremendous, Kimbrel very well could continue to slip another level in 2019 for whatever team he ends up with this winter.

Arodys Vizcaino: Ongoing shoulder trouble dogged Atlanta Braves closer Arodys Vizcaino throughout most of the 2018 season and while his numbers were good when on the mound (2.11 ERA, 1.17 WHIP. .213 BAA), he may have opened the door for setup man A.J. Minter to claim the closing role for the upcoming season. It is a clear trend that shoulder trouble tends to continually pop back up on a consistent basis and so on the health front alone, Vizcaino's 2019 status looks very shaky.

Wily Peralta: Anyone who thinks failed starter Wily Peralta has staying power as a closer for the Kansas City Royals is fooling themselves. While Peralta did a decent job during the second half of the 2018 season after moving into the role (14-for-14 in save chances, 3.67 ERA overall), ugly FIP (4.73) and XFIP (4.66) marks reflect how much luck the veteran received with his .279 BABIP. Add in a 6.03 BB/9 that is truly horrendous and it becomes clear Peralta is on borrowed closing time in 2019.

2019 FANTASY BASEBALL POSITION ELIGIBILITY

When it comes to the exercise that is the annual fantasy baseball draft, being aware of position eligibility among the player pool is an extremely important batch of information you need to be completely aware of. Stating the obvious, the more positions that a hitter qualifies at, the more overall value his annual fantasy baseball stock takes on. So with that said, below is our annual list of key players who have eligibility at more than one position and we divided this group into one that the typical 20 games threshold. Adjust your rankings accordingly.

Brian Anderson: 3B, OF
Javier Baez: 2B, SS, 3B
Tim Beckham: SS, 3B
Cody Bellinger: 1B, OF
Alex Bregman: SS, 3B
Jay Bruce: 1B, OF
Kris Bryant: 3B, OF
Matt Carpenter: 1B, 3B
Charlie Culberson: SS, 3B, OF
Ian Desmond: 1B, OF
Aledmys Diaz: SS, 3B
Wilmer Difo: 2B, SS
Adam Frazier: 2B, OF
Joey Gallo: 1B, OF
Marwin Gonzalez: 1B, 2B, SS, OF
Brock Holt: 2B, SS
Trey Mancini: 1B, OF
Ketel Marte: 2B, SS
Russell Martin: C, 3B
Jose Martinez: 1B, OF
Whit Merrifield: 2B, OF
Wil Myers: 3B, OF
Eduardo Nunez: 2B, 3B
Hernan Perez: 2B, SS, 3B, OF
Chad Pinder: 2B, OF
Jose Pirela: 2B, OF
Jurickson Profar: 1B, SS, OF
Daniel Robertson: 2B, SS
Miguel Rojas: 1B, SS, 3B
Pablo Sandoval: 1B, 3B

Travis Shaw: 1B, 2B, 3B
Yangervis Solarte: 2B, 3B
Cory Spangenberg: 2B, 3B
Blake Swihart: C, OF
Chris Taylor: SS, OF
Gleyber Torres: 2B, SS
Eric Thames: 1B, OF
Joey Wendle: 2B, 3B
Ben Zobrist: 2B, OF

2019 FANTASY BASEBALL TOMMY JOHN REPORT

When it comes to the annual exercise of projecting/analyzing pitchers for spring fantasy baseball drafts, studying K/9 rates, walk totals, and chances for victories typically get most of the attention with regards to deciding which guys to target. As we do every year in this space though, identifying the pitchers who possess the classic traits of those who often succumb to Tommy John surgery also needs to be front and center in your analysis. Having reached epidemic proportions over the last decade as pitchers throw harder and more often than ever before while coming up the developmental ladder, the two biggest characteristics of such a surgical victim include the following:

-1.) the pitcher in question is younger than the age of 28

-2.) the pitcher throws an average fastball 94 mph or higher.

With a pitcher's arm/elbow/shoulder not considered fully developed until generally reaching the age of 28, the previous year's almost always contain the majority of Tommy John cases. Add in the crazy velocity we are seeing out of today's pitchers and UCL's are snapping at a rate never seen before. Just to further drive home the point, here are those major league pitchers who underwent Tommy John last season and their average velocity and age:

Jharel Cotton: age 26, 93.6

Johnny Cueto: 32, 90.5

Jose De Leon: 26, 91.8

Brent Honeywell: 23, 95.5

Ben Heller: 27, 94.8

Dinelson Lamet: 26, 95.2

Keynan Middleton: 25, 96.7

Rafael Montero: 28, 94.3

Jordan Montgomery: 25, 91.1

Shohei Ohtani: 24, 94.4

David Phelps: 32, 94.8

Now in looking at the list above, 8 of 11 pitchers were under the age of 27 and 7 of the 11 had an average fastball over 94.0. So using these same metrics, let's see which young and hard-throwing hurlers you should be a bit more leery of this season (those who qualify for both are in bold).

Blake Snell: 25, 96.5

Noah Syndergaard: 26, 98.1

Luis Severino: 24, 97.9

Jose LeClerc: 24, 95.7

Aaron Nola: 25, 93.3

Trevor Bauer: 27, 95.0

Roberto Osuna: 23, 95.7

Walker Buehler: 24, 96.7

Felipe Vazquez: 27, 98.5

Corey Knebel: 26, 97.4

Jose Alvarado: 23, 97.9

Seranthony Dominguez: 23, 98.4

German Marquez: 23, 95.7

Mike Foltynewicz: 27, 96.8

Jose Berrios: 24, 93.8

Edwin Diaz: 24, 97.9

Sean Newcomb: 25, 93.5

Robbie Ray: 27, 94.1

Jack Flaherty: 23, 93.8

Luis Castillo: 25, 96.4

Joey Lucchesi: 25, 91.1

Carlos Martinez: 27, 95.6

Shane Bieber: 23, 93.4

Freddy Peralta: 22, 91.4

So as you can see, some prime fantasy baseball ace-level starters (Severino, Thor, Snell, Bauer, Buehler) qualify for BOTH in having an average fastball of 94 or higher and also being under the age of 28. Severino and Syndergaard in particular serve as major investment risks since their average fastball velocities come in OVER 97.0 which is some extreme pressure being placed on their elbows. Then you have a closer fraternity chock full of red flag pitchers such as Edwin Diaz, Roberto Osuna, Jose LeClerc, Seranthony Dominguez, Corey Knebel, and Jose Alvarado who all hit both marks as well to put them into scary territory for the 2019 season. So while we won't say to avoid all of these guys outright, there is almost no doubt that some will become the latest Tommy John statistic this season. The trends are just too stark to ignore and so going into your draft digesting all of this information can only serve to help you tip-toe around these potential landmines.

2019 FANTASY BASEBALL POSITION RANKINGS AND ANALYSIS

******* (PLAYERS WITH ADDITIONAL ELIGIBILITY ARE NOTED NEXT TO THEIR NAMES.)**********

CATCHERS

Draft Strategy: A year ago at this time, we went against our tried-and-true method of never drafting a catcher in the early rounds by making an exception for New York Yankees backstop Gary Sanchez as the slugger came off two monster seasons with the bat at the offensively-starved position. Maybe we should have stuck to our original guns as Sanchez flopped horribly as his bat hovered under or around the .200 mark all year and injuries were a constant problem. As a result, we are now 100 percent returning to our mantra to look for value at catcher in the middle-to-late rounds and 2018 brought such productive options through this strategy in the form of Kurt Suzuki, Francisco Mejia, Wilson Ramos, and Wellington Castillo.

*****Evan Gattis no longer carries catching eligibility to begin the 2019 season. ****

J.T. Realmuto: Meet the new number 1 catcher for 2019 fantasy baseball! With previous top options Gary Sanchez of the New York Yankees and Buster Posey of the San Francisco Giants both coming off a bad year to differing degrees in 2018, it was the Miami Marlins' J.T. Realmuto who set the bar offensively at the position last season by reaching career-highs in home runs (21), RBI (74), and runs (74); while also batting a solid .277 in the magical age-27 campaign. While Realmuto had to deal with a severe lack of support in the Miami lineup, he continues to reach new offensive levels every season which is the path you want your prospective fantasy baseball players to be traversing. The fact Realmuto can combine a good batting average with 20-home runs power makes him extremely valuable due to the utter lack of offensive contributors at the position but of course, the debate about using an early-round pick on a catcher is one of the more pronounced discussions each spring. By now you all know that our stance is firm in suggesting not to use an early round pick on a catcher and we only have to see the hurt that Posey and Sanchez put on their fantasy baseball owners the year prior as evidence of the risks in making such a move. With that said, Realmuto is the guy you take if you do choose to go that route and since he is just getting into his prime, there should be nice offensive stability here despite the high risk of injury when manning the tools of ignorance. About the only other quibble we have outside of the injury factor is that Realmuto's days of running already appear to be over as he swiped just 3 bags in 531 at-bats last season. After swiping 12 bases in 2016, Realmuto has sharply declined in that area in taking just 8 the following season and last year's 3. Considering how unmatched the rest of Realmuto's numbers are at the position compared to the rest of the catchers, this is not a major deal by any means in terms of the guy's 2019 value.

2019 PROJECTION: .279 19 HR 75 RBI 77 R 4 SB

Salvador Perez: Always lauded for his extreme durability and above-average offensive numbers at a thin position, it was a bit of a tough go for the Kansas City Royals' Salvador Perez in 2018. As a bit of a back-story here, we have spoken for a number of years now how Perez' massive workloads behind the plate would at some point result in sliding offensive numbers and maybe some injuries as well. We got a bit of both in 2018 as Perez' .235 average was a career-worst by a sizable margin and his K/9 has now been above 19.0 each of the last three years after habitually being in the mid-teen range previously. Despite those negatives (not to mention a ridiculously poor 3.1 BB/9 rate), Perez cracked 27 home runs for the second season in a row and it is clear he has reached his power prime at the age of 28. So in terms of what we can anticipate moving forward, the power seems here to stay for another few seasons despite Perez being an "older" 28 given all those innings squatting behind the dish. Where the latter is becoming an issue is in the sliding average and so after years of being a .260 hitter, we now could be looking at .245 being the new norm. As long as you accept that development going in, Perez should once again be a solid investment.

2019 PROJECTION: .248 26 HR 78 RBI 54 R 1 SB

Gary Sanchez: Oh my word was that brutal to watch! Serving as perhaps the biggest fantasy baseball bust of the 2018 season, New York Yankees catcher Gary Sanchez was as bad as a player could possibly be in terms of his downright disgusting performance. First, there was the unfathomable .186 batting average which made Sanchez the worst everyday hitter in the game in terms of that category last season. In addition, there were two separate DL stints due to an injured groin that kept Sanchez to just 374 at-bats and in the process putting a major hurt in the counting numbers. Finally, there was the truly horrific performance defensively behind the plate as Sanchez was a passed ball machine. Things have gotten so bad on the latter front that it is possible 2019 will be the last season Sanchez is an everyday catcher as the Yanks feel the pressure to move him to DH full-time given his well-earned reputation for being a defensive liability. In the end, Sanchez royally burned his fantasy baseball owners after going on average

in the second round last spring and his outlook for 2019 is as muddy as can be given the level of futility a year ago. Now in terms of any semblance of a positive, Sanchez' 18 home runs, 53 RBI, and 51 runs were actually very good totals considering he got just the 374 at-bats. Sanchez' power is undeniable and if he gets 500 at-bats this season, you can put 25-30 home runs and around 90 RBI down in ink. It is the batting average that has become the major concern here outside of the injuries but even on that front, there is at least some optimism. A brutally unlucky .197 BABIP did a ton of damage to Sanchez' average to say the least and since he drew a high number of walks (12.3 BB/9); it stands to reason he is headed for a sizable jump in that department for 2019. Keep in mind that Sanchez batted .290 and .278 his first two years in the majors with similar BB/9 and K/9 numbers but his BABIP in both of those campaigns was slightly north of .300. So if you were to take all of those factors into account, Sanchez' 2018 looks quite fluky given all the poor BABIP luck. That actually makes Sanchez a very good bounce-back candidate for 2019 fantasy baseball given the average comeback that is anticipated and on the very stable power. If you can look past all the ugly memories of 2018, you would see a very good buy-low opportunity is at hand with the slugging catcher.
2019 PROJECTION: .267 27 HR 84 RBI 77 R 1 SB

Buster Posey: In one of our more pointed and accurate critiques heading into the 2018 fantasy baseball season, we labeled annually overrated San Francisco Giants catcher Buster Posey as the latest Joe Mauer in terms of the former MVP continually losing almost all of his power and also succumbing to increasing injuries as he continued to move into his 30's. While no one can take away how great a hitter Posey has been in his career, the fact of the matter is the guy has been trending the wrong way statistically since 2014; with the ravages of catching having a lot to do with that. It was during the 2014 season when Posey reached the 20-home run mark for the second time in his career with 22 but since then his totals in that category have slipped from 19 to 14 to 12 and then all the way down to just 5 in 448 at-bats a year ago. That is as clear a trend as you can get and it doesn't even touch on how Posey's health has increasingly gone into the toilet. When it comes to the latter, Posey was forced to undergo hip surgery last September and given the six-month recovery timetable, there is no guarantee he will be ready to go for Opening Day 2019. So like we noted in our original point, Posey is the new Joe Mauer (but still carrying catcher eligibility unlike his former backstop counterpart) with regards to being capable of posting a useful but ultimately empty batting average; while also spending more and more time in the trainer's room. Again, we are not taking away from the fact that Posey can still hit (BB/9 and K/9 rates remain in line with the career trends) but you will be lucky to get more than 8-10 home runs here at this stage of the game and that is only if the guy can stay healthy which is becoming quite the challenge as shown by the hip surgery. Eventually, even the biggest name brand players need to be passed over for good and Posey has reached that point in our opinion.

2019 PROJECTION: .286 9 HR 73 RBI 74 R 1 SB

Yadier Molina: One of these years St. Louis Cardinals catcher Yadier Molina will get old. Or maybe not as the future Hall of Famer showed zero signs of decline in 2018 as he hit 20 home runs, drove in 74, and batted .261 in 503 at-bats. The 20 homers represented only the second time (and first since way back in 2012) that Molina reached that level of power and the 74 RBI were the second straight season he went over 70 which is like 90 at any other position given the dearth of offensive players at catcher. Be that as it may, Molina will turn 37 in July and perhaps the .261 average (his lowest since 2010) is an initial sign that age is slowly starting to do its thing to the veteran's production. In the end, though, Molina's price tag will never be overly expensive given the fantasy baseball communities yearly spring tradition of writing him off due to the advancing age. That means you should be able to snag him at a nice draft cost which we fully sign off on for at least one more season.

2019 PROJECTION: .263 16 HR 73 RBI 57 R 3 SB

Wilson Ramos: If you were to take out the never-ending injury problems that have plagued his very underrated career to this point, free agent catcher Wilson Ramos would universally be looked at as a top option at the position in almost all fantasy baseball leagues each spring. The fact of the matter though is that Ramos' well-documented history of getting hurt has made him nothing more than a mid-round pick each season but if you were to follow our lead like we annually suggest in these pages, you took the plunge here anyways given the vast upside. None other than the forward-thinking Rays made such a choice and were rewarded with a performance out of Ramos that served as the impetus for them to flip him to the Philadelphia Phillies at the July 31 deadline for solid prospect haul. In terms of the numbers, Ramos hit 15 home runs, drove in 70, and batted a collective .306 to finish as one of the best catchers in 2018 fantasy baseball. So while we currently don't know what type of ballpark Ramos will be hitting in this season as of this writing, we can confidently say that the 31-year-old will hit for a very good average for a catcher (above .300 two of the last three seasons) and supply around 15-20 home runs. Yes, the injury risk remains high but Ramos has few peers right now at the position this season.

2019 PROJECTION: .288 17 HR 74 RBI 53 RBI 0 SB

Wilson Contreras: After doing nothing but hit at a very solid rate since coming to the majors as a universally acclaimed prospect, the fantasy baseball hype for Chicago Cubs catcher Wilson Contreras reached a fever pitch as 2018 drafts got underway. This was a somewhat understandable development after Contreras hit 21 home runs and batted .276 for the Cubs the year prior and so projections of 25-30 long balls began to circulate among the experts given the fact the kid had done nothing but hit at every level of his development. Well as we see all too often (and especially among catchers) when the hype gets a bit out of hand, Contreras went the other way as he struggled for large segments of 2018 and saw almost every single offensive category (both surface and advanced) head sharply downward. The end result was just a pitiful 10 home runs, 54 RBI, and a .249 average and also a feeling that it is back to the drawing board when projecting the kid for the upcoming season. Now in terms of the advanced numbers, Contreras almost matched his K/9, BB/9, and BABIP rates from the previous season which means those were not the cause of the struggles. What seemed to be at the root of the problems was Contreras' hard-hit rate plummeted sharply; with both his slugging and isolated slugging rates taking a firm dive. This suggests that while Contreras stayed patient in terms of walks and wasn't hacking away given the stability of the BB/9 and K/9 rates; opposing pitchers were not giving him as much to drive compared to a year ago. More off-speed pitches went Contreras' way instead of the high number of fastballs he saw in 2017 and the weaker contact primarily caused the decline in homers/RBI/average. So while we can take solace in how Contreras' overall approach matched his very good 2017, we have to hope he can adjust back this season with regards to being able to unleash the power on a more consistent basis with the off-speed pitches. Still just 26-years-old and only a year removed from being considered a top catching prospect, Contreras' depressed draft price this spring should be taken advantage of given the skills that remain under the surface. At the catcher position, you always want to maximize as much value as you can and Contreras could pay off more than most on that front this season.

2019 PROJECTION: .272 17 HR 70 RBI 55 R 5 SB

Yan Gomes: With top catching prospect Francisco Mejia breathing down his neck and coming off a couple of underwhelming seasons, it looked like Cleveland Indians catcher Yan Gomes' days as the team's starter were numbered. Alas, Gomes took matters into his own hands in 2018 as he reported to spring training in tremendous shape and then proceeded to hit 16 home runs and bat a solid .266 in 435 at-bats. The Cleveland team brass was apparently impressed as they dealt Mejia to the San Diego Padres during the summer and openly expressed confidence in Gomes serving as the starter going into 2019. Still, only 31 as the new season gets underway, Gomes looks like a good backup catcher in leagues that use only one starter and a

moderate option for the two-catcher crowed. Despite being as boring as it gets in terms of investing in the guy, Gomes can be a help to a fantasy baseball roster this season at a position filled with volatility.
2019 PROJECTION: .257 15 HR 53 RBI 48 R 0 SB

Yasmani Grandal: Heading into free agency at the age of 30, power-hitting backstop Yasmani Grandal has cemented a reputation for being one of the very best power-hitting catchers in today's game. Consider that the 24 home runs Grandal hit in 2018 represented the third straight season of at least 22 in that category and he also chipped in nicely with 68 RBI and 65 runs scored. Of course, Grandal remains a batting average liability as he has not hit at least .250 since his 2012 debut and last season was more of the same there as shown by an ugly .241 mark. What is interesting is that Grandal has a very good eye at the plate in terms of walks (13.9 BB/9) but his strikeouts offset that skill by a decent amount (23.9 K/9). Since you won't find many catchers who can help you in batting average, we can overlook that struggle and embrace the very good power contributions here which will carry into the 2019 season.
2019 PROJECTION: .245 24 HR 71 RBI 63 R 1 SB

Francisco Mejia: With the Cleveland Indians looking to shore up a major bullpen weakness heading toward an expected playoff berth last summer, the team's trade for San Diego Padres All-Star closer Brad Hand made sense on a lot of levels. Unfortunately, the price was high in that the Indians had to part ways with the consensus number 1 catching prospect in all of baseball in the smooth-swinging Francisco Mejia. For Mejia, the move to San Diego is a good one in that he is expected to have the inside track over Austin Hedges to open the season as the team's starter at the position and this alone makes him the top sleeper among all catchers for 2019 fantasy baseball. In terms of Mejia's ability with the bat, the hype began to take off in 2017 when he batted .297 with 14 home runs in 383 at-bats at Double-A and it only grew as he hit at a very high level at Triple-A last season in both the Cleveland and San Diego systems before getting a late promotion by the Padres. While Mejia batted just .179 in that cup of coffee 21-game run, he drove the ball nicely with 3 long balls in hinting at future 20-plus home run power. Lauded for impressive natural hitting ability at every step of his development, Mejia should be included on all sleepers lists for spring drafts.
2019 PROJECTION: .279 15 HR 56 RBI 54 R 0 SB

Wellington Castillo: Long one of the more underrated hitting catchers in yearly fantasy baseball leagues, Chicago White Sox catcher Wellington Castillo attached a baseball Scarlett Letter to himself in 2018 by getting pinched for PED usage which cost him 80 games. Given that huge chunk of prospective at-bats being removed from the bottom line numbers, Castillo's .259 average and 6 home runs fell way short of expectations for those who looked to him as a cost-effective fantasy baseball catcher. With that said, Castillo is back as a starting backstop for the White Sox in 2019 and he stands a good chance of supplying his customary 15-20 home runs with around a .265 batting average which are numbers that still carry everyday status in the fantasy baseball world. Given that the PED suspension likely soured many on coming back to Castillo this season, he could be a dirt-cheap and semi-productive option if you choose to wait until the very late rounds to select your catcher.

2019 PROJECTION: .259 15 HR 56 RBI 43 R 1 SB

Jorge Alfaro: Appearing near the top of the catching prospect lists going into the last couple of seasons, the Philadelphia Phillies finally ran with Jorge Alfaro in bestowing upon him the starters job heading into 2018. While Alfaro outdid himself in terms of his expected high strikeout rate (36.6 K/9), he generally was solid in hitting 10 home runs and batting .262 in 377 at-bats. With that said, Alfaro's completely unsustainable .406 BABIP last season was primarily responsible for him hitting .260 and one would figure with such an insane strikeout rate, the guy is likely headed for .230 in 2019 when the batted ball luck likely moves back toward average levels. Even the much-talked-about power that was supposed to be a highlight of Alfaro's offensive game has not really materialized and so projecting him for anything more than 15 or so home runs this season would be foolhardy. A seriously flawed overall hitter who could go into the statistical gutter due to all the strikeouts, Alfaro is not a recommended play in our view.

2019 PROJECTION: .235 14 HR 44 RBI 38 R 2 SB

Kurt Suzuki: It has been a nice late-career renaissance for veteran catcher Kurt Suzuki who over the last two seasons batted .283/.271 and swatted a combined 31 home runs in a timeshare with Tyler Flowers on the Atlanta Braves. With both guys headed toward free agency, it is up for debate about whether one, both, or either guy will re-sign with the club but at the advancing age of 35, Suzuki apparently has some more offensive juice left in the tank. What really makes Suzuki a unique catcher with the bat is his annually impressive K/9 rates (11.1 in 2018) and that stands out immensely at a position filled with hackers. What it all comes down to here is whether or not Suzuki can get another 300-plus at-bat this season to maintain his decent numbers from 2017-18 and if so, he would represent a terrific second catcher in leagues that use two starters. Even in single-catcher formats, Suzuki would serve as a nice backup as well.

2019 PROJECTION: .273 14 HR 50 RBI 43 R 0 SB

Francisco Cervelli: While it was another season interrupted by rampant injury trouble, Pittsburgh Pirates catcher Francisco Cervelli once again proved he is one of the better players with the bat at the position as shown by him hitting 12 home runs, collecting 57 RBI, and batting .259 in 404 at-bats. What helps Cervelli post some useful numbers throughout his career has been an ability to draw walks (12.6 BB/9) but ongoing trouble staying healthy continues to undermine the guy on a yearly basis. Cervelli's absences from the lineup last season also opened the door for backup Elias Diaz to hit 10 home runs and bat .286 in just 277 at-bats which could usher in a timeshare for 2019. Given the youth and obvious ability of Diaz, Cervelli's outlook for the upcoming fantasy baseball season is looking quite murky at the moment and so even in two-catcher formats we would actually prefer the understudy's upside if we take a stab at the Pirate backstops.
2019 PROJECTION: .267 7 HR 48 RBI 37 R 4 SB

Mitch Garver: Ever since Joe Mauer was removed from catching duties a few seasons ago, the Minnesota Twins have been searching in vain for some stability behind the dish. While the jury is still out, the team may have something in Mitch Garver who opened some eyes by hitting 7 home runs, collecting 45 RBI, and batting . 268 in 335 at-bats in 2018. Having hit .291 with 17 home runs at Triple-A the year prior, Garver seems like he can handle the bat which is all that matters for prospective fantasy baseball owners going forward. With a history of drawing walks, Garver only has to keep his strikeouts under control in order to be a possible upside play in 2019. Not the worst way to spend a last round pick.
2019 PROJECTION: .266 11 HR 56 RBI 44 R 0 SB

Mike Zunino: Another season and another all-or-nothing campaign put forth by Seattle Mariners catcher Mike Zunino in 2018. Already carrying the reputation for being one of the most pronounced strikeout-prone hitters in the game, Zunino's 37.0 K/9 last season was laughable and the corresponding .201 average was predictably terrible. The real shame of Zunino's high-K approach is that it almost completely overshadows some very impressive power as the former third overall pick in the 2012 MLB Draft has cracked 25 and 20 home runs the last two seasons. Unfortunately, we just can't stomach the brutal average under a level of strikeouts that make even Joey Gallo recoil with disgust.
2019 PROJECTION: .205 23 HR 57 RBI 44 R 0 SB

Russell Martin (3B): Perhaps the only interesting part of what was a disastrous season for Toronto Blue Jays catcher Russell Martin is that the former All-Star picked up eligibility at third base. Turing a very old for his age 36 this February Martin hit a career-worst .194 with 10 home runs and 25 RBI in 352 at-bats. While the Blue Jays are saying publicly they anticipated Martin opening up the 2019 season as their starting catcher, it is also no secret they have held many trade talks with other teams in order to try and get out of the last year of his contract. In terms of whether or not Martin can be salvaged for at least one more season with regards to fantasy baseball, there is no doubt his .234 BABIP was extremely unlucky and the walk rate (15.9 BB/9) remained terrific. With that said, Martin is older than dirt for a catcher and hitting even 10 home runs again could be a huge challenge. Despite the very underrated career, Martin is done contributing to a fantasy baseball roster.

2019 PROJECTION: .228 9 HR 45 RBI 55 R 1 SB

Jonathan Lucroy: Now off of a second straight listless season with the bat (.241, 4 home runs, 51 RBI) after years of being a top-five guy at the position, it is not a stretch to say Jonathan Lucroy's days of contributing in fantasy baseball are finished. As he heads into free agency at the age of 32, Lucroy looks like your classic case of a catcher losing his offensive game after turning 30 given the rigors of catching on a daily basis. As a result, Lucroy can be ignored even if he re-signs with the Oakland A's or takes hold of a starting catcher gig somewhere else.

2019 PROJECTION: .248 7 HR 57 RBI 46 R 1 SB

THE REST

Brian McCann: Age claimed another hitting victim in 2018 and this time it was former perennial All-Star catcher Brian McCann. With his offensive numbers already in decline going into the season, McCann put forth his worst performance with the bat yet as he hit just .212 with 7 home runs in 216 at-bats. Given how obvious McCann's struggles were, the Houston Astros had him on the bench quite often in favor of both Martin Maldonado and Max Stassi and so his days of being a starter could be finished at the age of 33. Even if McCann were to get hold of a starting gig somewhere, he would likely just yield value in NL-or-Al-only leagues.

Austin Hedges: After a 2017 rookie debut that had some positive aspects (18 home runs in 417 at-bats) but also some stark negatives (a .214 average and ghastly 29.3 K.9), the anticipation of some sophomore improvement kept San Diego Padres catcher Austin Hedges as a speculative late-round pick in 2018 fantasy baseball drafts. Alas, Hedges pretty much remained the same on a per game basis in terms of power (14 home runs in 326 at-bats) but showed at least a mild average improvement (.231, 27.6 K/9). Those numbers certainly don't elicit much fantasy baseball excitement in mixed leagues and now Hedges has to deal with the arrival of top catching prospect Francisco Mejia who came over last summer from the Cleveland Indians at the July 31 trade deadline. With Mejia likely getting the first crack at the starting catcher's gig, Hedges looks destined for backup duty on the Padres going forward. In that case, Hedges would have almost zero fantasy baseball value.

Robinson Chirinos: We bet you didn't know that veteran catcher Robinson Chirinos belted a combined 35 home runs over the last two seasons and collected 103 RBI during the same span. On the surface, you would have thought those numbers would be that of an annual upper-tier fantasy baseball catcher but the truth is that Chirinos has generally been an undrafted player who gets picked up and dropped numerous times during the course of a season when injuries/slumps strike down the starters. The reason Chirinos slips through the cracks though is due to some annually ugly averages (.222 in 2018, .233 for the career) due to a boatload of K's (32.9 K/9) and also as a result of the guy never really getting an extended run as a starter. Now turning 35 this June, Chirinos may have a tough time grabbing hold of anything more than a backup spot for 2019 as he explores being a free agent. If Chirinos were to sign on as a starter, then bump him up a few spots to low-end status in two-catcher formats. If not, then you can ignore him again like always.

Travis D'Arnaud: Enough already. That simple statement would have to be the mantra for anyone in the fantasy baseball community who at one time had an interest in former top catching prospect Travis D'Arnaud who has proven only to this point in his career that he simply can't EVER stay healthy. Having been given yet another chance by the New York Mets to salvage his already fledgling status, D'Arnaud didn't even make out it out of April before he suffered a torn UCL in his elbow that required Tommy John surgery. Even prior to the procedure, D'Arnaud hit just .200 with a home run in 4 games and you have to go back to 2015 to find a season where he batted over .260. Even though hitters come back from Tommy John quicker than a pitcher does (an April return is possible in 2019), it is time to stop chasing the quickly vanishing potential.

John Hicks: Getting semi-consistent starts both at catcher and first base during the course of the 2018 season, the Detroit Tigers' John Hicks caught some attention primarily through his eligibility behind the dish when he hit .260 with 9 home runs in 288 at-bats. That modest line of production spoke more to the utter absence of any offensive contributions from the catching fraternity last season and less about what the 29-year-old Hicks was able to accomplish. With both starting catcher James McCann and first baseman

Miguel Cabrera expected to enter into the 2019 season as starters at those two positions, Hicks is not likely going to play enough early on to be worth your attention at the draft table even in AL-only leagues.

Elias Diaz: If not for the continued presence of veteran Francisco Cervelli, we would be much more excited regarding the 2019 fantasy baseball prospects of backup Pittsburgh Pirates catcher Elias Diaz. With Cervelli once again missing a bunch of time with injuries last season, Diaz took full advantage of the increased playing time by hitting .286 with 10 home runs in 277 at-bats. While a very intriguing performance on the surface, Diaz' advanced metrics were impressive as well given the below-average 14.4 K/9 rate and neutral .302 BABIP speaking to how legitimate his overall numbers were. While Cervelli is expected to begin the season as the Pirates' starter in the last year of his contract, Diaz needs to be watched closely if a trade of the former opens up the gig for him outright in 2019.

Tyler Flowers: Hitting a very solid .270 and .281 with a total of 20 home runs from 2016-17 in his return to the Atlanta Braves was a nice homecoming story for catcher Tyler Flowers and that performance gave the team the impetus to pick up his option for 2019. Unfortunately, Flowers' production declined as he batted a woeful .227 and at the same time battled injuries seemingly throughout the year. While 8 home runs in 296 at-bats for a catcher is not terrible by any means, Flowers heads into free agency at the age of 33 amid questions regarding whether he can be a starting backstop anymore in the majors. Even though it was an impressive mid-career uptick in production for Flowers the last few seasons overall, investing in a catcher who has passed the age of 32 and with a high amount of mileage on his body is not a good idea.

Austin Barnes: Los Angeles Dodgers catcher/second baseman Austin Barnes caught some moderate fantasy baseball attention last spring based almost solely on the notion his multi-position eligibility and chance to play on a moderately consistent basis could make the guy into another Ryan Doumit. Even though Barnes did get 19 starts at second (costing him eligibility to begin 2019 by one game for those who use 20 as a benchmark), Barnes did little with the bat as he hit just .205 with 4 home runs in 238 at-bats. While Barnes will likely be used in much the same manner by the Dodgers in 2019, he should be ignored in drafts this time around as the onus goes on him to show he can hit enough to be a fantasy baseball asset.

Chris Iannetta: Entering into the second year of the two-year deal (with an option for 2020) that catcher Chris Iannetta inked with the Colorado Rockies prior to the start of last season, the outlook appears quite cloudy here on a number of fronts. The first issue was Iannetta showing little with the bat as he hit just .224 with 11 home runs in 360 at-bats despite calling Coors Field home. Additionally, the Rockies still have prospect Tom Murphy representing a possible heir apparent which could move this arrangement to a timeshare for 2019. Even if Iannetta retains the starting gig to begin the season, his obvious decline makes him someone to avoid.

Tucker Barnhardt: Finally unloading the annually disappointing Devin Mesoraco midway through the 2018 season, the Cincinnati Reds took the opportunity to give a long look to backup Tucker Barnhardt in order to see if he could handle being the starter going forward. On that front, it was a mixed-bag performance as Barnhardt walked quite a bit for a catcher (10.3 BB.9) and the strikeouts were not terrible either (18.4 K.9). However, just 10 home runs in 522 at-bats and a shaky .248 average speak to the underwhelming performance by Barnhardt last season and so at present time, he can't be counted on as anything but NL-only fodder and maybe a very low-end option in two-catcher formats.

Max Stassi: With Brian McCann getting old right before the team's eyes in 2018, the Houston Astros began to give more of a leash to backup catcher Max Stassi as the season went on. The righty hitter did put forth a mixed bag of numbers though as Stassi batted just .226 but was also able to crack 8 home runs in just 250 at-bats. Strikeouts are a major problem here (29.6 K/9) which is going to make batting even .230 a challenge but Stassi will be just 28 this March and has a chance to stake a claim to the starting catching job if the Astros don't pick up McCann's option as expected. Even if the latter happens, Stassi has a lot to prove before we try him out in any sort of league this season.

Nick Hundley: Despite turning 35 this past September, aging backstop Nick Hundley is still holding on to a smidge of fantasy baseball value after he smacked 10 home runs and batted .241 in 305 at-bats for the San Francisco Giants in 2018. Like with most catchers, Hundley is never going to help in the average department but he has now hit a total of 52 home runs over the last six seasons which counts for something in leagues that play two at the position. A free agent at press time, Hundley is likely going to either be in a timeshare arrangement or a backup this season which could make reaching 10 home runs again a challenge.

Martin Maldonado: Brought in by the Houston Astros last summer to help pick up the defensive slack behind the dish for the expected playoff push, veteran backstop Martin Maldonado proved to be on one of the better pitching staff managers in the game. Maldonado even contributed a bit with the bat as he hit a total of 9 home runs and collected 44 RBI in 404 at-bats last season but those numbers also came with a brutal .225 average. While Maldonado has the pop to supply some useful home runs, he is unlikely to find a starting opportunity in free agency to make him even somewhat useful in two-catcher formats.

Austin Romine: Given the insane struggles both on the health and hitting fronts of Gary Sanchez throughout the 2018 season, it should not be overlooked the fine year that New York Yankees backup catcher Austin Romine had. While the .244 average was not good by any means, Romine was able to hit 10 home runs and drive in 42 batters in just 265 at-bats; while also putting forth superb defense behind the dish. In fact, Romine was so solid all the way around that many were calling for Sanchez to be moved to the DH spot in order to accommodate his backup being an everyday guy. Even though such a development makes sense on the surface, there are currently no plans for such an arrangement which means Romine won't take hold of any fantasy baseball value as long as Sanchez is healthy.

Devin Mesoraco: Yeah those 25 home runs Devin Mesoraco hit back in 2014 will go down as one of the all-time outlier campaigns in recent memory. While it seemed at the end of that season Mesoraco had become a sudden hitting star at catcher, the following four years have been nothing but horrible numbers and rampant injuries which have the guy barely holding onto a major league gig. With just 17 home runs total since 2014, it would be a gross understatement to say that Mesoraco is pretty much worthless when it comes to fantasy baseball this season. Even though the 11 home runs Mesoraco cracked in 2018 in a year split between the Reds and the New York Mets were actually quite decent, the .221 average show the extreme limitations here. Since there is a slew of all-or-nothing catchers permeating the waiver wire, Mesoraco should not be drafted anywhere this spring.

Matt Wieters: After years of endless injuries (including a Tommy John surgery) that completely stunted what was looking like a very good early career with the Baltimore Orioles, aging catcher Matt Wieters heads into free agency with no guarantee of finding a starting opportunity as he comes off another listless season in 2018 where he batted just .238 with 8 home runs and 30 RBI in 271 at-bats with the Washington Nationals. It has now been four years since Wieters has reached the 20-home run mark and since he will be turning 33 in May, it will take the planets aligning for him to have much in the way of fantasy baseball value this season.

Manny Pina: For the second season in a row, the Milwaukee Brewers got a nice batch of numbers from catcher Manny Pina as the veteran played good defense and contributed 9 home runs and a .252 average in 337 at-bats. Even though nobody will jump in excitement over those offensive numbers, Pina can work as the second option in deeper two-catcher leagues given that his average won't be a total killer and he can contribute a few bombs.

John Ryan Murphy: Having already made his way through three MLB organizations, Arizona Diamondbacks catcher John Ryan Murphy still has not shown much of the ability that made him a second-round pick back in 2009. Major contact struggles (31.8 K/9) made Murphy into an all-or-nothing hitter in his 223 at-bats for the D-Backs last season (9 home runs, .202 average) and the fact he will already be 28 in May means he is moving past the prospect portion of his career as well. Even in NL-only leagues, you can completely look past Murphy in spring fantasy baseball drafts.

Blake Swihart (OF): After watching both Sandy Leon and Christian Vasquez embarrass themselves with the bat for long stretches of the 2018 season,. it made sense that the Boston Red Sox took a look at catching prospect Blake Swihart as the year went on. While Swihart did amass 207 at-bats in making starts both behind the plate and in the outfield, he failed to distinguish himself by hitting just .229 with 3 home runs and 6 steals. A 27.5 K/9 was a big problem and perhaps signified that Swihart was not yet ready to be a major league regular but the kid was a 2011 first-round pick for a reason so the jury is still out about whether he can develop into an offensive asset. Given that the pressurized Boston market is not in the habit of having young prospects work through struggles at the major league level, Swihart should only be treated as a guy to monitor in spring training.

FIRST BASEMAN

Draft Strategy: As always, first base is where monster offensive numbers are found and so you want to get a stud at this position before the end of Round 3 is possible. In addition, we always suggest double-dipping here as well for your CI or MI option but also keep in mind that potent options tend to emerge on the wire here like we saw in 2018 with Jesus Aguilar and Max Muncy.

Freddie Freeman: With both Miguel Cabrera and Joey Votto showing major signs of aging in 2018, the mantle of being the top hitting first baseman in fantasy baseball could very well be bestowed on the Atlanta Braves' Freddie Freeman. Finally avoiding the health trouble that took chunks out of two of his previous four seasons, Freeman was able to amass a staggering 707 at-bats a year ago which led to 23 home runs, 98 RBI, and a .309 average. When you add the 94 runs scored and 10 stolen bases to the ledger, Freeman served as the rare five-tool fantasy baseball first baseman which always carries an extra tier of value. If you were to nitpick, however, the 23 homers were a very disappointing total when you consider Freeman cracked 28 in 2017 with almost 200 fewer at-bats and also went for 34 the season before. One would figure Freeman would have easily cleared 30 home runs and maybe even make a run at 40 with such a high allotment of at-bats but that obviously didn't happen. When you look at Freeman's excellent walk (10.7 BB/9) and strikeout (18.7 K/9) rates, the light amount of home runs take on the stench of being an outlier however and likely can be thrown out when projecting him moving forward. While it seems like he has been around forever, Freeman will be just 29 when the 2019 season gets underway and his five-tool ability at first base is unmatched by anyone else at the position other than maybe Paul Goldschmidt. Be sure not to over think it here as the proper course of action is to snag Freeman with a pick halfway through the first round this spring.
2019 PROJECTION: .307 29 HR 98 RBI 104 R 9 SB

Paul Goldschmidt: Reaffirming how the fantasy baseball season is six months long and not three, we present to you the maddening 2018 campaign of Arizona Diamondbacks All-Star first baseman Paul Goldschmidt. A locked-in superstar who has been an incredibly dominant five-tool fantasy baseball monster for years, Goldschmidt was almost universally seen as one of the most stable prospective first-round picks given the fact he remained flat in his prime at the age of 30 and also possessed uncanny durability. What happened next almost defied comprehension though as a slow start to the season in March/April (.273, 4 HR, 30.3 K/9) soon morphed into a comically inept May (.144, 3 HR, 31.5 K/9) which actually elicited outlandish talk Goldschmidt was going through a premature decline or that he was maybe on steroids previously. While we were as shocked as anyone about how poorly Goldschmidt was swinging the bat, patience was preached from this peanut stand given his youth and for the fact, the veteran was simply fighting through an extended slump which happens to everyone at various times. Thus, it was no shock when Goldy proceeded to go absolutely nuclear with the bat from that point onward as he batted .364 in June, .317 in July, and .356 in August to completely re-establish himself as a premier first baseman in fantasy baseball. Despite those rough first two months, Goldy still ended up with another overall dominant campaign as he batted .290 with 33 home runs, 95 runs, and 83 RBI while making it four seasons in a row accruing at least 665 at-bats. In terms of the advanced metrics, Goldschmidt's K/9 went up a bit to 25.1 but that was skewed by the 30.0-plus marks the first two months of the season. The remaining four months saw Goldy back to around career norms which means there is no need to say there are some growing holes in his bat. Really, the only quibble we have with Goldy was the massive drop in stolen bases as he swiped just 7 in 2018 (down from 32 and then 18 the two years prior) but this is no shock when you consider that bigger-bodied players like the D-backs slugger tend to lose their speed quickly when they reach the age of 30. So while we need to project the loss of steals in Goldy's price tag moving forward, he is still top-shelf in the other four categories which place him again in first-round territory.

2019 PROJECTION: .295 34 HR 107 RBI 104 R 8 SB

Anthony Rizzo: While Arizona Diamondbacks first baseman Paul Goldschmidt got the lion's share of negative attention during what was a rough beginning to his 2018 season, it was no picnic for those owning stock in the Chicago Cubs' Anthony Rizzo. Looked at as one of the most dependable first-round options during spring drafts, Rizzo saw a major spike in strikeouts which led to a terrible .149 average in March/April and just a .249 mark during the first half of the season. Given that he was still in the early phase of his prime, it was no shock when Rizzo caught fire during the second half as he hit .329 and by the end of the season all was forgiven as he batted .283 with 25 home runs and 101 RBI. Now there were some clear negatives here that were a bit unexpected such as Rizzo losing 25 runs scored from the year prior (99 to 74) and he also failed to extend to three the number of seasons he swatted 32 home runs. Beyond that though, Rizzo was pretty much the same slugger that earned him first-round status in the first place as both his BB/9 (10.5) and especially K/9 (12.0) rates were terrific. Still, just 28 as the 2019 season gets underway, Rizzo is absolutely worthy of hearing his name called at the end of Round 1 in drafts and if he drops to Round 2, even better. Just beware that Rizzo didn't make a single appearance at second base in 2018 which removes the ridiculous eligibility he had there in some leagues that season.

2019 PROJECTION: .284 107 RBI 95 R 5 SB

Cody Bellinger (OF): The sophomore slump police claimed another victim during the 2018 fantasy baseball season as Los Angeles Dodgers first baseman/outfielder Cody Bellinger took a firm step back in his numbers almost across the board after going on average in the early second round of spring drafts. Bellinger's first half was in particularly poor which made his owners quite antsy but by the end of the year, the 23-year-old posted a decent .260 average with 25 home runs, 84 runs, 76 RBI, and even 14 stolen bases. All but the steals declined compared to Bellinger's beyond awesome rookie debut (.267/39 HR/97 RBI/87 R/10 SB) and that was with an extra 184 at-bats. Some growing pains had to be expected however as Bellinger made it look way too easy as a rookie but the kid still made some gains worth mentioning on the advanced statistics front which should not be overlooked. Perhaps most important was Bellinger lowering his K/9 rate from 26.6 as a rookie to a better 23.9 a year ago. If Bellinger can continue to knock down that number again this season, we may be able to remove the batting average red flag he currently carries around. For now, though, Bellinger looks like a very good bounce-back candidate for 2019 fantasy baseball and revisiting those superb rookie numbers with a slightly better average seems well within reach. Also, keep in mind Bellinger once again qualifies both at first base and the outfield for 2019.

2019 PROJECTION: .270 34 HR 93 RBI 88 R 11 SB

Jose Abreu: For the first time in five MLB seasons since coming over from Cuba, Chicago White Sox first baseman Jose Abreu went down as a fantasy baseball disappointment. Having established himself the previous four years as one of the most consistent players in the game, Abreu saw his offensive numbers fall across the board as a barren White Sox lineup lent little support and health woes that cropped up during the second half of the season furthered the trouble. In the end what we got out of Abreu were just 22 home runs, 78 RBI, and a .265 average which all went down as career-low totals for the slugger. While those numbers fell short of what was anticipated, some perspective is needed here on a number of key fronts as we look toward his potential impact for the upcoming fantasy baseball season. For one thing, Abreu will still be just 32 when the 2019 season gets underway which still represents prime years for a power-driven player. In addition, Abreu's advanced metrics show a hitter who is still the same guy he has always been since making his debut in 2014 when he slammed 36 home runs, collected 107 RBI, and batted .307. Both Abreu's BB/9 (6.7) and K/9 (19.7) rates were in the middle range of his historical performances in those categories and one of the main reasons the batting average fell to .265 last season (after previously never going under .290) was due to the fact his .294 BABIP was a major outlier compared to those career norms. Digging into that crucial last point a bit more, Abreu's BABIP during his first four years in the majors ranged from .327 and .356 which right there tells you last season's .294 was a primary cause for the batting average tumble. Taking this a step further, if you were to throw out the highest and lowest BABIP's of Abreu's five-year career (see you later .294 and .356), the remaining three marks would be .333, .327, and .330 which are almost clones of one other. So it stands to reason that Abreu's typical BABIP is around .330 which is a sizable leap from the .294 of a year ago and this also means a batting average uptick in 2019 to around .290 is likely. What will also help the average and the rest of Abreu's counting numbers would be good health and that was not part of the equation for the first time in his career last season as well. Having previously never had a season without at least 622 at-bats, Abreu's paltry 553 total in 2018 compared to his career norms is an easy to spot indicator of why he fell away from the 30-HR/100-RBI mark. In the midst of what was his best hitting stretch of the season during the month of August, Abreu first was forced to undergo emergency surgery for a strangled testicle (it hurts just typing this). Things then got even more bizarre in mid-September when Abreu was hospitalized due to complications from an ingrown hair and that proved to be the final nail in the coffin for his 2018 season. So as you can see, Abreu's injuries were not of the baseball variety and really were as fluky as can be which means we don't have to worry about him being a constant source of DL frustration going forward. With Abreu hopefully having better luck on the freaky injury front, the counting totals should rebound to where they should be. So in putting this all together, it is easy to make a case that Abreu will go right back to the upper-tier fantasy baseball first baseman he historically has been before his very difficult 2018 clouded the picture a bit. With some very unlucky health and a tough BABIP combining to do an unfair number on Abreu a year ago, our advice is to take advantage of the draft discount this spring and dive back in here without hesitation.

2019 PROJECTION: .288 26 HR 98 RBI 84 R 1 SB

Matt Carpenter (3B): St. Louis Cardinals first baseman/third baseman Matt Carpenter did almost the impossible during the course of 2018 as he was deemed to be finished as a prime MLB hitter early in the year and by its conclusion, was talked up as a possible MVP. It was that kind of a roller coaster ride for Carpenter's fantasy baseball owners as they watched with mouths agape when hitting just .155 in March/April elicited chatter that back and shoulder injuries the previous few years had robbed him of strength and the ability to turn on the baseball. Well, Carpenter decided instead to go nuclear with the bat the remaining five-plus months of the season as home runs seemingly went out on an everyday basis and the MVP talk became rampant by the of the year. In the end, Carpenter looked worthy of the lofty award as he hit a cumulative .257 with a career-best 36 home runs and 111 runs scored. Add in 81 RBI and Carpenter had his best overall season at the age of 32. By now it is old news how Carpenter successfully transformed himself from a .300-plus slap hitter who was lucky to crack double-digit home runs to an absolute monster in the power categories at the expense of the average. It is no secret that Carpenter is more of a hacker now than he ever has been (career-worst 23.3 K/9 last season) but he still walks like a leadoff man (15.1 BB/9). Despite some recent health trouble, Carpenter looks stable enough to be counted on for another similar season in 2019 but keep in mind he carries eligibility at just first and third base (losing second). **2019 PROJECTION: .263 29 HR 86 RBI 108 R 3 SB**

Miguel Cabrera: While no one will ever take away the fact Detroit Tigers first baseman Miguel Cabrera may be one of the greatest sluggers AND pure hitters of all-time, his body is starting to completely give out on him as he only played in just 38 games last season. Serving as another example of a big-bodied slugger who began to quickly deteriorate once past the age of 32 (along the same lines as Carlos Lee, Prince Fielder, and Ryan Howard), Cabrera suffered a torn biceps tendon in early June that required season-ending surgery and it marked the third time in the last four years the veteran has missed extensive time due to health woes. Injuries aside, Cabrera has also lost some luster as a hitter/slugger as shown by the fact his slugging percentage dipped under .500 each of the last two seasons and also as evidenced by a home run per game rate that has taken a dive during that same span as well. Ill health, age. and declining offensive numbers all go hand-in-hand and the fact Cabrera will be 36 in April means more trouble is likely going to be on the way. While we wouldn't be surprised if Cabrera still hit for average (he was at .299 before the biceps tear last season), his declining power and constant health issues make him nothing more than a UTIL or CI bat at best at during the latter stages of his career. **2019 PROJECTION: .284 19 HR 73 RBI 65 R 1 SB**

Jesus Aguilar: More than any other hitting position in yearly fantasy baseball leagues, first base becomes a spot where some terrific out-of-the-blue values can be found on the waiver wire given the power-centric abilities of the players involved. 2018 saw a big one emerge in the form of the Milwaukee Brewers' Jesus Aguilar who finally received everyday at-bats for the first time in his career and then proceeded to put forth a season that was worthy of some MVP votes as he batted .274 with 35 home runs and 108 RBI. Perhaps we should have seen this explosion coming as Aguilar did bat

.265 with 16 home runs in just 311 at-bats in part-time duty with the Brewers the year prior but either way, the 28-year-old is now worthy of being talked about as a supreme power first baseman for 2019 fantasy baseball. In trying to get a read on how repeatable Aguilar's 2018 performance was, the advanced metrics are pretty positive as he accumulated a near-neutral .309 BABIP, drew a nice amount of walks (10.2 BB/9) and didn't strike out at an overly obscene rate (25.3 K/9) for someone who was involved in his first full MLB campaign. Since there will be some Aguilar doubters among the fantasy baseball community this spring, the draft cost is unlikely to be overly pricey which means the risk is not great even if there is a slight jog back on the numbers. Count us as believers.

2019 PROJECTION: .277 33 HR 102 RBI 84 R 0 SB

Ian Desmond (OF): Some guys just get maligned by the fantasy baseball community each and every season no matter how underrated their numbers may be and serving as a poster boy for such an unwanted group would undoubtedly be Colorado Rockies first baseman/outfielder Ian Desmond. While Desmond is getting a bit long in the tooth at 33, he comes off a 2018 campaign where he posted his FIFTH career 20/20 campaign with 22 home runs and 20 stolen bases. While the .236 average was unacceptable considering Desmond played home games at Coors Field, his 82 runs scored and 88 RBI made him a very good four category contributor who would go down as one of the top fantasy baseball values considering the very depressed 2018 draft price. The reason why Desmond's price tag was so cheap last spring in holding a persona non grata tag was due to the fact he somehow figured out a way to bomb offensively as a member of the Rockies during his first season with the team in 2017. Managing just 7 home runs, 15 steals, and a .274 average while dealing with constant injuries, Desmond became a guy nobody actively sought to own the following season. That narrative should change this time around though as Desmond has held the power/speed game despite moving closer to his mid-30's. Even Desmond's ugly .236 average was of the fluke variety as his .279 BABIP centered into unlucky territory and also when you consider the guy has historically been in the .330 range with that number, a sizable average uptick is likely going forward. So, in essence, we could be looking at a very affordably priced 20/20 hitter who possesses eligibility at both first base and the outfield, plus likely showcasing an average that is likely going to move northward. While we usually try to shy away from veteran hitters who have passed the age of 32, there are exceptions to be made when the price is right and the numbers still work.

2019 PROJECTION: .266 20 HR 90 RBI 84 R 19 SB

Joey Votto: Say it isn't so Joe! Even one of the greatest pure hitters of all-time (the advanced metrics say so) in Cincinnati Reds first baseman Joey Votto could only hold off the ravages of age for so long as the former All-Star endured what can only be described as a brutal 2018 campaign. Just one season removed from arguably his second-best career performance (just slightly behind an otherworldly 2010), Votto looked completely shot almost overnight as he managed just 12 home runs, 67 RBI, and a .284 average in 623 at-bats. What is even more disturbing is that those numbers would have been worse if not for Votto putting forth a very good finish (a .291 average with 3 home runs in September/October). While Votto endlessly claimed during the course of the year he was simply going through an extended slump, we are not buying that notion one bit considering the type of A-list hitter we are talking about here. What is really interesting is the fact that from an advanced metrics perspective, Votto's numbers were pretty much in line with career norms. Yes, his strikeouts spiked a bit in going from 11.7 in 2017 up to 16.2 a year ago but the latter was the "norm" number in terms of Votto's career rates in that category. In addition, Votto's .333 BABIP went right along with his customary output there as well. The only thing that jumped out though was Votto's drastic drop in slugging as he went from .578 in 2017 all the way down to .419 last season. Often drops this sharp from an aging hitter are an indication of erosion and with Votto now 35-years-old and with a history of knee trouble, we could very well be looking at the decline phase of his career unfolding before our eyes. While some will say the slugging drop in 2018 belongs in the outlier bin, we can't do such a thing when a hitter is at the age Votto currently is and so we need to project that into his outlook for the approaching fantasy baseball season. With Votto fitting into the always sketchy category of an aging/eroding "name brand" player, we would regretfully say to take a pass.

2019 PROJECTION: .298 22 HR 78 RBI 77 R 4 SB

Edwin Encarnacion: While the effects of an advancing age continued to take a chunk out of the offensive numbers for Cleveland Indians first baseman Edwin Encarnacion in 2018, the veteran still maintained some of the best power numbers in the game as he hit 32 home runs and drove in 107 batters in 579 at-bats. When looking at the totality of Encarnacion's production last season, however, it was easy to see that air continues to leak out of the statistical tires. Specifically speaking, Encarnacion's shoddy .246 batting average was the third straight season he saw a decline there and it became FIVE consecutive campaigns where the K/9 increased (up to a career-worst 22.8). Those two metrics are very clear indicators of age and/or a slowing bat and those trends should only continue to grow into 2019. Making matters even more concerning was Encarnacion's runs scored number taking a major tumble, going from 96 in 2017 all the way down to just 74 last season. So in essence what we have here now is a guy who no longer can hold down an everyday first base spot in mixed fantasy baseball leagues and instead Encarnacion belongs in the UTIL or CI spot. While the power remains very potent, Encarnacion is really just a 2 category guy now and he also faces the additional risk of getting hurt given the advancing age. All in all, this is another "name brand" former early-round star that should be avoided if possible this season.

2019 PROJECTION: .245 30 HR 104 RBI 77 R 1 SB

Ryon Healy: On a 2018 Seattle Mariners team that hit home runs like they were going out of style, new first base arrival Ryon Healy did his part in slugging 24 long balls and driving in 73 batters in 524 at-bats after coming over the previous winter from the Oakland A's via a trade. Having hit 25 home runs with 78 RBI the year prior, Healy has established a baseline of what we can expect moving forward in terms of fantasy baseball and that is of a two-category staple that also carries along some issues in the other categories. Driving the latter point home is the fact that the slow-footed Healy only scored 66 and 51 runs his first two MLB seasons and he obviously won't contribute on the base paths either (zero career steals). Then there is the batting average which seemed to be a bright spot as a 2017 rookie (.305) but then last year not so much (.235). In comparing the two seasons on the average front, it really all came down to BABIP as Healy went from a lucky .319 in 2017 down to a rough .257 last season. That means Healy is likely going to end up somewhere in the middle going forward and so a .270 mark sounds about right. Considering Healy's solid 21.6 K/9 suggests someone who is not a pure hacker, he may even be able to go a smidge higher if the luck stays neutral. Since he turned only 27 this past January, Healy also has a chance to tap into even more power as he reaches his prime this season. Finally, since Healy is already a bit off the fantasy baseball radar, the guy is presenting himself as a very nice buying opportunity. Just be sure you realize Healy no longer qualifies at third base this season before cutting the check.

2019 PROJECTION: .267 26 HR 79 RBI 57 R 0 SB

Max Muncy: It took until his age-28 season for power-hitting first baseman Max Muncy to finally receive an extended MLB look but perhaps the wait was worth it as the former 2012 fifth-round pick became an overnight sensation as he clubbed 35 home runs, collected 79 RBI, and batted .263 in 481 at-bats for the Los Angeles Dodgers in 2018. Clearly, Muncy caught opposing pitchers unfamiliar with his game off guard the first half of the year when he batted .271 with 22 of the 35 homers (dropping to .255 and 12 respectively during the second half) but that type of power played well for those who made the add early on in the year. Now in terms of whether Muncy can sustain such a level of production going forward, we do have concerns about his high-K approach (27.2 K/9) which could lead to extended cold spells that may make the Dodgers antsy in looking for a replacement at some point given the lack of a track record. On the other hand, it is encouraging Muncy draws a very high level of walks (16.4 BB/9) and that his neutral .299 BABIP suggested the average was quite stable. What we need to be most concerned with here is that often out-of-the-blue power explosions from the first base position (which Muncy qualified as a year ago) can just as quickly vanish back into fantasy baseball Siberia the next year once opposing pitchers zone in on the batting weaknesses. Muncy could very well go down this same route as his second-half struggles last season might attest to oncoming trouble and that threat alone makes him nothing more than a late-round UTIL/CI option for mixed fantasy baseball leagues.

2019 PROJECTION: .255 28 HR 74 RBI 73 R 2 SB

Justin Smoak: Despite not falling off the statistical map, Toronto Blue Jays first baseman Justin Smoak did undertake a sizable decline in his offensive numbers last season as most pundits predicted. On the latter point, it seemed obvious to surmise Smoak's 2017 career-year (38 homers, 90 RBI, .270) belonged in the outlier bin when you gazed at the fact he only once previously reached 20 long balls (right on the number in 2013) and never ONCE having hit over .240. So it went as Smoak jogged back to just 25 homers, 77 RBI, and a .242 average last season and it is around those numbers that we expect him to remain moving forward. As of this writing, it was unknown whether the Blue Jays would pick up Smoak's option but obviously his fantasy baseball value would be a bit more pronounced operating in the homer-haven that is Rogers Center. Even if he were to move on to another locale, however, Smoak is just a backup/borderline UTIL/CI bat to begin the 2019 fantasy baseball season.

2019 PROJECTION: .249 26 HR 75 RBI 73 R 0 SB

Eric Hosmer: While Eric Hosmer had to be elated beyond belief to net an eight-year deal worth a staggering $144 million in what was a dormant free agent market for veteran hitters last winter, the fact he moved to another prime pitching park going from Kansas City to San Diego meant additional chances for underwhelming numbers for a guy who had posted some serious duds previously in his career. So really it was no surprise when Hosmer went out and had his worst year as a pro since 2012 as he batted .253 with 18 home runs and 69 RBI in 157 at-bats. While Hosmer did lack in lineup protection on the forever rebuilding Padres, he certainly bore responsibility for spiking his K/9 rate up to 21.0 last season. Hosmer also shows no sign of ever going back to being the double-digit stolen base guy he was earlier in his career which helped elevate his fantasy baseball stock a bit above where it really should have been. No longer in his prime after turning 28 last October, Hosmer has ceded daily starting first base status to begin the 2019 fantasy baseball season and in actuality, looks like quite a boring UTIL or CI option as well.

2019 PROJECTION: .284 19 HR 75 RBI 77 R 5 SB

Matt Olson: With the 2018 Oakland A's seemingly doing the impossible in winning the second AL Wild Card despite having the major leagues' lowest payroll, it stood to reason that a batch of the team's prospects had to come up big to make such a leap. This, in fact, did wind up taking place as the A's got multiple contributions from their farm system and this included first baseman Matt Olson who was originally just a 16th round pick of the team back in 2012. Despite the lack of draft pedigree, Olson's power bat was very impressive last season as he smashed 29 home runs, drove in 84, and scored 85 runs in quickly becoming one of the team leaders. So on a club that stressed the long ball and high OBP's (.335), Olson more than fit in with the A's last season. However, from a fantasy baseball front, he was much less valuable. Given the extreme proliferation of power in today's game, Olson's 29 home runs were not as valuable as you may think and the .247 average that went along for the statistical ride took some shine off that number as well. So you can pretty much classify Olson as another grip-it-and-rip-it hitter who draws some more walks than similarly skilled guys one may find on the wire (10.6 BB/9) but all in all, this puts him mostly as a backup first baseman in mixed leagues.

2019 PROJECTION: .253 27 HR 86 RBI 83 R 1 SB

Luke Voit: One of the bigger puzzles when projecting 2019 fantasy baseball first baseman centers on New York Yankees sudden "star" Luke Voit. We put the word star in quotes due to the fact that the Yankee faithful pretty much canonized Voit during his second-half run with the team when he went bonkers with the bat to the tune of 14 home runs and a .333 average after coming over from the St. Louis Cardinals in a deal that was mainly for international pool money. While Voit did hit an additional homer with the Cards in a limited time period for the team prior to the trade, we really must look only at his Yankee numbers in terms of trying to figure out where this goes. At the very least, we can say Voit is the favorite to start Opening Day at first base for the Yankees given how horrible Greg Bird performed last season and operating in the homer-haven that is Yankee Stadium will only help to keep the momentum going for the slugger. What we also like about Voit is that he draws walks (10.6 BB/9) which will help ward off the expected average decline (he is not a .322 hitter) that is anticipated for 2019. A 26.7 K/9 is on the high side though and given the lack of any sort of track record, Voit could easily slide back into irrelevancy if he doesn't adjust back to opposing pitchers who will likely have a better plan to attack him this season. At the very least, Voit needs to be drafted as a mid-to-late round pick given his home park and the possible breakthrough we saw in his magical 2018 campaign.

2019 PROJECTION: .284 25 HR 84 RBI 73 R 1 SB

Yuli Gurriel: Having arrived in the majors out of Cuba already at a back-end prime stage of his career, Houston Astros first baseman Yuli Gurriel will be turning 35 this June which on the surface is a decent-sized concern for his immediate fantasy baseball prospects. With that said, Gurriel remains a very useful UTIL or CI bat who has already proven to be a .300 hitter and also possesses moderate 15-20 home run power if he accrues enough at-bats. Showcasing uncanny contact skills for a first baseman (just an 11.0 K/9 a year ago), Gurriel should be good for another .300 average this season; along with good counting stats in runs and RBI while operating in a stacked Astros lineup. As long as you accept there won't be much in the way of power, Gurriel can be an underrated support player for your team this season.

2019 PROJECTION: .295 15 HR 79 RBI 74 R 4 SB

C.J. Cron: Free from the maddening lineup machinations of former manager Mike Scioscia during his tumultuous Los Angeles Angels days, DH/first baseman C.J. Cron found new life with the Tampa Bay Rays in 2018. Having gone on record as being a fan of Cron's swing going back to his early days with the Angels, even we were a bit shocked at how much power the guy showed last season as he cracked 30 home runs and drove in 74 batters in 560 at-bats. Unfortunately, the power was really the only aspect of Cron's season that was impressive from a fantasy baseball angle as he batted just .253, didn't walk much (6.6 B/9), and struck out at a higher rate that we would be comfortable with (25.9). Now into his prime years as he turns 29 in January, Cron is best left as your CI or UTIL bat based almost solely on the power.

2019 PROJECTION: .259 28 HR 78 RBI 67 R 2 SB

Brandon Belt: In what has become the theme for his so-far disappointing career, San Francisco Giants first baseman Brandon Belt had another season marked with somewhat intriguing offensive promise being almost completely undermined by a severe inability to stay healthy. At one time a top hitting prospect while coming up the Giants' minor league ladder who debuted back in 2011, Belt was being talked about as a future .300 hitting/25-home run impact player who would play well in yearly fantasy baseball leagues. Now 8 seasons later, we are still waiting for Belt's first 20-homer season and his once-lauded batting average potential has become nothing but a rumor as he batted just .241 and .253 the last two years. Already having suffered numerous concussions in his still young (30 years old) career, Belt dealt with chronic knee trouble throughout the course of the 2018 season that led to surgery in September. The real shame of it all is that Belt teased us again during the first half of the year when he smacked 13 home runs and batted a solid .287 in reigniting talk that maybe he was ready to realize his sizable past potential as a classic post-hype sleeper. Alas, the knee trouble pretty much destroyed Belt's second half (1 home run, .155 average) to end the year on another sour note. Getting back to the numbers, there is no doubt that Belt's power prior to the All-Star Break was his best per game rate of his career and he also controlled the strike zone nicely in posting a tidy 10.7 BB/9 rate which helped in the batting average department as well. If the knee problems didn't arise, it is entirely possible Belt would have finally reached 20 home runs but even discussing reaching that modest power mark from a fantasy baseball first baseman makes it clear we may be wasting our time here in the first place. With the average dipping into shoddy territory the last two years, the health being an annual crisis, and with you as a fantasy baseball participant needing so much more power from the first base position, it is clear we have reached the point where we can finally stop chasing this annual tease.

2019 PROJECTION: .263 19 HR 70 RBI 77 R 5 SB

Albert Pujols: Having just completed his 18th MLB season, Los Angeles Angels first baseman/DH Albert Pujols can walk into the Hall of Fame if he chose to finally hang up his cleats after a career that's included some of the most mindboggling offensive numbers ever seen. Still, with three years and $87 million left on his deal with the Angels, Pujols is not ready to put his bat away just yet after smacking a very solid 19 home runs and driving in 64 batters in 498 at-bats in 2018. Now in terms of where Pujols stands with regards to today's fantasy baseball, he has not been anything more than a UTIL, CI, or backup first base option in mixed leagues since 2015 as the batting average really began to erode and the bat began to slow a bit. Like most aging sluggers, the home runs and RBI become the only categories where such a player can help in fantasy baseball leagues and this is certainly Pujols' standing since his .245 average last season was ugly and represented the third time in the last four seasons he has fallen under the .250 mark. Add in the typical injury problems that annually arise with an older big-bodied player such as Pujols (he missed the entire last month of 2018 after needing a debridement of his left knee) and it becomes crystal clear that he is just barely holding onto being a useful player in fantasy baseball for 2019.

2019 PROJECTION: .248 20 HR 80 RBI 67 R 1 SB

Yonder Alonso: Another hitter who the fantasy baseball community felt the regression police would drag down during the course of the 2018 season was Cleveland Indians first baseman Yonder Alonso but it was sort of a mixed bag on that front. While Alonso did take a jog back on the power as anticipated (going from 28 homers in 2017 to 23 a year ago), the lefty swinger posted a career-high 83 RBI in the stacked Cleveland lineup. Beyond the homers and RBI, however, Alonso was a liability as he batted just .250, scored 64 runs, and had a bagel in steals. It does need to be said that Alonso has at least cemented 20-25 home run power after serving mostly as a doubles first baseman during the first 7 seasons of his career and an unlucky .283 BABIP last year did help to depress the average a bit below where it should have been. With that said, Alonso only nets starting usage as a UTIL or CI bat in mixed leagues as guys with his profile can be had at a dirt cheap rate.

2019 PROJECTION: .264 24 HR 79 RBI 65 R 1 SB

Jose Martinez (OF): Anyone who owned St. Louis Cardinals first baseman Jose Martinez during the course of the 2018 fantasy baseball season was struck by the notion he got a raw deal from the team. While Martinez hit over .300 for the second year in a row with the Cards (.305), the team's trade for Matt Adams at the July 31 deadline turned him unfairly into a part-time player the rest of the way. What is interesting is that while Martinez hit 13 of his 17 home runs during the first half, his .318 average in the second half was better than a .297 mark prior to the All-Star Game. A classic late bloomer who had to work his way through four other MLB organizations before getting his big break, Martinez should have a chance to reclaim the first base job all to his own this spring now that Adams is expected to depart in free agency. While no one knows exactly how the Cards view Martinez as of this writing, we now have two straight seasons of underrated hitting and moderate power than can work nicely in your CI or UTIL spot.

2019 PROJECTION: .304 16 HR 77 RBI 65 R 2 SB

Carlos Santana: Annually in the running as the most boring veteran hitter to own in fantasy baseball, it was another typically uninspiring season for Philadelphia Phillies first baseman Carlos Santana in 2018. Santana went along with his career trends of hitting for good but not great power by posting 24 home runs and 86 RBI; while at the same time recording another ugly batting average of .229. It has now been five straight seasons where Santana has failed to bat at least .260 and his power has dropped off a clear level the last two years as the home runs totals have both been under 25 in each year during that same span. Like with Minnesota Twins catcher Joe Mauer, Santana lost a ton of his fantasy baseball value once catcher eligibility fell by the wayside and honestly you really should strive to do better here for your backup first baseman.

2019 PROJECTION: .254 23 HR 88 RBI 84 R 4 SB

Ryan Zimmerman: If you knew anyone who believed to be legit the tremendous production Washington Nationals first baseman Ryan Zimmerman put forth in 2017, try selling that individual a bridge while you're at it. While no one can take away what were some very good early season performances from a much younger Zimmerman, his out-of-the-blue numbers bonanza last year when he hit 36 home runs, drove in 108, and batted .303 looked destined for the outlier bin the moment the final at-bats were put in the books. After all, Zimmerman had not hit more than 16 home runs since 2013 and his never-ending health woes made the guy as unreliable a player as there was in the game. So it certainly was no shock to the system when Zimmerman went right back to his very mediocre ways in 2018 as the injuries returned in earnest (missing almost three months with a serious oblique strain), the numbers plummeted (just a .264 average with 13 home runs and 51 RBI), and he got another year older (turned 34 last September). Still, with another year and an option left on his deal with the Nats, Zimmerman will likely be opening the 2019 season for the team at first base. Even though the Nats may be stuck with Zimmerman, you don't have to be.

2019 PROJECTION: .262 17 HR 67 RBI 65 R 1 SB

Matt Adams: In the case of first baseman Matt Adams, you can apparently go home again. After stalling somewhat as a St. Louis Cardinals prospect, the team traded Adams to the Washington Nationals during the course of 2017 in a clear signal they were fed up waiting for the physically impressive hitter to finally crack even 20 home runs in a single season. Given the fresh start with the Nats, Adams would do just that as he hit the number right on the nose; while also batting .270 and collecting 65 RBI. While those statistics were far from elite, it perhaps suggested the light bulb finally went off for Adams to be a decent UTIL or CI bat in yearly fantasy baseball leagues. Well like everything else that went wrong for the Nationals in 2018, Adams struggled for long stretches of the year and he was soon sent right back to the Cardinals at the July 31 deadline given the latter's need of another bat for the stretch run. So in terms of the numbers, Adams actually did set another career-high in home runs with 21 (which came in only 337 at-bats) but his .239 average left a lot to be desired. With just a pathetic career .208 hitter versus lefties suggesting Adams belongs in a platoon, his free agency outlook is not looking overly promising as well. The fact that Adams can swat 21 homers in just 337 at-bats does show power that could maybe approach the 30 mark if he were to push the plate appearances up to around 500 but the drastic righty/lefty splits will make this unlikely. Also having batted less than .250 three straight seasons, Adams is overall just a backup first baseman (he loses outfield eligibility for the start of 2019) who is quite boring in nature.

2019 PROJECTION: .248 20 HR 63 RBI 45 R 0 SB

Greg Bird: New York Yankees catcher Gary Sanchez had some company in terms of his colossal bomb of a season in 2018 as first baseman Greg Bird tried to outdo his teammate in every way. Already carrying with him a well-earned label of being injury-prone (missing all of 2016 due to shoulder surgery), Bird didn't even make it out if spring training before being forced to undergo surgery on his ankle for the second season in a row (this time to remove a bone spur). Upon his return to the team at the end of May, Bird proceeded to hit like he didn't even know how to hold a bat. Things got so bad during the summer that the Yankees turned to summer acquisition Luke Voit who almost immediately began smacking baseballs all over and out of the park on a nightly basis. By the time the playoffs arrived, Bird was not even included on the Yankees' postseason roster as Voit became the undisputed starter. In the end, Bird only managed a .199 average with 11 home runs in 311 at-bats and he entered into the winter with no outward path to consistent playing time to at least begin the 2019 season. Once lauded as a supreme power-hitting prospect who was very impressive during his 2015 debut (.261 with 11 home runs in 178 at-bats), Bird has now hit just .190 and .199 the last two seasons which is obviously not going to cut it. It is entirely possible Bird's massive slumps are at least partially a product of a young player missing a ton of developmental time due to serious injuries but either way, he is not even worth drafting in AL-only leagues unless a trade grants a new start somewhere else.

THE REST

Ryan McMahon: When you are a Colorado Rockies hitting prospect at any position on the diamond, you almost automatically have a place on annual fantasy baseball sleeper lists due to the offensive-dimensions of Coors Field. First base prospect Ryan McMahon certainly was included in this group as he caught some attention in drafts last spring amid rumors he would have a chance to break camp with the team and for the scorching .326 (Double-A) and .374 (Triple-A) averages he put forth in the minors in 2017. Unfortunately, like Tom Murphy before him at catcher, McMahon failed to do much in his 202 at-bats with the Rockies last season as he struggled to make contact (31.7 K/9) and generally gave off the impression he was not ready to be a major league hitter just yet. With that said, McMahon still has the smooth-swing and 20-25 home run power to be a factor at some point and he will likely get a chance again this spring to finally latch on with the Rockies for good. This classifies McMahon as a monitor priority during the exhibition slate and a guy you need to move up your cheat sheets by a decent margin if it looks like he will make the Opening Day roster.

Tyler White: Mostly a forgotten prospect in the beyond stacked Houston Astros farm system the last few seasons, first baseman Tyler White looked destined to be a Quad-A guy as 2018 got underway. Originally just a 2013 33rd round pick, White failed to make much of a positive impression with the team when given cup of coffee looks both in 2016 and 2017. Undeterred, White proceeded to hit very well at Triple-A (.333, 14 HR in 313 at-bats) which basically forced the Astros to promote him in June. Despite serving part-time duty the rest of the regular season, White continued hitting at a nice clip as he batted .276 with 12 home run and that earned him the starting first base job by the time the postseason got started. Now in terms of 2019 fantasy baseball, White more than likely did enough good things last season to at least serve as the backup to Yuli Gurriel to begin the year but a timeshare could also be possible as well given the power advantage the former brings over the latter. With White showing very impressive bat control/discipline a year ago (10.1 BB/9, 20.7 K/9), the hulking slugger should be watched during spring training to see what in fact his role will be this season.

Tyler Austin: While he may not have gotten a completely fair shake with the New York Yankees since debuting in the majors back in 2016, all is well now for first baseman Tyler Austin after he received new baseball life after being dealt to the Minnesota Twins last summer. Serving as an everyday member of a lineup for the first time in his career, Austin showed some intriguing power as he finished the season with 17 home runs and 47 RBI in 268 at-bats. Unfortunately, the high strikeout rates that perhaps made the Yankees leery of Austin's long-term potential followed him to Minnesota as he put forth a terrible 35.4 K/9 which resulted in just a .230 average. With Austin also not showing the greatest eye in terms of walks (7.1 BB/9), we could be looking at an annual batting average struggle which would then place him squarely into AL-only starting territory. Even though the power is intriguing, there are a ton of ugly average sluggers with a similar profile to Austin permeating your league's waiver wire.

Jake Bauers: Whenever the Tampa Bay Rays promote a prospect, you always have to take notice given their extreme success in developing pitchers and hitters and so first base farmhand Jake Bauers entered into the fantasy baseball consciousness when summoned last June. While Bauers struggled mightily at times (.201 average), he did post an 11/6 split in homers/steals in just 388 at-bats which is somewhat intriguing and a 13.9 BB/9 was quite encouraging as well. Bauers did struggle with strikeouts

(26.8 K/9) but that really was no shock since the kid was just 22 when debuting in the majors last season. Since Bauers has shown himself to be a decent power/speed guy while coming up in the minors and during his rookie MLB campaign, he should be kept in play as a possible late-round upside pick in deeper formats. Also, keep in mind Bauers is eligible in the outfield which adds to the interesting outlook.

Josh Bell: After coming out and surprising the fantasy baseball establishment by hitting 26 home runs in 2017, Pittsburgh Pirates first baseman Josh Bell was under an unsaid mandate to prove such an out-of-the-blue number (compared to previous minor and major league rates) was not a fluke. Well, Bell ultimately failed at such a venture in 2018 as he slumped to just 13 home runs and even added an ugly .261 batting average as well. At one time at least a semi-intriguing prospect when coming up the Pittsburgh system due to a string of .300 averages, Bell has become more strikeout-prone since arriving in the majors and his power has been below-average for what is needed from a fantasy baseball first baseman. Even though he won't turn 27 until August, Bell is not a very inspiring late round draft pick by any means.

Joe Mauer: By now even the biggest Joe Mauer apologist would have to admit the former All-Star batting champ has almost zero value left when it comes to fantasy baseball as the former top-five catcher has been nothing but a low-end backup first baseman since moving out from behind the dish a number of years ago. Save for the king of all outlier campaigns back in 2009, Mauer has mostly been an empty batting average since as he annually struggled to reach double-digits in home runs and injuries began to crop up in earnest as well. 2018 was a new low for Mauer as he managed to hit just 6 home runs in 543 at-bats; while also recording poor RBI (48) and run (64) totals. While Mauer's .282 average remained solid as always, he will now be 36 in April which will only exacerbate the red flags in his declining offensive game.

Matt Davidson: Now two full years into his MLB career, Chicago White Sox first baseman Matt Davidson won't make the fantasy baseball establishment forget how good Paul Konerko once was for the team as he put forth another seriously flawed campaign that included a .228 average and just 20 home runs in 496 at-bats. The holes in Davidson's swing are of the gaping variety as shown by a sickening 33.3 K/9 a year ago and so batting over .230 will be a tremendous challenge given how often the guy strikes out. Despite the power being decent enough, Davidson is even a borderline option in AL-only leagues this season.

Ronald Guzman: The Texas Rangers continued unloading veterans both before and during the course of the 2018 season as a full rebuild got underway and that opened the door for the team's prospects to get an early look against major league opposition. This included slugging the first baseman Ronald Guzman who showed the power by swatting 16 home runs and collecting 58 RBI in 428 at-bats but also proved to be far from a finished product as he hit just .235 and posted a horrid 28.3 K/9. While Guzman has every right to improve as he gains more experience, he seems like another all-or-nothing home run hitter who is a dime a dozen in today's baseball.

Wilmer Flores: After cracking 18 home runs in just 362 at-bats while having eligibility all over the infield in 2017, the New York Mets' Wilmer Flores appeared to be on the verge of becoming a possible upper-level hitter going forward. Unfortunately, Flores never found any traction during the course of the 2018 season as he gave back numbers across the board despite having even more at-bats (429). Perhaps most disturbing was the paltry total of 11 home runs Flores hit and since he has never been a friend to the batting average category (the .271 from last season serving as a career-best), the drop in power made the guy tough to own even in NL-only formats. Making matters worse for Flores in terms of potential 2019 fantasy baseball value is the fact he now only carries eligibility at first base and even there he may not start to begin the year due to the fact the Mets plan to have Jay Bruce work primarily at the position. Given all of the question marks from above, Flores is best left to the waiver wire in all leagues to begin the season.

Mitch Moreland: They don't get much more boring than Boston Red Sox first baseman Mitch Moreland when it comes to yearly fantasy baseball and the veteran managed to hold onto this classification despite playing the last two years with the Boston Red Sox. Still with one more year left on his Red Sox deal, Moreland became just a part-time player for the team once Steve Pearce came over in a summer trade. With a just a career .241 mark versus lefties, Moreland could go right back to a platoon in 2019 if the Red Sox bring back Pearce in free agency or land someone else to compete with him. So with Moreland already not looking at a full allotment of at-bats, his mediocre 15-HR/.245 average from 2017 looks like around what we should expect going forward with regards to the numbers and that doesn't engender much in the way of possible fantasy baseball interest.

Steve Pearce: Serving as some sort of an AL East hired gun (having logged time with each of the five respective teams in the division), first baseman Steve Pearce showed he can still turn on a fastball last season as he batted .284 with 11 home runs in 251 at-bats split between the Toronto Blue Jays and Boston Red Sox. Turning 36 in April, Pearce is a more valuable real-life MLB player than a fantasy baseball one and so he should be avoided in almost all leagues.

Justin Bour: Generally a solid power-hitting first baseman who grabbed hold of some backup or NL-only value the last few years, first baseman Justin Bour took the wrong time to have a terrible season as he heads into free agency this winter. In a year split between the Miami Marlins and Philadelphia Phillies, Bour batted a career-worst .220 and only managed 20 home runs and 59 RBI in 501 at-bats. Still just 30-years-old, Bour's chronic struggles versus lefties (.219 career mark) severely limit any possible upside going into 2019 and so he is going to have a tough time finding a starting job on the market coming off such an ugly season. Even for the AL or NL-only crowd, Bour is looking as shaky a potential fantasy baseball option as ever.

Mark Reynolds: Ageless slugger Mark Reynolds is like the MLB version of "Where's Waldo?" in that you never know which team he will show up on each season and then immediately begin smashing home runs at his customary above-average pace. It is good work if you can find it as Reynolds has been that guy since coming into the league and his home run binges usually put him in the fantasy baseball conversation at least once or twice a season. In 2018 it was with the Washington Nationals where Reynolds cracked 13 home runs and drove in 40 in just 235 at-bats as the veteran's power showed no signs of eroding any time soon. Of course, Reynolds' 27.2 K/9 and .248 batting average also went along with career trends which speak to the overall limitations the guy brings to the fantasy baseball table. While it remains a fun story, Reynolds should be handled as just a mid-season add only when he gets hot with the power.

Lucas Duda: Turning 33 in February, free agent first baseman Lucas Duda is now becoming a journeyman right before our eyes. While Duda did some good things during his days with the New York Mets, he likely is going to have to settle for either a one-year deal or even a minor league invite to spring training as he comes off a 2018 season where he hit just .241, struck out at a 27.8 K/9 clip, and slugged 14 home runs in 367 at-bats. Given his long history of being completely useless versus lefties, Duda will also need to be in some sort of a platoon if he does stick in the majors in 2019. Even though he hit 30 home runs as recently as 2017, you want to try and do better for your backup first baseman even in AL or NL-only leagues.

Logan Morrison: Despite coming off a career-year in 2017 when he set personal bests in home runs (38), RBI (85), and runs (75); first baseman Logan Morrison found little interest in the free agent market due to the plethora of similarly-skilled sluggers who were also available. As a result,

Morrison was forced to settle for a one-year deal (with an option) worth $6.5 million from the Minnesota Twins. The Twins had to be thankful they didn't open the vault any more than they did for Morrison as the 31-year-old was downright brutal in batting just .186 with 15 home runs in 95 games for the team before he was forced to undergo season-ending hip surgery. Now it needs to be said that Morrison suffered from epic bad luck with the batted ball as shown by his .196 BABIP (..300 is average) but the guy still has hit under .250 each of the last three seasons while offering nothing but power to his fantasy baseball owners. Since 2017 is now looking like a gross outlier, Morrison should not be drafted this spring.

Hanley Ramirez: Despite having a past being a consensus number 1 overall pick in fantasy baseball leagues during his early Florida Marlin days as the team's five-tool superstar, the final chapters of Hanley Ramirez' career are already tough to watch. Even though the veteran roared out of the 2018 gates by hitting .330 with 3 home runs while mostly manning the DH spot for the Boston Red Sox in March/April, Ramirez went into a horrific slump in May that put the wheels in motion for the team to designate him for assignment at the end of the month. Making matters a bit more absurd, Ramirez then found himself connected to reports he was involved in an expansive drug ring that likely scared off any other team from picking him up even after eventually being cleared of the matter. Having turned 35 in December, Ramirez will need to likely settle for a minor league deal from an American League team to serve as a part-time DH and nothing more given the almost complete loss of athleticism here. While Ramirez' advanced metrics are still somewhat decent (7.2 BB/9, 17.9 K/9 last season), his days of being a fantasy baseball asset are finished for good.

Brad Miller: If you really are interested in possibly owning Brad Miller for 2019 fantasy baseball, you should probably just put this book down and go do something else. After engineering one of the biggest outlier campaigns we ever saw in 2016 when Miller cracked 30 home runs for the Tampa Bay Rays, the following two seasons were nothing short of a disaster as he batted .201 and .248 respectively with a total of 16 long balls during that span. With an insane 32.3 K/ rate last season showing little clue at the dish, you can make the case Miller is probably already shot as a major league hitter at the age of 29.

SECOND BASE

Draft Strategy: All of a sudden second base has exploded with top-tier offensive options as consensus top-five pick Jose Altuve is now joined by 2018 monsters Jose Ramirez, Ozzie Albies. Javier Baez, and to a lesser extent; Scooter Gennett and Whit Merrifield. Given the fact that tremendous depth has emerged here, using a pick in the top three rounds here is not exactly necessary. You can certainly do just fine with a Gennett or a Merrifield in the middle rounds while stocking up on the other positions with your prime selections.

Jose Altuve: While Los Angeles Angels outfielder Mike Trout once again was the consensus number 1 pick in most 2018 fantasy baseball leagues, there was a case to be made that Houston Astros second baseman Jose Altuve was worthy of such a distinction as well. After all, Altuve was coming off what could only be described as a statistical bonanza the previous season when he won his third career batting title with a .346 mark; while also adding 24 home runs, 112 runs scored, 81 RBI, and 32 steals. Also, while it seemed like Altuve has been around forever, he was actually just reaching his prime years in turning 28 that May. So with Altuve's blockbuster five-tool ability well-established, those who did tab him number 1 overall likely didn't hear much of an argument from their league. While Altuve was certainly fully deserving of not lasting past at worst the second pick in drafts last spring, the pint-sized dynamo actually had a bit of a tough time during the course of the 2018 season. The biggest issue was Altuve being placed on the DL for the first time in his career with an injured knee and his 599 at-bats represented his lowest total since breaking in as a rookie in 2011. Fewer at-bats meant fewer counting stats as Altuve came in at 13 home runs, 61 RBI, 84 runs scored, 17 steals, and a .315 average. All five of those categories were sizable declines from not only 2017 but 2016 as well and there are multiple talking points to look at here. The first is that Altuve's power decline is something to watch going forward as the 20-plus homers he hit in 2016-17 seemed a bit beyond what he was capable of given the advanced indicators. In addition, any slip in stolen bases (Altuve lost 15 from 2017 to last season) need to be looked at closely given the trend of players losing some speed as they approach 30. While Altuve will just be turning 29 in May, he has quite a bit of wear and tear on him already given the massive amount of plate appearances and games played he has undertaken since arriving with the Astros in 2011. Perhaps the least concerning from this peanut stand was the average dip as .317 is still an excellent number and both Altuve's walks (9.2 BB/9) and strikeouts (13.2 K/9) remained right with career levels. It very well could be the bum knee negatively impacted Altuve even when he did return from the DL last season and so a mini-mulligan could be given for his "disappointing numbers last season. When you break it all down, we still think Altuve is every bit at the top of his game and should not last past the top five picks in all 2019 drafts this spring.

2019 PROJECTION: .329 16 HR 84 RBI 115 R 28 SB

Javier Baez (SS, 3B): Since he was first promoted by the Chicago Cubs at a very young age, there were some stark growing pains that super utility infielder Javier Baez had to fight through before unleashing the massive potential that was talked about since he was selected 9th overall in the 2011 MLB Draft. Strikeouts and impatience were the major issues holding Baez back and were overshadowing what was a very potent power/speed game burgeoning under the surface. Fast forward to the 2018 season and Baez more than made the quantum leap to superstar status as he engineered a true five-category campaign in setting career-bests in all FIVE standard ROTO categories; highlighted by 34 home runs, 111 RBI, and 21 stolen bases. Just as potent were Baez' 101 runs scored and .290 batting average; in particular, the latter given some earlier troubles in that category due to the elevated K rate. Blessed with some of the most top-end natural ability of any player in baseball, Baez just like that becomes an early-round stud who at the age of 26 is just now entering into his prime. Now in terms of the advanced metrics, Baez remains underwhelming with the walks (4.5 BB/9) and strikeouts (25.9 K/9) but at least the latter has declined from 28.3 the year prior. Always producing BABIP's well into the lucky range given his speed, Baez should be able to ward off any major average hit even if the lack of walks and high K's remain. Qualifying also at shortstop and third base, Baez is shaping up as a terrific second-round pick in drafts this March.

2019 PROJECTION: .286 32 HR 105 RBI 103 R 20 SB

Ozzie Albies: Boy do the Atlanta Braves have some sick young hitting talent and that generation is highlighted by second baseman Ozzie Albies who began the 2018 season on an epic tear and finished right up among the top-tier of players at the position as we move towards spring training. While Albies was no secret in fantasy baseball drafts last spring given his very impressive minor league performances and future five-category potential, the multi-talented dynamo decided to speed up the statistical clock right from the jump in coming out in March/April by hitting 9 home runs and batting .293 as his owners were jumping for joy at their fortunate luck. While Albies obviously couldn't keep up that extreme level of hitting, he did successfully fight through some typical rookie ebbs and flows to indicate he is the rare prospect who could stay on top of what opposing pitchers were trying to exploit. In the end, Albies would finish with 24 home runs, 101 runs scored, 72 RBI, and 14 steals and he seems set to stay locked-in as the team's number 2 hitter until further notice. About the only knock we can put on Albies last season was a bit of an ugly .261 average but that had more to do with a lack of walks (5.3 BB/9) than strikeouts (solid 17.0 BB/9). The previous statement is an important one in that walks can be remedied much more easily than fixing strikeouts and so Albies still has a potential future as a .300 hitter based on what these rates are saying. Driving home this point even more was the fact Albies' .285 BABIP was in the unlucky zone and even more so for a guy with his type of above-average speed. So while we can easily put in ink another 25 homers and 15 steals, we may also soon be able to place useful averages in there as well beginning in 2019. Amazingly just 22 when the new seasons gets underway, Albies is every bit the stud we anticipated he would be.

2019 PROJECTION: .284 25 HR 77 RBI 110 R 16 SB

Whit Merrifield (OF): Qualifying under the premise of "his season turned out better than I thought it had been" was undoubtedly Kansas City Royals second baseman Whit Merrifield who has now put forth back-to-back years of top-notch production that gets somewhat overlooked given the small market/rebuilding team he plays for. After bursting onto the fantasy baseball scene the year prior when he hit 19 home runs, stole 34 bases, and batted .288; many in the community were curious to see if Merrifield was a one-year anomaly or in fact a second baseman they could depend on going forward. Count the latter being the case as Merrifield was terrific again in 2019 as he hit another 12 home runs, stole a very potent 45 bags, and batted .304. Add in 88 runs scored on a bad team and 60 RBI from the leadoff spot and Merrifield helped across all five categories. Now while some may get on him for losing 7 home runs last season despite receiving an additional 77 at-bats, we would point out Merrifield never profiled as a big power guy and in fact likely caught opposing pitchers off guard in 2017 given their unfamiliarity with his approach. So in our opinion, any home runs Merrifield contributes are a bonus and instead the focus should be on the 45 steals which is extremely valuable in today's game given the declining numbers in that category around the league. Merrifield certainly does the leadoff batter thing nicely as he doesn't strike out a ton (16.1 K/9) and draws enough walks to stay competitive there (8.6 BB/9) which will only help him churn out more .300 batting averages and 80-plus runs scored campaigns as well. While Merrifield will already be 30 by the time the 2019 season gets going given his late MLB start, we can cease worrying about any stolen base declines for another year or two and instead should embrace a guy who is the real deal in terms of being a very underrated fantasy baseball multi-category contributor.

2019 PROJECTION: .298 14 HR 65 RBI 90 R 37 SB

Gleyber Torres (SS): It was certainly worth the wait for the New York Yankees to finally unveil top infield prospect Gleyber Torres in 2018 after he missed almost the entire previous season due to Tommy John elbow surgery and based on what was a terrific rookie debut, top-tier status could very well be in the offing going forward. Already universally lauded as one of the best prospects in baseball before he was traded by the Chicago Cubs to New York in the Aroldis Chapman deal back in 2016, Torres's natural power and overall hitting skills seem to be a perfect fit for Yankee Stadium as the kid posted 24 homers, 77 RBI, and a .271 average in 484 at-bats last season. Even though there were some injuries (a lengthy summer DL stay due to a hip problem) and typical rookie slumps, Torres is only scratching the surface of what he is capable of accomplishing. Already drawing walks at an impressive level (8.7 BB/9), Torres just needs to cut down on the K's a bit (25.2 K/9) before we get the entirety of the vast potential. About the only negative is that Torres doesn't run much for a middle infielder (6 steals in 2018) but that is no reason to keep him out of the early round discussion for spring drafts.

2019 PROJECTION: .282 27 HR 86 RBI 70 R 8 SB

Dee Gordon: A longtime favorite in these pages despite the moronic PED bust a few years ago, things did not go swimmingly in Dee Gordon's first season with the Seattle Mariners in 2018. A fractured toe sent Gordon to the DL for a bit early on in the year and perhaps that issue dogged him the rest of the way as he wound up stealing just 30 bags in 588 at-bats. While 30 steals is phenomenal for 99 percent of the players in the game, it was about half of what was anticipated for Gordon whose annual fantasy baseball price is overly impacted by what he accomplishes in that category. In addition to the steals dip, Gordon hit .268 for the second time in three seasons and just 62 runs scored meant he was a letdown in the three areas where almost 100 percent of his value was tied into. That being said, we are willing to give Gordon a mulligan on his season since he is still extremely valuable as a major running weapon in today's stolen base-depressed era and for the fact he will be fronting another loaded Mariners lineup. While Gordon is inching up toward the Danger Zone for a speed-oriented player as he turns 31 in April, we gladly would dive right back in here in the early rounds of the draft once again.

2019 PROJECTION: .288 2 HR 34 RBI 95 R 48 SB

Scooter Gennett: Anyone who took a look at overall 2018 fantasy baseball drafts would have quickly realized there was very little respect coming Cincinnati Reds second baseman Scooter Gennett's way after what was an impressive career-year performance the season prior when he smacked 27 home runs, drove in 97, and batted .295. What likely stirred this trend was Gennett absolutely sailing past his previous norms in the power categories as he served mostly as a doubles hitter who could post decent averages but also not steal bases while working the middle infield. While Gennett still doesn't steal bases, his power game was in fine working order again in 2018 as he clubbed 23 home runs, drove in 92, and posted a .310 average in 638 at-bats. The numbers don't lie here and they read Gennett cementing himself as a mid-20's home run guy who also is capable of posting 80-plus marks in runs/RBI, and an average hovering around .300. That type of four category production works nicely on any fantasy baseball roster despite the small demerit of not contributing much in the way of steals from a position you like to get a decent total from. Still, only 28 as 2019 arrives, Gennett became a classic case of a hitter who put it all together when the prime years arrived. Stamp him as 100 percent legit folks and take advantage of any league that overlooks him again.

2019 PROJECTION: .304 25 HR 93 RBI 84 R 6 SB

Rougned Odor: Based on tools alone, few middle infielders can hold a candle to Texas Rangers second baseman Rougned Odor. Having posted HR/SB ratios of 30/15 and 18/12 the last two seasons, Odor has the look of a fantasy baseball monster lying just under the surface. That surface is filled with poor plate discipline and ugly batting averages that have seriously derailed the overall progress though. Despite Odor's K/9 rates not being obscene (23.7 last season), his tendency to swing at early pitches in the count have caused the average to come in over .270 just once in five MLB campaigns. Now some perspective is certainly needed here as Odor was no doubt rushed to the majors before he was ready (promoted at the age of 20 in 2014) and being forced to learn how to hit major league pitching on the fly is a big chore for any prospect. So it shouldn't be a total shock that Odor has posted some ugly averages and underwhelming advanced metrics since his debut and just only now is getting close to reaching his prime ages, a major explosion like we saw out of a similar case in Javier Baez last season could very well occur here. In fact, the parallels are very close between the two and Odor even has been the better player both in walks and strikeouts to this point. With an unfathomably poor .224 BABIP serving as the main impetus resulting in Odor's much-criticized .204 average in 2017 going down as an all-time fluke, it is time to fully jump back on the bandwagon here given the obvious skills in play. A 30/15/.270 season is just waiting to happen for Odor and those smart enough to realize it will benefit the most this season.

2019 PROJECTION: .267 27 79 RBI 84 R 14 SB

Brian Dozier: Former All-Star second baseman Brian Dozier chose a bad time to have a horrific season as he heads into free agency off a truly terrible

2018 that saw him bat .215 and post 21 home runs in 632 at-bats. While no stranger to ugly batting averages, it seemed like Dozier's days of being a sub-.250 guy was a thing of the past after posting marks of .268 and .271 from 2016-17. Unfortunately, Dozier was one big mess at the dish throughout last season and getting traded by the Minnesota Twins to the Los Angeles Dodgers failed to spark him much. With that said, Dozier was actually not as bad a hitter as the surface numbers may indicate as a trip into the advanced metric world would indicate. Primarily speaking, Dozier's .240 BABIP was comically unlucky and when you also see that his walks (11.4 BB/9) and strikeout (20.4 K/9) rates were excellent, it stands to reason he should have actually been more of a .270 guy if the batted ball number was more neutral. That is a good sign moving forward for Dozier on the average front and the fact he still is running a bit (12 steals) is another feather in his 2019 statistical cap. While Dozier's overall outlook will be impacted some by wherever he winds up in free agency, we think there is a decent buy-low opportunity here for a guy who was dreadfully unlucky last season.

2019 PROJECTION: .259 26 HR 93 RBI 97 R 11 SB

Daniel Murphy: Already facing an initial stint on the DL to begin the 2018 season as he recovered from very scary micro fracture knee surgery, aging second baseman Daniel Murphy was stamped firmly on our "DO NOT DRAFT" list in these pages last spring. As it turned out, Murphy didn't return to the Washington Nationals until mid-June and it wasn't until the second half of the season where the All-Star finally began to show the smooth-hitting skills that made him a mid-career renaissance story. Having been traded to the Cubs once the Nats waved the white flag in August, Murphy finished with another solid average (.299) and still managed 12 home runs in 351 at-bats after working off the rust coming back from the surgery. As he heads into free agency in his age-34 season, there are valid questions about whether Murphy is now into the decline phase of his career. What we can say is that perennial .300 hitters like Murphy tend to hold onto this skill as they begin to age and so we have no qualms saying the guy should post another good number there in 2019. Also, with walk and strikeout rate that remain right along career norms, Murphy is not really showing outward signs of dropping off as a hitter. The real question mark centers on health and this is where things may get dicey as Murphy has long had knee trouble which took a rougher turn when he had the micro fracture surgery. It is imperative that the threat of more health trouble is factored into whatever draft price Murphy comes attached with this spring but on the flip side, an expected drop in ADP also makes him somewhat of a bargain as well. As long as you can get Murphy in the middle rounds and not any earlier, we are willing to sign off on one more season of usage.

2019 PROJECTION: .294 20 HR 88 RBI 89 R 2 SB

Robinson Cano: Clearly not learning from the stupidity of Seattle Mariners teammate Dee Gordon getting suspended 80 games for PED's a few years prior, the team's veteran perennial All-Star first baseman/second baseman Robinson Cano unbelievably got pinched himself for testing positive for a banned substance that resulted in him being sat down for the same amount of time. What became really crazy about the whole situation was that usually those who get busted for PED's are younger players who are looking for an edge to keep them in the game and not someone who already became well-established as one of the best hitters among his generation like Cano. Be that as it may, a firm stain has been attached to Cano's resume and the PED bust also clouds his fantasy baseball outlook to a large degree going into 2019. Now in terms of the numbers, Cano still hit quite well last season in batting .303 with 10 home runs in 348 at-bats but the fact he turned 36 this past October means a decline is imminent. With Cano also conceivably off the juice this season, 20 home runs are no longer the lock it always had previously been. So while the advanced metrics in 2018 don't show much deviation for Cano compared to previous norms, we suggest moving on for good here given the age and all that has recently transpired.
2019 PROJECTION: .294 22 HR 90 RBI 75 R 1 SB

Cesar Hernandez: Earning a designation as a quality but underrated fantasy baseball second baseman the last couple of seasons has been the Philadelphia Phillies' Cesar Hernandez and 2018 was no different as the leadoff man hit 15 homers, stole 19 bags, and scored 91 runs. The 15 homers represented a career-high and at the age of 28, Hernandez likely has grown into some more power as he reached his prime years. The uptick in power went nicely with the stolen bases as Hernandez has swiped 15 or more bags for five years running and he shows no signs of slowing down there just yet. While his average did decline to a shaky .253, that was mainly due to Hernandez' BABIP dropping sharply compared to established career norms. So in essence what we have here is a four-category producer who is flat in his prime years and carries a very affordable draft price tag. Sounds to us like a bargain worth investing in this season
2019 PROJECTION: .290 11 HR 55 RBI 89 R 17 SB

Joey Wendle (3B): The always impressive Tampa Bay Rays prospect pipeline continued unabated in 2018 as the team unleashed second baseman/third baseman Joey Wendle on the majors to predictable acclaim. Garnering a high amount of Rookie of the Year attention, Wendle hinted at five-tool potential as he hit 7 home runs, stole 16 bases, and batted .300 in 545 at-bats. A late-blooming prospect (already turning 29 in April) who took some time getting his game in gear, Wendle's impressive 17.6 K/9 rate last season shows a guy who knows how to handle the bat and so more .300 averages are likely to be on the way. Also possessing the speed to help in the steals category, about the only remaining unknown is how much power Wendle will hit for. So far we have not seen much of an uptick there in terms of Wendle's minor and major league indicators and so it probably is a good idea not to project a big increase there for 2019. Even if the power stays below-average, Wendle offers enough in the other four categories to be a nice mid-round pick.

2019 PROJECTION: .296 10 HR 75 RBI 78 R 19 SB

Jeff McNeil: When the New York Mets let longtime second baseman Daniel Murphy depart in free agency for nothing in return a few years back, they were deservedly destroyed when the guy went out and put forth nothing but blockbuster numbers for two-plus seasons with the rival Washington Nationals. Luckily for the Mets, they may get a do-over at the position as their second base prospect Jeff McNeil looks like a Murphy clone with his high-contact hitting approach that suggests he could be a major upside play moving forward. While it was only a 63 game sample size, McNeil wowed both the Mets and those who took a stab in fantasy baseball as the 26-year-old batted .329 with 3 home runs and 7 steals in 248 at-bats. Already running better than Murphy ever did in terms of steals, McNeil has the extreme contact rate (posting a ridiculously good 9.7 K/9 rate last season) down pat which allowed for such a high average. Having also hit 19 long balls combined at Double-A and Triple-A prior to his promotion indicates McNeil could be a 20-25 home run guy as soon as this season. Still off the fantasy baseball radar given the late summer debut when many already threw in the towel on their teams, McNeil is a major sleeper who should be targeted heavily in the middle rounds of drafts.

2019 PROJECTION: .315 16 HR 65 RBI 75 R 11 SB

D.J. LeMahieu: Carrying the tag of being a Colorado Rockies hitter always counts for a little extra something when evaluating a fantasy baseball hitter but that designation still doesn't move the interest meter much when it comes to second baseman D.J. LeMahieu. While a solid and effective player, LeMahieu has settled into being mostly a low-end starter/top-end backup at the position who in a given season helps in just 2-3 categories. In 2018 that was just homers as LeMahieu hit a career-high 15 and runs scored as the leadoff man crossed home plate on 90 occasions. The rest of the statistical package was lacking as LeMahieu stole just 6 bags, batted .276, and drove in only 62 batters which reinforces his moderate standing for 2019 fantasy baseball. Now that he is turning 31 in July, LeMahieu's days of running look to be almost finished as he went from 23 steals in 2015 down to just the

6 a year ago. Also, LeMahieu has only reached double-digits in home runs twice in his 8-year MLB career despite the advantages of Coors Field. While we do see a batting average revival this season after LeMahieu's BABIP dropped over 50 points from his previous norms, the entirety of his offensive output remains lacking. Add in the fact the Rockies declined a qualifying offer for LeMahieu last October which ensures his departure and the outlook is as murky as ever.

PROJECTION: .297 12 HR 63 RBI 92 R 5 SB

Josh Harrison: Now down to just second base eligibility after years of carrying up to three positions, veteran Josh Harrison loses a major chunk of his previously moderate fantasy baseball value as 2019 quickly approaches. While Harrison has had some quality seasons in the past, he comes off a rough 2018 campaign that saw him spend a chunk of the year on the DL with a fractured hand and hit a mediocre .250 with 8 home runs and 3 steals in 374 at-bats. What does need to be said is that without the vast amount of games missed due to the broken hand, Harrison likely would have been around the 16/12 split he put forth in homers/steals the year prior and that is where he should be graded for at least one more season as he is aging just a bit at 31. Also, Harrison's .286 BABIP was down by around 40 points from previous norms which means an average uptick is likely as well. Even though Harrison is not the worst way to spend one of your last draft picks, his somewhat boring numbers and loss of third base and outfield eligibility for 2019 doesn't make him overly attractive either.

2019 PROJECTION: .270 14 HR 53 RBI 67 R 11 SB

Jonathan Schoop: Already with a reputation for posting numbers which are all over the statistical map, Milwaukee Brewers second baseman Jonathan Schoop burned most of his fantasy baseball owners a year ago in enduring an almost season-long batting slump that severely eroded his offensive output. This just one year removed from Schoop cracking 32 home runs, driving in 105 batters, and hitting .293 for the Baltimore Orioles which suggested he was one of the next wave of high-end fantasy baseball middle infielders. While we knocked Schoop for his utter lack of stolen base ability, we were also fine owning him as long as the homers kept flying out and the average remained respectable. Well, none of the above happened a year ago as Schoop saw his homer total dip to 21, the RBI's slide to 61, and the average sink into the gutter at .233. The Orioles showed just how much they thought of Schoop as well by dealing him to the Brewers over the summer despite the fact he was only 25. Granted a fresh start with the Brewers for 2019, Schoop stands a decent chance of at least bringing his power numbers up a bit this season now that he remains in one of the best home run parks in the majors but the average is certainly up for debate due to some approach struggles that need refining. For one thing, Schoop's utter lack of patience (3.8 BB/9) is a major problem for the average prospects and that makes a somewhat high 23.0 K/9 stand out even more. Yes an unlucky .261 BABIP helped drive down the average a bit but Schoop is now looking like he can go over .260 with his current advanced metrics. Since Schoop won't be doing any running, this makes him very dependent on home runs, RBI, and runs which increases the bust risk yet again this season. Since we always suggest getting a decent amount of steals from your middle infielders, Schoop has too many inherent flaws right now to really justify a draft selection.

2019 PROJECTION: .257 25 HR 84 RBI 86 R 1 SB

Jonathan Villar (OF): After we correctly predicted that second baseman/outfielder Jonathan Villar would completely bomb out in 2017 coming off a tremendous outlier season the year prior, this peanut stand pivoted the other way last spring when the guy's draft cost sank into the gutter. This is where one of the tenets of winning fantasy baseball reveals itself as every player has value based on their draft cost given the possible upside payoffs and that is where Villar gained intrigue last season. While the guy was never the .285 hitter his fluky average showed in 2016, the solid power/speed/runs scored skills were very much stable. So while Villar was traded from the Milwaukee Brewers to the Baltimore Orioles in a clear dump last summer, the guy produced nicely as he hit 14 home runs, stole 35 bags, and batted .260. A 26.8 K/9 rate indicates Villar will never make inroads with his strikeout-heavy approach but again the power/speed game remains quite valuable. Also possessing eligibility both at second base and the outfield, Villar can be a terrific late-round pick that is capable of filling in nicely at either spot when needed.

2019 PROJECTION: .260 16 HR 59 RBI 74 R 28 SB

Jed Lowrie: Despite being clearly on the back nine of his career, second baseman Jed Lowrie became the rare player to engineer a career-year at the age of 35 in 2018 when he set personal bests in home runs (23), RBI (99) and runs scored (78); while also posting an adequate .267 average. Having fought injuries throughout his career, Lowrie remains a capable fantasy baseball second baseman who has much more value in deeper mixed or AL/NL-only formats. Earning a career red flag as a middle infielder who doesn't steal bases (0 swiped bags last season), Lowrie is unlikely to match his 2018 numbers given his checkered health history and advancing age.

2019 PROJECTION: .263 17 HR 74 RBI 73 R 0 SB

Daniel Robertson (SS): On a Tampa Bay Rays team that historically have quickly pushed their prospects toward claiming everyday major league jobs, utility infielder Daniel Robertson acquitted himself nicely in 2018. The

2012 first-round pick was clearly not ready to stick in the majors in 2017 when he batted just .206 in 254 at-bats but he improved his average to a solid .262 last season with 9 home runs in 88 games while playing all over the field. Unfortunately, Robertson suffered a thumb injury while sliding into a base at the start of August and season-ending surgery was needed. As far as the offensive output is concerned, Robertson has 20-homer potential and he draws walks (12.6 BB/9) which should help him post a decent average. Keep in mind though there is also almost no speed here which is a clear negative when talking about a potential middle infield fit. Add in eligibility at second, third, and shortstop however and Robertson has a certain value as a prime backup with remaining upside in mixed fantasy baseball leagues.

2019 PROJECTION: .278 17 HR 59 RBI 67 R 4 SB

Yoan Moncada: Another frustrating case of a player who is blessed with otherworldly natural speed and strength but can't get their careers going due to lacking in the art of pure hitting would be Chicago White Sox second baseman Yoan Moncada. The prize return when the White Sox traded ace pitcher Chris Sale to the Boston Red Sox, Moncada's much-discussed power and speed brought forth visions of him quickly becoming a five-tool monster. Alas, you need to be able to hit to unleash those skills and Moncada has really been lacking on that front as he has now batted just .231 and .235 his first two years in the majors. The biggest problem has been Moncada's brutal strikeout rate as he posted K/9's of 32.0 and 33.4 during that same span and those utterly ridiculous numbers are a tremendous red flag for his prospective 2019 fantasy baseball value. If you squinted close enough you could see 17 homers and 12 steals and envision more where that came from but until Moncada gets some sort of control of the strikeouts, he can be nothing but a late-round upside pick at his current level of production.

2019 PROJECTION: .243 19 HR 65 RBI 79 R 15 SB

Starlin Castro: Once the New York Yankees traded him to the Miami Marlins in the Giancarlo Stanton deal last winter, second baseman Starlin Castro lost about 25 percent of his prospective fantasy baseball value due to the massive downgrade in ballpark and lineup protection. This was not an insignificant development by any means as Castro had performed well with the Yankees and became a useful fantasy baseball option at the position during his tenure there. So it went however as Castro still did his best to have a nice year (.278, 12 homers, 6 steals) but he was more or less just a backup player in most mixed leagues. Still, with one more year (and an option) left on his deal with the Marlins, Castro is headed for a repeat of his 2018 numbers unless he mercifully gets dealt out of town. If that were to

happen, bump Castro up your rankings a bit as he will still be just 29 to begin the 2019 season and his overall offensive game remains quite solid.
2019 PROJECTION: .279 14 HR 55 RBI 79 R 5 SB

Ketel Marte (SS): At one time an intriguing speed-oriented prospect while coming up the Seattle Mariners system, it took second baseman Ketel Marte getting traded to the Arizona Diamondbacks to finally get an extended chance to show his ability. On that front, it was a mixed bag as Marte did impress by hitting 14 home runs and stealing 6 bags in 580 at-bats last season. The downside was just a .260 average which became the second year in a row Marte posted that exact mark. Some perspective is needed on the latter though as Marte's advanced metrics point to someone who should have finished with a much higher number in that category. For one thing, Marte's contact rate was excellent (13.6 K/9) and he drew walks at an impressive clip as well (9.3 BB/9). In most cases, positives in both of these categories usually mean an average north of .275 but an unlucky .282 BABIP last season helped destroy that trend for Marte. So instead you should focus on the decent power/speed game, the still youthful age as he turned just 25 last October, and the expected average uptick to convince yourself to buy low on this solid talent.
2019 PROJECTION: .273 15 HR 65 RBI 75 R 8 SB

Dustin Pedroia: The ravages of playing the physically demanding second base position continued to take a major toll on Boston Red Sox former MVP Dustin Pedroia in 2018 as he began the season on the DL while recovering from knee surgery the previous October. Pedroia's return in late May lasted all of three games (with one hit in 11 at-bats) before a new bout of knee soreness sent him right back to the DL for what would turn out to be the remainder of the season. Just to show you how serious the knee situation is, Pedroia required yet another cleanup procedure in July which proved to be too much for him to come back from. Now having turned 35 this past August, Pedroia looks completely shot in terms of being a contributing major league player and even before the knee trouble, his speed and power both had left the statistical station (just 7 homers and 4 steals in 463 at-bats in 2017). This is another classic case of a big-time "name" player who simply doesn't have it anymore and who should be completely ignored in spring drafts.
2019 PROJECTION: .280 5 HR 45 RBI 59 R 2 SB

Ian Kinsler: The end is drawing near for former All-Star second baseman Ian Kinsler as one of this generation's greats goes into free agency this winter off a bit of a tough 2018 campaign that saw him bat just .240 but also post a tidy 14/16 mark in homers/steals. Turning 37 this July, Kinsler is clearly playing on one of the last holes on the back-nine of his career but the fact he was able to still hit 14 homers and steal 16 bases at least shows the guy has kept himself in good enough shape to contribute some useful numbers. Still, Kinsler has hit just .236 and .240 the last two seasons and he is likely going to have to settle for a one-year deal somewhere with no guarantee of a long leash. What needs to be noted though is that Kinsler's advanced metrics in contact rate (12.0 K/9) and walks (7.5 BB/9) remained very impressive. Also a brutally unlucky .250 BABIP did its part of help drag the average down as well. So for those who take part in deeper mixed leagues, don't automatically toss Kinsler out of consideration as a backup second baseman.

2019 PROJECTION: .257 12 HR 50 RBI 63 R 14 SB

Asdrubal Cabrera: While everyone in the fantasy baseball community wants to write him off every season, veteran infielder Asdrubal Cabrera continues to produce on a yearly basis. Still holding eligibility at second, third, and shortstop; Cabrera goes into free agency at the age of 33 still holding onto some of his offensive skills. Primarily this would be power as Cabrera matched a previous career-high of 23 home runs last season and the accrued 75 RBI were his most since 2011. The downside is that Cabrera is getting more strikeout-prone than ever before (20.1 K/9) and the walks plummeted as well in 2018 (6.9 BB/9) as opposing pitchers took more liberties with his swing. With the steals having left the station years ago, Cabrera is strictly just a home run and RBI guy now who has the added bonus of multi-position eligibility.

2019 PROJECTION: .266 20 HR 73 RBI 65 R 1 SB

THE REST

Howie Kendrick: Now into the twilight of his career at the age of 35 and coming off a 2018 season that ended in late May as a result of a ruptured Achilles tendon, veteran Washington Nationals second baseman Howie Kendrick will likely serve as a utility man for the team during the last year of his contract. Prior to snapping the Achilles, Kendrick showed he could still handle the bat as he hit .303 with 4 home runs in 160 at-bats but it is tough to see the guy being fantasy baseball relevant in 2019 given his current status on the Nats. Still chasing the batting title that many said was part of his destiny, Kendrick is a much better real-life player than a fantasy baseball one at this stage of the game.

Luis Urias: The San Diego Padres took a look at second base prospect Luis Urias late in 2018 in order to see if he could be a possible option for them at the position going into next year but it was tough to get an idea of whether this was feasible since the kid only got into 12 games before suffering a season-ending hamstring injury. Prior to the promotion, Urias batted a solid .296 with 8 home runs and 2 steals in 533 at-bats at Triple-A but he really profiles as a guy who has a good eye (12.6 BB/9) that will enable a .300 batting average with little in the way of power or speed. That won't move the needle much in the fantasy baseball world and so Urias is really just for the NL-only crowd.

Cory Spangenberg (3B): It was another season where San Diego Padres second baseman Cory Spangenberg showed the ability to both hit home runs and steal bases (posting a 7/6 split in just 329 at-bats) but the .235 average continued an overall trend of too little in the way of pure hitting. Having been given a slew of previous chances to finally take hold of a starting spot and ultimately, failing to do so at every turn, Spangenberg looks like an old news story to us.

Alen Hanson: Having now put forth two partial seasons in the major leagues where he posted home run/stole base ratios of 4/11 and 8/7 respectively, it may be time to give a longer leash for San Francisco Giants second baseman Alen Hanson. While he is already 26, Hanson's ability to hit for some power and run a bit always will be something that catches the attention of the fantasy baseball community and so his spring status should be looked at in terms of potential playing time for the start of the 2019 season. While Hanson has shown almost no patience so far (just a comical 2.9 BB/9 last season), there are tools here which could serve as a help down the road.

Hernan Perez (SS, 3B, OF): Milwaukee Brewers jack-of-all-trades veteran hitter Hernan Perez has solidified himself as a multi-positional bench asset in mixed fantasy baseball leagues over the last few seasons given the value of having someone who can literally qualify all over the diamond (2B, SS, 3B, OF) to put into your lineup in a pinch on light schedule days or when injuries strike down a starting option. It also helps that Perez can put up some useful numbers as well since he hit 9 home runs, stole 11 bases, and batted .253 in 2018. In the end though, you are only looking at a very late round pick in deeper mixed leagues or even a waiver wire guy who gets picked up and dropped multiple times throughout the season.

Nico Goodrum: Longtime minor league second baseman Nico Goodrum finally got his big break in 2018 when the rebuilding Detroit Tigers gave the former 2010 second-round pick 292 at-bats to show what he could do. While Goodrum's reputation from the minors of being a batting average drain continued at the major league level (.245), he did show some interesting power/speed ability by smacking 16 home runs and stealing 12 bases. Already entering into his age-27 season in 2019, Goodrum has little margin for error in terms of sticking with the Tigers and so some work needs to be done on his 26.8 K/9 rate so the average has a chance of somewhat improving. On the strength of his power/speed ability, Goodrum remains on the AL-only radar.

Jason Kipnis: If he weren't still under contract with the team at least through the 2019 season, it is likely the Cleveland Indians would be done with fading second baseman Jason Kipnis. While he is still just going to be 32 this April, Kipnis has looked shot the last two seasons in batting .232 and .230 respectively; while also dealing with constant injuries. Once Kipnis lost his speed after stealing as many as 31 bases back in 2012, his fantasy baseball value dropped precipitously and after just 18 homers and 7 steals in a massive 601 at-bats in 2018, there is very little reason to go back to the well here anymore.

Eduardo Nunez (3B): Likely to have his 2019 option picked up by the Boston Red Sox given his usefulness as a backup infielder on the team the previous year, Eduardo Nunez will then likely have a tough time gaining much of a fantasy baseball impact under such a scenario. Having turned himself into a very solid player from 2016-17 as he hit for average, popped a few homers, and stole a bunch of bases; Nunez' upside is not great as a semi-regular with the Red Sox as shown by him hitting just 10 home runs, stealing 7 bases, and batting .265 in 502 at-bats last season. Turning 32 in June, Nunez needs more consistent at-bats for us to take a closer look here again and so you really just need to keep tabs on the guy if injuries should, in fact, open up a more regular gig.

Brock Holt (SS): Solid Boston Red Sox utility man Brock Holt goes into the 2019 fantasy baseball season losing quite a bit of luster given the loss of both outfield and third base eligibility, which is no small thing since a major dose of his value comes from being able to qualify all over the diamond. This is because Holt is not an impact offensive player (.277, 7 home runs, 7 steals in 2018) and so he should be left to the waiver wire where you can feel free to add him again later on if the eligibility improves.

Joe Panik: When you are primarily known in the fantasy baseball world for being a batting average asset and then go out and hit .254 in 2018, the discussion ends in terms of any possible usage going forward. With Panik still having never hit more than 10 home runs or stolen above 5 bases in a given season, there is not much to talk about here as the guy should rot on the waiver wire in almost all leagues.

Devon Travis: Ill health and Toronto Blue Jays second baseman Devon Travis go hand-in-hand and last season it was a bum knee that kept him to just 378 ineffective (.232, 11 home runs, 3 steals) at-bats. It is now getting well past the time where Travis looked like a future asset at the position for the fantasy baseball community and things don't ever seem like they will change for the better. Avoid.

Kolten Wong: We are now well past the time where St. Louis Cardinals second baseman Kolten Wong held even moderate fantasy baseball value and that won't change after the 28-year-old hit just .249 with 9 home runs and 6 steals in 407 at-bats last season. What is frustrating here is that Wong has terrific contact skills (14.7 K/9) and the speed to be a weapon on the bases but for one reason or another it simply has not happened for the guy. At some point, you always got to cease waiting for a prospect to finally figure things out and this is where Wong currently resides in fantasy baseball terms.

Wilmer Difo (SS): Possessing at least some mildly intriguing power/speed ability, Washington Nationals infielder Wilmer Difo failed to impress when given the chance to play down the stretch last season once the team decided to surrender their quest for a playoff spot. While a 7/10 split in homers/steals became semi-useful, Difo's .230 average showed the limitations here. As a result, it is unlikely the Nats will give Difo a starting spot to open the 2019 season which means he should be ignored in drafts.

Ben Zobrist (OF): Sometimes you get some out-of-the-blue category upticks from aging veteran players given their experience and ability to change some things on the fly as opposed to a prospect and this was seen with Chicago Cubs infielder/outfielder Ben Zobrist batting .305 last season. While it was a completely empty number (9 home runs, 3 steals, 58 RBI), the average at least made Zobrist somewhat serviceable when it came to fantasy baseball after looking like he was done on that front the year prior. Turning an ancient 38 in May, Zobrist is still squarely a better real-life player than a fantasy baseball one.

Christian Arroyo: Tampa Bay Rays second base prospect Christian Arroyo remains on the train between the minors and the major leagues as his offensive game is still not to the point of being worthy of an everyday player at the highest level just yet. While he received 20 games with the Rays last season, Arroyo batted just .264 with a single home run and zero steals in 59 at-bats. While Arroyo has a patient approach at the dish (10.2 BB/9), he is also a bit strikeout-prone (27.1 K/9) which speaks to the limitations here so far. With a glove that is already terrific, Arroyo only has to make some more gains with the bat to finally carve out a firm spot on the Rays in 2019. Until we see this take place, Arroyo should be avoided.

SHORTSTOPS

Draft Strategy: Like with second base, the shortstop position has seen a major infusion of young and very potent talent the last two-plus seasons and that starts with first-round stars Manny Machado and Francisco Lindor. Don't hesitate to draft either one in the middle of Round 1 and then pivot to 1B and your first outfielder by the end of Round 3.

Francisco Lindor: Well I guess the power is legit. When Cleveland Indians shortstop Francisco Lindor went out in 2017 and smashed 33 home runs (which was a massive increase of 18 from the previous year), the skepticism ran high regarding whether or not the All-Star could keep up that kind of power level. Lindor would have none of this talk however as he went out last season and not only further IMPROVED his home run total by hitting 38 but put forth a blockbuster campaign that had him square in the MVP running. In addition to the now solidified monster power, Lindor drove in 92, scored 129 runs, stole 25 bases, and batted .277. All but the average joined Lindor's 38 homers as career-highs and at the age of only 25, he is absolutely a locked-in top-five fantasy baseball pick for 2019 drafts. In digging into the numbers a bit more, Lindor did, in fact, change his swing angle prior to 2017 which likely accounted for the power uptick (dropping his groundball rate by around 10.0 and increasing the fly ball mark by the same number). Since Lindor has hit over 30 home runs two years running with this approach, we can fully buy into its legitimacy. The flip side of Lindor hitting more fly balls is that the once .300 average has dropped to the .275 range but that is the price of doing home run business. Still, with remaining excellent walk (9.4 BB/9) and strikeout (14.4 K/9) rates, it is very possible Lindor can still go back to being a .300 hitter with his current fly ball tendencies given the previous two metrics going well into the positive range. Finally., Lindor's uptick in steals from 15 in 2017 to last season's 25 is big since it shows he is still interested in running despite his new status as a prime power hitter. So in the end what we have here is one of the brightest offensive stars in fantasy baseball and Lindor should be treated as such by going as high as the third pick overall behind Mike Trout and Mookie Betts this spring.
2019 PROJECTION: .284 34 HR 95 RBI 119 R 20 SB

Manny Machado: By the time you read this, free agent shortstop Manny Machado may be a very rich man as he heads into the open market at the height of his talent and also entering into just his age-27 season when the prime years typically begin. The former third overall pick in the 2013 MLB Draft certainly deserves whatever riches come his way as Machado is widely considered one of the best offensive players in the game on the strength of true five-ability. Machado had all those skills working in 2018 as he clubbed 37 long balls, drove in 107 batters, scored 84 runs, stole 14 bags, and batted .297 as prospective teams began salivating thinking about what it would be like to have him on their roster. Earlier comparisons of a young Miguel Cabrera with better speed certainly are applicable here given the fact Machado's walk (9.9 BB/9) and strikeout (14.7 K/9) rates are tremendous as well. As an added bonus, Machado's 14 steals were his most since going for 20 back in 2015 and so that is another statistical feather in his cap. Since Machado is actually just now arriving at his prime, there is no doubt he will be right there or even perhaps slightly better his 2018 numbers if it can be believed. This secures Machado's mid-first round fantasy baseball grade for at least the next few seasons and at the same time, make him a truly fantastic investment even at such a lofty price tag.

2019 PROJECTION: .298 35 HR 104 RBI 95 R 10 SB

Trevor Story: Boy was this some page-turning Story. Pardon the pun here but it was a beyond ridiculous 2018 season for Colorado Rockies shortstop Trevor Story as he ironed out some previous struggles and in the process become a monster five-tool player who likely tipped the scales in many leagues. For the price of what was only on average a mid-round pick, Story proceeded to post career-bests in ALL FIVE standard ROTO mixed league categories and those insane numbers read as follows: 37 home runs, 108 RBI, 88 R, 27 SB, and a .291 average. Yes, this was the same Trevor Story who crashed and burned just the year prior when he batted .239 with 24 home runs and struck out at a very disturbing 34.4 K/9 rate; while also serving as a human stop sigh on the bases as well with just 7 steals in 555 at-bats. That rough performance is ultimately what made Story's 2018 go beyond comprehension but he also certainly looked another classic case of a talented hitter who successfully smoothed out his game to unleash the entire potential. In cases such as this, a trip into the advanced metrics world is needed to determine the legitimacy of the numbers and even on this front, there is optimism. The biggest issue was Story's strikeouts as he successfully carved into his previously nasty rates in that category to lower the K/9 to a much more acceptable 25.6 last season. In addition, Story decreased his fly ball rate a bit (47.9 in 2017, 43.1 in 2018), which in turn, increased the line drive tally (18.4 to 22.7 respectively). Fewer fly balls and more line drives mean more hits falling in and when combined with fewer empty plate appearances ending in strikeouts, serve as nice batting average boost. Now a very lucky .345 BABIP certainly helped on the average front but keep in mind Story's worst previous number in that category had been a similarly lucky .332 which means he is one of those guys with good speed who can beat the curve there a bit. Now in terms of the stolen bases, Story has good speed as we already noted and the fact he was likely feeling so much better about himself as a player with his tremendous work with the bat likely gave him the confidence to run more freely. Counting on another 27 steals may be pushing it for 2019 but 20 seems very possible. So when you look at the total package here, Story just has to keep working on the strikeouts for him to be able to be in the same statistical neighborhood for 2019 and at that level, he makes the late first-round/early second-round grade.

2019 PROJECTION: .286 35 HR 110 RBI 89 R 19 SB

Trea Turner: The hype machine went into overdrive when it came to the 2018 fantasy baseball draft prospects of Washington Nationals shortstop Trea Turner as the five-tool dynamo evoked visions of a 20-HR/60-steal/.300 season that resulted in him being picked on average in the middle of the first round in spring drafts. We see so often though that drafting a player so high based a great deal on potential have a way of not working out and we got some of that from Turner last season on a few fronts. While 19 home runs and 103 runs scored were nice on paper, the fact he only added 8 more long balls (compared to the 11 he hit the previous year) in an extra 293 at-bats was in actuality a disappointment. Also, while Turner's 43 steals were a tremendous number, they came in around 17 short from what was predicted given the insane amount of speed the guy has. Finally, Turner batted just .271 and this followed another so-so .284 mark the season before which fell quite a bit short of the predicted .300. So, in essence, Turner did not yield first-round numbers last season but the allure of the remaining massive stolen base potential and overall five-tool ability could have him once again going in the first round of 2019 drafts. Again, we are as big a fan of Turner's potential as anyone else out there but a first round pick seems a bit rich in our view. If Turner maintains his current pace of numbers, he will still be a supreme player in 2019 fantasy baseball but even more so if priced properly this spring.

2019 PROJECTION: .295 20 HR 75 RBI 107 R 45 SB

Carlos Correa: Amazingly having turned just 24 this past September, Houston Astros shortstop Carlos Correa's status as a top-tier fantasy baseball talent is completely secure despite a somewhat difficult 2018 campaign caused mainly due to a lengthy DL stint for a back problem. Missing a month-and-a-half during the summer as a result of the injury wound up causing Correa's offensive numbers to plummet since his reduced 468 at-bats came out to just 15 home runs, 65 RBI, and a very ugly .239 average. Before going into why we remain so high on Correa off such a rough year, let's get the remaining negatives out of the way first. One such issue concerns Correa completely applying the brakes on the running game as he has now stolen a total of just 5 bases in the last two seasons combined. It is strange that Correa has already kicked this part of his game to the curb given his youth but perhaps injuries have caused him to re-think the risk the whole exercise brings. Beyond the decline in steals, Correa's power has been of the good-but-not-great variety as he has yet to hit more than 24 home runs in four MLB seasons. So while we again can go back to the youth as a reason why Correa may not have grown into his power peak just yet, it should be noted he is not in the class of Manny Machado, Francisco Lindor, or Trevor Story on this front. With all that said, Correa's present and future remain very bright as he operates toward the top of the very potent Astros order and it was only in 2017 where he batted .315 with 24 home runs and 84 RBI for the team. As far as the average dip a year ago, Correa dealt with an unlucky .282 BABIP that was way down from .328 and .352 tallies from 2016-17 and so a rebound there seems likely. So once you take into account the remaining upside and the likelihood Correa will have better health/batted ball luck this season, a strong case can be made of him being a decent second-round pick this spring in your draft.

2019 PROJECTION: .288 27 HR 88 RBI 89 R 4 SB

Corey Seager: For the second season in a row, former fantasy baseball first-round pick Corey Seager of the Los Angeles Dodgers dealt with injuries but unlike the year prior, the severity was much worse in 2017 as a torn UCL which led to Tommy John surgery in his elbow ended things for the 24-year-old shortstop after just 26 games. Making matters even more disturbing on the health front was the revelation that Seager was also forced to undergo arthroscopic surgery on his hip last August as well. Despite the fact he will turn just 25 last July, Seager's magnificent breakthrough in 2016 (.308, 26 HR, 105 R, 72 RBI) is already being overshadowed by the health woes. While the latter is troubling, Seager still possesses some of the best pure hitting skills in all of baseball and on talent alone, he could easily go right back to his 2016 numbers with positive health. Keep in mind how Seager is still a year or so away from reaching his prime and that his likely depressed ADP for 2019 will make him that much more of a value/upside investment. Expected to be ready for the start of the season since position players have a much shorter recovery period from Tommy John, Seager is shaping up to be some bargain.

2019 PROJECTION: .300 24 HR 77 RBI 98 R 4 SB

Xander Bogaerts: A bit of a volatile presence in yearly fantasy baseball leagues since first arriving in the majors for good back in 2014, Boston Red Sox shortstop Xander Bogaerts had his best overall season yet in 2018 by setting career-bests in home runs (23) and RBI (103) as a new level of power was reached. We are still looking for some consistency out of Bogaerts since his offensive numbers have been a bit all over the map and injuries have interrupted chunks of previous seasons but the fact he turned just 26 last October means the guy is just now reaching his statistical prime. Now in digging into the numbers a bit more, Bogaerts could already be signaling that his days of running may be nearing an end as he swiped just 8 bases in 580 at-bats last season but on the flip side, his 72 runs scored were a fluky low number considering the potent lineup he was in the middle of. Making matters more positive is that Bogaerts is a solid career .284 hitter and very much capable of reaching a .300 average in 2019 considering the very good walk (9.5 BB/9) and strikeout (17.6 K/9) rates. While injuries do remain a concern, Bogaerts is right there on the border of being a top-five fantasy baseball shortstop this season.

2019 PROJECTION: .293 24 HR 107 RBI 88 R 10 SB

Jean Segura: Ever since departing the Arizona Diamondbacks via a trade to the Seattle Marines, shortstop Jean Segura has been one of the most underrated offensive players in all of baseball as he posted a second straight supreme season out West in 2018. Fully reaffirming his status as a five-tool fantasy baseball star after some earlier inconsistency with the Brewers, Segura batted .304, scored 91 runs, and posted a 10/20 mark in homers/steals in 632 at-bats. What has always been interesting about Segura is the fact he combines an almost complete aversion to walks (5.1 BB/9) with one of the best contact abilities in the game (10.9 K/9) which help him supply the yearly .300 averages (three straight seasons above that mark). While Segura doesn't blow up home runs and steals, the fact he contributes in both at shortstop while helping everywhere else make him a nice value play once again for 2019 fantasy baseball. Turning 29 in March, Segura is pretty much cemented into his current numbers for the time being but that is still a decent place to be for your possible starting shortstop option.

2019 PROJECTION: .307 11 HR 65 RBI 95 R 23 SB

Adalberto Mondesi: For the kid once known as "Raul Jr.", it is not an understatement to say that Kansas City Royals shortstop prospect Adalberto Mondesi will be among the most-hyped "have to have him" players entering into 2019 fantasy baseball drafts. While Mondesi's ugly hitting struggles prior to last season were well-documented, it appeared that a change in his stance at the dish while in the minors have unlocked what can only be described as tremendous pure physical talent. It is very rare to find a player who is built both for high-end power and speed like Mondesi is and his 75-game run with the Royals a year ago (.276, 14 home runs, 32 stolen bases) was a league-clincher for many who were lucky enough to pick him up off waivers. Even though it is far from an exact science, extrapolating Mondesi's half-season run with the Royals last season would result in absolutely silly numbers and that will fuel the hype train as 2019 drafts arrive. So in terms of what to do with Mondesi in such a crazed environment, it is would be an impossible sell to avoid paying what is expected to be a very high price for the power/speed marvel this spring but we also need to remind you of the endless cases of guys with similar half-year explosions falling on their faces the following year. It is under this conservative breath where you need to really focus in on the fact that despite all the beautiful surface numbers last season, Mondesi's plate approach remain very ugly as his 3.8 BB/9 was pathetic and the 26.5 K/9 were nothing to write home about either. So that .276 Mondesi hit last season is unlikely to be repeated going forward if those advanced metrics don't improve and remember this is still the same guy who hit .170 and .185 during trial looks with the team from 2016-17. In the end, you really don't want to get caught up in the craziness that will be Mondesi's 2019 draft cost because the jury is still out here on what kind of overall offensive player he can be.

2019 PROJECTION: .253 23 HR 65 RBI 77 R 44 SB

Jose Peraza: Despite losing both outfield and second base eligibility for 2019 fantasy baseball, Cincinnati Reds shortstop Jose Peraza can more than hold his own at the shortstop position as he comes off a terrific career-year where the speedster set or matched personal bests in homers (14), runs (85), RBI (58), and steals (23). Add in the very solid .288 average and all of a sudden we have a new five-tool option to include toward the top of the shortstop rankings. While it took Peraza a few years to hit his stride, he is actually only going to be 25 for the start of the 2019 season which means another level of offensive production could be in the offing. Even if Peraza stays at his 2018 rates, that would still leave him as a smart cost-efficient option for the position and a guy who you can plug in and never have to worry about. We're buying.

2019 PROJECTION: .286 15 HR 55 RBI 88 R 24 SB

Jurickson Profar (1B, OF): Anyone who was familiar with the insane amount of injuries that former number one Texas Rangers infield prospect Jurickson Profar was forced to endure from 2014-16 had to feel happy for the kid when he finally made his mark in the majors last season. Finally finding some semblance of health, Profar at least gave a reminder of the skills that once made him such a highly-acclaimed prospect a few years earlier as he hit 20 home runs, stole 10 bases, and literally played all over the field to give him eligibility at first, shortstop, and third base for 2019 fantasy baseball. While the .254 average came out not so hot, Profar's .269 BABIP was very unlucky and doubly so for someone who possesses his type of speed. When you also add in some excellent walk (9.1 BB/9) and strikeout (14.8 K/9) rates, Profar should have been hitting .280 or above. What is really amazing is that through all of the injury trouble, Profar will only be 26 this season and so he has a smidge of upside remaining before reaching the prime years. Overall, there is quite a bit to like here which makes Profar a very smart mid-round pick.

2019 PROJECTION: .279 23 HR 80 RBI 88 R 11 SB

Didi Gregorius: Talk about a classic case of irony. Having represented the winning run in sliding into home plate to give his New York Yankees team a walk-off wild-card clinching victory, All-Star shortstop Didi Gregorius in the process tore cartilage in his wrist almost ended his regular season in its tracks. That gigantic bit of misfortune was not a fitting end to what turned out to be another excellent season by the man who did the impossible in more than adequately replacing Derek Jeter however, as Gregorius batted .268 with 27 home runs, 86 RBI, and 10 steals. The 27 homers set a Yankees team record and placed Gregorius right on the cusp of top-tier status at the position in terms of fantasy baseball. When he was first acquired by Yankees GM Brian Cashman prior to the start of the 2015 season, Gregorius arrived into town with the reputation for being a light-hitting/slick-fielding shortstop who the team hoped would maybe grow into some power down the line. Boy did that wish come true as Gregorious's 9 home runs in 2015 were followed by an uptick to 20 the following season, and then all the way up toward 25 and 27 the last two years. In addition to the power, Gregorius has cemented a reputation for being a high-contact hitter (12.1 K.9) who saw his average dip down to a somewhat shaky .268 last season due to a large extent the effects of an unlucky .259. As an added bonus, Gregorius improved some career-long aversion to walks by upping his BB/9 to a solid 8.4 last season and even added in 10 steals to complete the very potent fantasy baseball picture. What is interesting here is that the 10 steals notwithstanding, Gregorius tends to drop in yearly fantasy baseball drafts due to the fact he doesn't usually swipe a high number of bases and this is a form of discrimination in the game that never seems to cease since we all want our middle infielders to supply around 20 thefts at those positions if it is possible. Be that as it may, there is no longer any debate that Gregorius is not one of the top shortstops in the game and the fact he will be turning just 29 in February means he is still in the early stages of his prime. Unfortunately, a damaged UCL tendon in Gregorius' elbow suffered during the team's Game 1 loss to the Boston Red Sox in the ALCS led to Tommy John surgery when the series was through and he is not expected to be ready to go when the 2019 season gets underway. Early projections are that Gregorius could return sometime in July but that still represents a major chunk of lost counting numbers. As a result of the surgery, Gregorius needs to be dropped down more than a bit in 2019 fantasy baseball shortstop rankings but he is certainly capable of being a sizable difference-maker when he does return to game action sometime during the summer.

2019 PROJECTION: .275 28 HR 88 RBI 86 R 7 SB

Tim Anderson: If there was no such thing as batting average, Chicago White Sox shortstop Tim Anderson would be much more acclaimed for his annually underrated power/speed game. Anderson took those skills to another level in 2018 as he set career-highs in home runs with 20 and steals with 26 which followed a 17/15 campaign the year prior. In addition to the power/speed game, Anderson also posted personal bests in runs scored with 77 and RBI with 64. On but that batting average. It is in this category where Anderson has had major trouble as his .240 mark last season stole some thunder from the rest of the offensive haul. With a high 24.6 K/9 rate and literally no patience at the dish as shown by a comical 5.0 BB/9, Anderson's approach is far from textbook. This is a real shame in that Anderson's ugly .281 OBP gives team management reason not to place him in the leadoff spot where of course the counting stats would be even more potent. So even though Anderson won't be 26 until June, it is imperative he make at least some inroads with the shoddy walk and K rates in order to improve on his modest fantasy baseball standing. In terms of the big picture, Anderson's very affordable yearly draft price does make him one to target given the excellent power/speed game but having to cover for the average adds another annoying wrinkle to the investment.

2019 PROJECTION: .255 23 HR 67 RBI 79 R 24 SB

Marcus Semien: Helping to drive the bus for the Oakland A's as the team with MLB's lowest payroll eventually clinched one of the AL Wild Card spots was underrated shortstop Marcus Semien. While Semien deservedly gets knocked in yearly fantasy baseball leagues due to batting average struggles (.255 last season), the guy has also proven to be a useful power/speed guy as he showed a year ago by hitting 15 home runs and stealing 14 bases in 703 at-bats. What is interesting about Semien's average struggles are the fact that both his walk (8.7 BB/9) and strikeout (18.6 K/9) rates were solid last season and should have resulted in a mark around .270 or higher. That bodes well for some improvement going forward and when paired with the 15/15 ability, makes Semien a nice mid-round pick that no one is focusing on.

2019 PROJECTION: .267 16 HR 74 RBI 86 R 11 SB

Andrelton Simmons: Already known as arguably the best infield defender in the major leagues, Los Angeles Angels shortstop Andrelton Simmons should be lauded for developing his offensive game to the point that he is now an interesting fantasy baseball stock. Finally taking advantage of his good speed and growing power, Simmons has now posted ratios of 14/19 and 11/10 in the home run/steal categories the last two years; while his average has come in at .278/.292 during the same span. Also possessing absolutely tremendous contact ability (7.3 K/9), Simmons's .337 OBP is a great indicator of how good of an offensive player he has developed into. Even though it may feel boring to draft Simmons, the numbers suggest you should be more pumped about the investment.

2019 PROJECTION: .284 13 HR 73 RBI 75 R 11 SB

Elvis Andrus: Serving as a long-time critic in these pages of Texas Rangers shortstop Elvis Andrus, we screamed to the rafters last spring about how his 2017 offensive production belonged completely in the outlier bin. Having never hit more than 8 home runs since coming to the majors back in 2009, the 20 long balls Andrus cracked last season were a complete fluke and so were the 88 RBI that went along for the ride. Most fantasy baseball veterans had the same gut feeling however and so nobody was surprised when Andrus went back to being a single digit home run hitter in 2018 with just 8 and the RBI total of 33 fell completely off the map as well. Even more troubling was Andrus sliding to just 3 stolen bases and a horrid .256 average which were both career-lows. Yes, Andrus deserves some slack since he missed a chunk of the season with a fractured right elbow but it is not like his legs were impacted with regards to the lack of steals. Already the Rangers are trying their best to get out from under Andrus' ridiculous contract (a criminal 8 years for $120 million) but they have about as good a chance of doing that as the guy has of ever going near those 2017 numbers again.

2019 PROJECTION: .273 8 HR 57 RBI 78 R 23 SB

Chris Taylor (OF): When the Los Angeles Dodgers began to give infielder/outfielder Chris Taylor an everyday spot in the team's lineup early in the 2017 season, opposing pitchers were caught a bit off guard in not knowing the tendencies of the 2012 fifth-round pick. Given this setup, Taylor opened eyes in the fantasy baseball community by hitting 21 home runs, stealing 17 bases, and batting .288 while qualifying at second base, shortstop, and the outfield. As solid a performance as that was, we threw shade at Taylor in these pages a year ago in identifying his ugly 25.0 K/9 and very lucky .361 BABIP as sizable red flags not to be overlooked for 2018. So it went as pitchers possessing more of a scouting report on Taylor went to town on the holes in his swing and the result was an increase in the K/9 to a horrid 29.5, a drop in the average to .254, and just a mediocre 17/9 home run/stolen base performance. Already 28-years-old, Taylor is no longer a prospect and he loses second base eligibility to begin the new season which serves as yet another negative. While a useful player to have on your bench, Taylor should not classify as anything more.

2019 PROJECTION: .257 19 HR 67 RBI 88 R 12 SB

Lourdes Gurriel: Knowing full well they were in the midst of a rebuild and a clear notch or ten below the New York Yankees and Boston Red Sox in the AL East, the Toronto Blue Jays began taking a long look at their future which included giving 263 at-bats to infield prospect Lourdes Gurriel last season. A bit off the prospect radar after a rough 2017 showing at Double-A, Gurriel did nothing but hit both at that level and later at Triple-A which gave the Blue Jays the impetus to see what they had in the kid. Despite battling a bunch of injuries (ankle, concussion, and finally a hamstring that finished his season early), Gurriel acquitted himself nicely by hitting .281 with 11 home runs and 35 RBI in 65 games. The 22.4 K/9 was not awful considering it was Gurriel's first crack at major league pitching but he has to do significantly better than a pathetic 3.4 BB/9 to not fall prey to ugly batting averages. Also, Gurriel is no speedster by any means and so stolen bases will not be part of the equation. At this point, the Jays plan on having Gurriel serve as their everyday shortstop to begin the 2019 season and the kid also carries eligibility at second base to put himself into play as a late-round upside pick.

2019 PROJECTION: .266 17 HR 65 RBI 54 R 4 SB

Amed Rosario: Pretty much going along with everything else that has dogged the franchise of late, it appeared the New York Mets had grossly overhyped the prospect abilities of shortstop Amed Rosario as the smooth-fielding speedster floundered to a horrendous .246 average with 4 home runs and 6 steals during the first half of the 2018 season. It certainly didn't help that the Mets buried Rosario down in the 8th spot in the order which is death for an NL hitter but this story would change for the better once the All-Star Game was in the books. It was during the second half of the season where Rosario really began to put all these impressive tools together and once the hits began falling on a nightly basis, the Mets did the smart thing in moving him all the way up to the top of the order. The result was Rosario almost overnight turning into a true leadoff disrupter as he batted .268 with 5 home runs and a massive 18 steals. While Rosario's composite .256 average was quite ugly, the 9/24 ratio in homers and steals were very much intriguing. So even though the Mets haven't yet publicly stated whether or not they intend to have Rosario lead off to begin 2019, count on that development as a strong possibility given what we saw during the second half of 2018. Now Rosario does still have his flaws such as an utter lack of patience (4.9 BB/9) which doesn't really jive for leadoff duty but it needs to be stressed the kid is just 23 and a good 3-4 years from his prime. Growing pains will still be a part of the picture this season but the talent is really beginning to surface.

2019 PROJECTION: .270 12 HR 55 RBI 79 R 27 SB

Scott Kingery: While he was probably a bit rushed when the Philadelphia Phillies summoned him to the majors early in the 2018 season, shortstop prospect Scott Kingery still retains some very interesting upside after hitting 8 home runs and stealing 10 bases as a rookie. All you have to do is look at Kingery's 18/19 mark in homers/steals in 2017 at Double-A to get an understanding of the talent that is bubbling under the surface here and so this is a name to absolutely store away for your late-round upside picks.
2019 PROJECTION: .275 16 HR 54 RBI 77 R 14 SB

Paul DeJong: It was literally a smashing debut for St. Louis Cardinals shortstop prospect Paul DeJong in 2017 as the slugger cracked 25 home runs and batted .285 for the team in 108 games but the performance really just set the stage for us to label him a prime bust candidate for the following season. Including DeJong squarely on the "Do Not Draft" portion of our guide last spring, we centered our argument on the fact the guy's inflated .349 BABIP helped him bat the .285 and also the ugly 28.0 K/9 rate would be exposed by opposing pitchers as well. Fast forward to the end of 2018 and our predictions more than came true as DeJong's average sank all the way down to a brutal .241 and his home run total also jogged back to 19 despite receiving an extra 47 at-bats. With no speed to speak of to offset the average hit, DeJong has been revealed to be just a mediocre overall hitter who is a backup at best in 2019 mixed fantasy baseball leagues.
2019 PROJECTION: .254 20 HR 65 RBI 63 R 1 SB

Freddy Galvis: Heading into free agency at the age of 29, veteran shortstop Freddy Galvis will try to talk up his decent power/speed game to prospective MLB teams this winter. On that front, Galvis has proven to be quite effective as his home run/stolen base numbers the last three seasons have read as follows: 20/17, 12/14, and 13/8 while with the Philadelphia Phillies and San Diego Padres. What Galvis will try to avoid discussing are his annually shoddy batting averages which have come in at .241, .255, and .248 during that same span. With Galvis having also never scored more than 71 runs or 67 RBI, he can be considered nothing more than a backup shortstop in mixed leagues or a borderline starting option in AL or NL-only.
2019 PROJECTION: .249 14 HR 65 RBI 67 R 10 SB

Brandon Crawford: Just three years into a six-year deal worth $75 million, you got think the San Francisco Giants are already having major regrets for bestowing such a commitment to flawed shortstop Brandon Crawford. Serving as the definition of boring and limited, Crawford's 14 home runs, 4 stolen bases, and .254 average last season was almost a carbon copy of his numbers in those categories the previous year (.253, 14 homers, 3 steals). This means Crawford is another "he is who he is" guy in terms of the numbers not moving much in either direction at the age 32 to begin the 2019 season and so Crawford is strictly just for the NL-only crowd.

2019 PROJECTION: .255 15 HR 56 RBI 65 R 2 SB

Dansby Swanson: After completely bombing at the dish as a rookie amid some pronounced fantasy baseball hype in 2017 (.232, 6 homers, 3 steals), Atlanta Braves shortstop Dansby Swanson was a mostly ignored commodity when drafts got underway last spring. With the often profitable post-hype sleeper tag in play on Swanson for 2018, the former 2015 first overall pick was only moderately better as he batted .238 with 14 home runs and 10 stolen bases. When digging into the numbers a bit more, Swanson actually showed decent plate skill as he drew a solid amount of walks (8.3 BB/9) and the strikeouts were not obscene for someone who was just 24 last season (22.9 K/9). Given the fact Swanson is still a few years from reaching his prime, incremental improvement is anticipated again for 2019. In Swanson's case, that means only a run at about 17 homers and 12 steals to go with maybe an average jumping up to around .260. Those numbers certainly don't make one run out to secure Swanson's fantasy baseball services this season and so he should be graded as just a backup shortstop with a small level of upside.

2019 PROJECTION: .258 16 HR 65 RBI 63 R 11 SB

THE REST

Willy Adames: While the glove was clearly ahead of the offensive game, Tampa Bay Rays shortstop prospect Willy Adams is a name to keep tabs on during spring training this March given the sizable upside he brings to the fantasy baseball table. Having some decent power/speed numbers while coming up the Rays' minor league ladder, Adames acquitted himself nicely as a rookie in 2018 when he hit 10 home runs, stole 6 bases, and batted .278 in his first taste of major league action. That is a nice floor to begin with and given the success the Rays have always had with developing their farmhands, Adames should be in consideration as a late-round sleeper.

Orlando Arcia: Simply put, nothing went right for Milwaukee Brewers shortstop prospect Orlando Arcia during the 2018 season. Drafted as an upside player at the position given the terrific minor league numbers and a very good 15/14/.277 performance for the team in 2017, Arica went through some pronounced slumps last season that got so rough he was eventually sent back to the minors for a spell to find his game. In the end, Arcia managed just a .236 average with 3 home runs and 7 steals in 366 at-bats but the upside still remains and in fact, the post-hype sleeper siren is blaring. Remember that Arcia is still just 24 and he wouldn't be the first prospect to stumble after some early success. The power/speed game remains very potent here and if Arcia can just learn some more plate discipline (4.1 BB/9, 23.8 K/9) the kid can really develop into a major value play this season.

Aledmys Diaz (3B): For the second time in three MLB seasons, shortstop Aledmys Diaz went above the 15-home run mark in 2018 by swatting 18 to go with a 55 RBI and a .263 average. Add in 55 runs scored and 3 steals and nothing Diaz did last season will generate much in the way of fantasy baseball interest. Maybe in AL-only leagues, Diaz can garner some attention but you should strive to do much better in mixed leagues for your backup shortstop this season.

Tim Beckham (3B): After years of underwhelming/disappointing numbers not befitting a former 2008 number 1 overall pick, it finally looked like shortstop Tim Beckham had gained some traction in his MLB career when he hit 21 home runs and batted .278 in a year split between the Tampa Bay Rays and Baltimore Orioles in 2017. With Beckham now having the opportunity to hit for a full year in the bandbox that is Camden Yards, expectations were on the optimistic side. Unfortunately, like everything else that went wrong for the Orioles last season, Beckham was a letdown as his ugly batting average history reared its ugly head again (.230) and he managed just 12 home runs in 402 at-bats. Still unable to take walks (6.7 BB/9), Beckham's strikeout-heavy approach (24.9 K/9) and lack of speed (just one steal last season) leave very little in the way of assets for the upcoming fantasy baseball season.

Nick Ahmed: Previously known for his defense, Arizona Diamondbacks shortstop Nick Ahmed added some pop to his game last season when he posted career-highs in home runs (16), runs (61), and RBI (70) in 564 at-bats. Unfortunately, those slightly above-average numbers came with a shoddy .234 average and all of 5 steals which speaks to the limitations of Ahmed when it comes to yearly fantasy baseball leagues. Turning 29 in March, there is not going to be much, if any, further uptick in Ahmed's numbers and so he is really reserved for the NL-only contingent.

Jorge Polanco: Another case of stupidity was seen in previously emerging Minnesota Twins shortstop Jorge Polanco who got busted 80 games last season for testing positive for PED's. The drug bust was a real shame given the fact Polanco's 13/13/.256 campaign the year prior seemed to hint at something intriguing in terms of fantasy baseball. So while Polanco did go 6/7.288 in just 333 at-bats last season, we take whatever he did there with a grain of salt given the steroid label. With that said, Polanco is still just 25 and who carries some decent walk (7.5 BB/9) and strikeout (18./6 K/9) rates that when combined with the power/speed game keep him somewhat interesting.

Addison Russell: Honestly the only reason we devoted any space in this book to Chicago Cubs shortstop Addison Russell is to blast him for being an outright pig for reportedly causing years of harm, and abuse to his ex-wife. For that Russell deserved the 40-game ban MLB handed down to him last September and no one would have argued if it were longer (especially this peanut stand). Just an overrated and at the same time ineffective hitter since coming to the majors in 2015, Russell has no place on a fantasy baseball roster all the way around.

Jose Iglesias: It was another year of solid but unspectacular play by perennial AL-only shortstop Jose Iglesias. The Detroit Tigers veteran has always been known for his excellent glove and decent speed (15 stolen bases) but the latter is pretty much all Iglesias offers to those in the fantasy baseball community since he batted just .269 with 5 home runs in 464 at-bats last season. Still in his prime, as he turned 29 in January, it should be more of the same for Iglesias in 2019 which keeps him only as a possible option in deeper AL-only formats.

Miguel Rojas (1B, 3B): It took to going through three MLB minor league systems for shortstop Miguel Rojas to finally reach the major leagues for good with the Miami Marlins in 2015. Despite struggling with the bat for a few years on the forever rebuilding Marlins, Rojas had sort of a mini-breakthrough in 2018 when he hit 11 home runs, stole 6 bases, and batted .252. In terms of fantasy baseball, Rojas is not really even worth drafting in NL-only leagues despite a very nice 13.1 K/9 rate last season.

THIRD BASEMAN

Draft Strategy: The third base position has become the weakest group of hitters among the four infield spots and that would have been unthinkable just a few seasons ago as second base and shortstop lagged. The fact of the matter is that this group saw some major disappointments from early-round picks such as Kris Bryant, Justin Turner, Travis Shaw, and Mike Moustakas and overall, third base is quite top-heavy led by Nolan Arenado, Manny Machado, and Alex Bregman. If you can snag any of the latter three then, by all means, do it but if not, come back here in the middle rounds while you fill out the rest of your middle infield.

Jose Ramirez: One of the major themes heading into fantasy baseball drafts last spring centered on whether or not the jump to 29 home runs for Cleveland Indians third baseman Jose Ramirez in 2017 was sustainable or not. Having made a jump from just 11 long balls in 2016 to the 29 the following season, this became a major topic of discussion since Ramirez was being selected in the very pricey Round 2-3 range. Well one MVP-type season later, we can firmly state that Ramirez is not only a power-hitting dynamo but also a complete five-tool monster as he absolutely went bonkers in all five standard ROTO categories. Taking another sizable leap in homers with 39, Ramirez also set career-highs with 106 RBI, 110 runs scored, and 34 stolen bases. Even though the average dipped a bit to .272, that was a fluke number due to Ramirez suffering from an unlucky .254 BABIP. Basically, no matter where you looked, Ramirez was exemplary and the fact he made a solid run at a 40/40 campaign speaks to how tremendous a player he has developed into. Already universally acclaimed for possessing one of the best hitting approaches in the game going into the year, Ramirez dazzled in the advanced metrics world as well with splendid 15.2 BB/9 and 11.5 K/9 rates. Really, the only issue was the average but we already talked about how unlucky Ramirez was there with the batted ball. Driving the latter point home, Ramirez has hit .312 and .318 the two seasons prior and with such exceptional patience/contact ability, there is no reason he can't go back to posting such an average again. So while Mike Trout and Mookie Betts are set as the 1-2 picks in 2019 fantasy baseball drafts, Ramirez is every bit in the discussion to go number 3.
2019 PROJECTION: .304 37 HR 109 RBI 115 R 27 SB

Nolan Arenado: When you combine hitting ability and defensive acumen, there may not be a better player in all of baseball than Colorado Rockies third baseman Nolan Arenado. The Gold Glove winner proved this yet again by posting his standard batch of massive offensive numbers in 2018 which were highlighted by 38 home runs, 110 RBI, and 104 runs scored.

Durability and dependability are both major selling points here as Arenado has amassed over 650 at-bats four years running and this is a crucial skill not to be overlooked considering his annual mid-first round price tag. Getting back to the numbers, Arenado is simply ridiculous with the power game as he has not hit less than 37 home runs or driven in fewer than 100 batters during each of the last four seasons. Want more? How about scoring between 97 and 116 runs and hitting at least .287 from this same span. While Arenado doesn't steal bases (just 2 in 673 at-bats last season), the guy is as safe a pick as you can possibly make given the continued youth (turning just 28 in April) and for playing half his games at Coors Field which just makes more pronounced the impeccable offensive game.

2019 PROJECTION: .298 37 HR 119 RBI 105 R 4 SB

Alex Bregman (SS): Whether you play him at shortstop (he qualifies there again for 2019) or third base, Houston Astros infield monster Alex Bregman makes the grade as a late first-round pick since he comes off a massive campaign last season which included posting career-highs in home runs (31), runs (105), RBI (103), and batting average (.286). Given the fact he was the second-overall pick in the 2015 MLB Draft, Bregman's explosion should not be a shock to anyone given the upper-level talent we are talking about here but the scary part is that the kid can even improve some more as he turns just 25 in March. Having successfully worked out some strikeout trouble when he first arrived on the scene in 2016 (lowering his K/9 from 24.0 to just 12.1 since), Bregman's patient-heavy approach (13.6 BB/9) should result in him making a firm run at a .300 average in 2019 to go with all of the potent power numbers. Serving as the icing on the statistical cake was Bregman stealing 10 bags last season to qualify him as a five-tool guy for the time being. In short, there is nothing troubling in any way, shape, or form regarding Bregman's 2019 fantasy baseball outlook and so he is absolutely worthy of hearing his name called among the first 15 or so picks this spring.

2019 PROJECTION: .289 33 HR 108 RBI 107 R 11 SB

Anthony Rendon: Nicely settled in his prime years, Washington Nationals third baseman Anthony Rendon has entered into the portion of his career where the offensive numbers will start settling in on a yearly basis. In Rendon's case this means something close to the 24 home runs, 92 RBI, and .308 batting average he posted in 2018 which keeps him squarely in the second tier of third baseman when it comes to the upcoming fantasy baseball season. While the 12 steals Rendon swiped in 2016 are never coming back (just 9 total over the last two seasons), the veteran does possess a batting average-friendly approach that centers on supreme walk (9.2 BB/9) and strikeout (13.7 K/9) rates. In actuality, there is very little volatility to speak of here when it comes to Rendon's immediate fantasy baseball outlook outside of some past injury trouble so feel free to draft with confidence.

2019 PROJECTION: .305 25 HR 96 RBI 90 R 4 SB

Eugenio Suarez: Already an underrated/affordable fantasy baseball third baseman coming into the 2018 season, the Cincinnati Reds' Eugenio Suarez took his game to a whole new level as his age-27 campaign predictably resulted in a career-best home run (34), RBI (104), and average (.283) totals. Add in a solid 79 runs scored and Suarez ended up being a terrific four-category contributor for those who paid little to secure his services the previous spring. That attractive draft price is not likely to remain in place for 2019 however given the uptick in power but Suarez is still someone who should be targeted given the impressive profile he has gathered of late. What has certainly helped Suarez reach new heights with his game was successfully upping his walk totals (going from a 4.3 BB/9 in 2015 all the way up to 10.6 a year ago) and a bit of an increase in line drive rate combined as boosters to the batting average. Since Suarez has always possessed impressive natural power, the home runs moving above the 30 mark are no shock at all. So even though Suarez may still get a bit overlooked when discussing the top slugging third baseman in today's game, don't you make the same mistake.

2019 PROJECTION: .280 32 HR 98 RBI 84 R 2 SB

Kris Bryant (OF): What on earth is going on here? Just two short years from being in consideration for a top 2-3 pick in fantasy baseball drafts and at a time when he is just reaching the prime years, Chicago Cubs third baseman Kris Bryant is in the process of trying to halt two straight years of declining offensive numbers. While it was bad enough Cubs manager Joe Maddon planted Bryant in the second spot in the team's order in 2017 (which robbed him of RBI chances), it is also concerning that he still saw declines in 4 out of the 5 standard ROTO categories (all but batting average) that were just the undercard to what became an even more horrifying performance a year later. Even though this publication and pretty much everyone else in the fantasy baseball community gave Bryant a mulligan for his 2017 dip, no one could have foreseen him hitting just .272 with 13 home runs and 52 RBI in 447 at-bats last season. Now right off the bat, it does need to be said Bryant was severely impacted by a persistent shoulder injury that lingered almost the entire second half of the year. Any shoulder ailment almost always negatively hurts prospective power and so Bryant's sizable decline in homers and RBI can at least partly be explained on that front. Bryant does need to take some blame though for striking out more often (K/9 going from 19.2 in 2017 up to 23.4 last season) and at the same time drawing fewer walks (14.3 BB/9 down to 10.5 during the same span).

Perhaps the extended slump Bryant dealt with contributed to him being more aggressive at the dish and falling out of his swing but the numbers were a complete letdown considering the spring cost. Finally, Bryant already seems done with stealing bases as he has now gone from a high of 13 in 2015 all the way down to just 2 a year ago. So after digesting all the negativity, what happens next? Well let's start with Bryant going into just his age-27 season in 2019 and we all know that is when the prime years begin and often the offensive numbers take off. We also firmly believe the shoulder was a big problem that both Bryant and the Cubs minimized to the public and was directly responsible for the numbers decline. So figuring Bryant enters into 2019 spring training with a clean bill of health, we could be looking at a return to around 30 homers, 100 runs/RBI, and an average that will be in the neighborhood of .290. That would certainly be a mighty valuable batch of numbers and be worthy of a second round pick in drafts. The best part is that Bryant may slip to Round 3 coming off such a tough season and we would not hesitate for a second jumping back into a fantasy baseball relationship with the guy at this price since the talent is just too obvious.

2019 PROJECTION: .288 28 HR 95 RBI 110 R 7 SB

Miguel Andujar: Brandon Drury who? Prior to the start of the 2018 season, the New York Yankees were planning on going with trade acquisition Brandon Drury to serve as the team's starting third baseman since it was felt top prospect Miguel Andujar needed a bit more seasoning before becoming an everyday member of the team. Fast forward to a bout of migraines that sent Drury to the DL in April and everything was put into place for Andujar to have what was one of the more impressive rookie campaigns in recent memory for the AL Wild Card winners. The much talked about smooth swing and high contact rate that made up Andujar's scouting report became obvious from the start as the hits began falling in abundance and before you knew it, Drury was shipped off to Toronto to make room for the team's newest star. A star Andujar certainly became as he set a team rookie record with 47 doubles, smashed 27 home runs, drove in 92 batters, and hit .297 in 606 at-bats. While Andujar's defense at the hot corner is passable at best, what he does with the bat is beyond impressive since he won't turn 24 until March. Adding even more hype to Andujar's outlook is the fact many of those 47 doubles will soon turn into additional home runs as he continues to add muscle in maturing physically. As a result, we could easily be looking at 35 home run 2019 campaign; with the .300 average and 90-plus runs and RBI going along for the ride as well. Even though Andujar needs to work on his patience (4.1 BB/9), he offsets that issue with a very impressive strikeout (16.0 K/9) rate. So no matter how you look at Andujar, in our opinion this is one of those guys who qualifies as a "the sky is the limit" hitter.

2019 PROJECTION: .310 33 HR 97 RBI 88 R 4 SB

Nick Castellanos: A big favorite of this publication last spring, Detroit Tigers third baseman Nick Castellanos rewarded our optimism when he hit 23 home runs, drove in 89 batters, scored 88 runs, and recorded a tidy .298 average at the age of 26 last season. While Castellanos did, in fact, give back 3 homers and 12 RBI from the previous year, this shouldn't dull you one bit on the guy's abilities in heading toward 2019 fantasy baseball. Remember that Castellanos will be reaching the magical age of 27 this March and so another uptick in numbers is likely. When you then take into account his annually affordable draft price, Castellanos suddenly becomes a great option at third base if you choose to address other positions earlier in the draft. You don't have to tell us how solid a player Castellanos is and so we will be strong buyers once again.

2019 PROJECTION: .295 27 HR 93 RBI 90 R 4 SB

Josh Donaldson: No this low of a ranking for free agent third baseman and former MVP Josh Donaldson is no misprint as the guy is now more name brand than actual impact offensive player at this stage of the game. Now an old 33 and breaking down physically after years of all-out play at the demanding third base position, Donaldson's offensive performance continued to plummet in 2018 when he hit all of 8 home runs, drove in 23, and batted a pathetic .246 in 219 at-bats. Yes missing so much time to injury played a major role in Donaldson's brutal season but even going back to 2017 the signs began to appear that trouble was ahead (K/9 increase, less isolated power). With Donaldson's K/9 now up to 24.7 last season and a neutral .302 BABIP showing he earned the mediocre offensive rates he put forth, it would take guts to draft the guy as your starting third base option for 2019 fantasy baseball. Sure the depressed draft cost will be somewhat attractive but don't get caught up in this potential trap.

2019 PROJECTION: .267 24 HR 80 RBI 74 R 2 SB

Matt Chapman: Oakland A's 2014 first-round pick Matt Chapman didn't take long to turn himself into a star for the 2018 AL Wild Card winners as a somewhat slow start to the season ended with the guy garnering some MVP attention due to excellence both offensively and defensively. Quickly showing himself to be a human vacuum glove at first base, Chapman was certainly no slouch with the bat either as he hit .278 with 24 home runs and 100 runs scored while working near the top of what became a powerhouse Oakland lineup. While the rest of Chapman's statistical haul was not overly impressive (1 stolen base, 68 RBI), there is every reason to believe he has another tier of production to reach given the fact he will turn just 26 in April. Typical of an Oakland hitter, Chapman does a nice job drawing walks

(9.4 BB/9) but in order for him to realize his optimal batting average potential, he needs to cut down a bit on the high 23.7 K.9 rate. Considering the usually affordable price tag for West Coast hitters due to the late night starts of their games on the East Coast, Chapman is shaping up to be a very nice value play with some remaining upside for those who smartly take a look here in drafts.

2019 PROJECTION: .284 26 HR 105 R 74 RBI 2 SB

Travis Shaw (1B, 2B): While there was some numbers volatility last season for Milwaukee Brewers third baseman Travis Shaw when compared to 2017, the slugger still managed another fine year as he hit 32 home runs, drove in 86, and even added eligibility at first/second base once the team acquired Mike Moustakas over the summer. The 32 homers represented the second straight season Shaw has reached the 30 mark and since he is in the early stages of his prime in turning 29 in April, it seems a safe bet that level will be reached again in 2019. As nice as the power, was, however, Shaw did lose 15 RBI from the previous year but that likely had to do with an incredibly unlucky .242 BABIP which also sent the batting average tumbling to a ghastly .241. For a guy who accumulated 587 at-bats last season, it is tough to post such a rough BABIP given all those plate appearances and so Shaw can be given a pass on the average since the batted ball was certainly not cooperating by any means. Adding more validity to this assessment is that Shaw's BABIP for the other three seasons of his MLB career finished between .299 and .312 and so since that range is an established benchmark, count on the average moving back up towards .270 in 2019 once the luck predictably regresses back a bit to the mean. Finally, Shaw's advanced hitting metrics were tremendous as both his walk (13.3 BB/9) and strikeout (18.4 K/9) rates point to someone who should be hitting for a much higher average. So as it stands, Shaw is carrying around some very solid value centered around underrated power, an expected rise in average, and an eligibility at three infield positions. When you also consider Shaw's annual draft price doesn't really ever come in on the expensive side, the buying opportunity at hand this spring looks immense.

2019 PROJECTION: .267 30 HR 93 RBI 83 R 4 SB

Justin Turner: Some guys just seem to find health trouble and a shining example of such an unfortunate trend would be Los Angeles Dodgers third baseman Justin Turner. The carnage in 2018 started in Cactus League play when Turner suffered a broken wrist after getting hit by a pitch which kept him on the DL from Opening Day all the way through mid-May. Turner would not be done with the DL though as he went back on the list in late July due to a strained groin. In between the two DL stints were additional stretches where Turner dealt with wrist and hip pain which firmly gives off the impression the 34-year-old is dealing with the effects of advancing age destroying his body. The real shame of all the missed time was the fact Turner remains a terrific hitter who batted .312 with 14 home runs and 62 runs scored in 462 at-bats. We have now seen Turner hit over .300 in three of the last five seasons (going as high as .340 in 2014) and with remaining excellent advanced metrics in walks (11.0 BB/9) and strikeouts (12.7 K/9), we understand fully the lure of coming back to the guy in spring drafts. Unfortunately, Turner is completely unreliable from a health standpoint and while he can still hit with the best of them, the threat of so many missed games costing his owners precious counting statistics is a major negative. Given that third base has become so deep the last few seasons, it is probably is a good idea to avoid the stress Turner typically supplies those who are invested.

2019 PROJECTION: .308 19 HR 78 RBI 79 R 2 SB

Rafael Devers: Given their recent track record for putting forth titanic hitting prospects (Mookie Betts, Andrew Benintendi, and to a lesser extent Jackie Bradley Jr. of recent note), the fantasy baseball community wasted little time diving in fully on 21-year-old third baseman Rafael Devers for drafts last spring. While Devers was far from overmatched as a very young everyday hitter during the second half of 2017, this only served to add to the hype the following spring. Well, youth/inexperience won out as Devers not only battled injuries last season but struggled for long stretches at the plate which resulted in a horrible .240 average but a more promising 21 home runs in 490 at-bats. Some major perspective/patience is certainly warranted here given that Devers just turned 22 this past October and so struggling a bit at such a young age in the pressure-cooker that is Boston is very understandable. The growing pains also should not dim Devers' potential in terms of fantasy baseball as the power looks to be a lock to reach the 30-home run mark possibly as soon as 2019 and the average will surely grow as well once the kid works through some impatience (7.8 BB/9) and strikeout (24.7 K/9) trouble. In the end, though, Devers' price tag in drafts this spring figures to be much cheaper as many will focus on the .240 average but smart players will take advantage of the buying opportunity considering the sizable upside.

2019 PROJECTION: .254 27 HR 75 RBI 71 R 7 SB

Maikel Franco: After years of endless waiting, Philadelphia Phillies third baseman Maikel Franco finally put forth some solid offensive production in 2018 by hitting 22 home runs, collecting 68 RBI, and batting .270. While far from difference-making numbers, Franco lowered his K/9 to a career-best 13.3 last season which helped improve the batting average a bit (up from .230 in 2017); while the home runs per game were at another personal high level (the 22 long balls came in just 465 at-bats). Even though Franco still needs to work on his utter lack of patience (6.2 BB/9), at least he is trending in the right direction with his overall production. With that said though, Franco is best left as a backup third baseman with a smidge of remaining upside.

2019 PROJECTION: .268 79 RBI 65 R 1 SB

Eduardo Escobar: Having just re-signed with the team for three years this past October, Arizona Diamondbacks third baseman Eduardo Escobar timed it perfectly in terms of posting his best season which went a long way for the former part-time player earning such a pact. In a season which began with the Minnesota Twins and ended wearing an Arizona Diamondbacks uniform (via a summer trade), Escobar was able to post career-highs in home runs (23), RBI (84), runs (73), and average (.272). While he doesn't run much at all (only 2 steals in 631 at-bats), Escobar contributed solidly in 3 categories (runs, RBI, homers) and was not terrible in a fourth (average). So while that may garner Escobar a decent deal in free agency, it really doesn't get anyone to jump up and down with excitement in the fantasy baseball community. Just a .257 career hitter with no speed, Escobar is very limited already before we even determine if the power uptick is legit. Now Escobar has reached his prime power years at the age of 29 which works in his favor regarding the home runs but 23 is certainly not a big number in today's game. Also when you consider Escobar's .308 BABIP was actually slightly on the lucky side, you see there is no much room for any average growth as well to help make the total statistical package more appealing. So while Escobar would work just fine as a backup infielder on your team (also qualifying at shortstop), drafting him as anything more would be an error in judgment.

2019 PROJECTION: .263 20 HR 77 RBI 74 R 4 SB

Mike Moustakas: Confronted with a completely dead free agent market last winter despite coming off a 38 home run season the year prior with the Kansas City Royals, veteran third base slugger Mike Moustakas gambled on his ability to repeat such a performance in 2018 by taking a one-year deal to return to the team. The subsequent results were a bit of a mixed bag as Moustakas saw his home run total drop to a still very good 28 but the batting average tumbling from 2017's .272 to last season's .251 was more troubling. On the flip side, Moustakas did set a career-high in RBI with 95 in a year split between the Royals and the Milwaukee Brewers (coming over to the latter via a summer trade). As he enters back into the free agent market at the age of 30 and off a total season that fell a bit short compared to 2017, Moustakas may not find much more of a market for his services this time around. Wherever he does end up, however, Moustakas at the very least has proven to be a good home run/RBI asset but the rest of the statistical package is lacking. A career .251 batting average and complete lack of speed show the limitations here and so Moustakas really classifies as a borderline 12-team mixed league starting option.

2019 PROJECTION: .257 27 HR 88 RBI 73 R 2 SB

Jake Lamb: When word came down late in spring training that the Arizona Diamondbacks would install a humidor at Chase Field to help buttress some of the home run tendencies of the park, the thinking was that this would impact the team's lefty sluggers such as third baseman Jake Lamb the most given the dimensions there. Unfortunately, we were not able to prove this theory due to the fact Lamb endured an injury-marred 2018 campaign that only allowed him to play in 56 ineffective (6 home runs, .222 average) games. Specifically speaking, Lamb battled shoulder trouble almost from the start of the year and it eventually led to season-ending surgery at the start of August when fraying in the joint was discovered. While Lamb will be just 28 once the 2019 fantasy baseball season gets underway, he remains a flawed slugger at third base which was seen more in his 2017 campaign when he smacked an impressive 30 home runs but with just a .248 average. Now having hit under .250 in four of his five MLB campaigns, Lamb is best served as a backup in mixed leagues for the upcoming season.

2019 PROJECTION: .253 25 HR 90 RBI 84 4 SB

Adrian Beltre: Already with a closet full of Gold Gloves, 3,000-hits in the bag, and sitting just 23 shy of 500 career home runs, borderline Hall of Fame third baseman Adrian Beltre may not be ready to hang up his cleats just yet as he openly mulled a return for 2019. It has been nothing short of a remarkable career for Beltre who still was a productive player in 2018 when he hit 15 home runs, drove in 65, and batted .273 for the Texas Rangers in 481 at-bats. While it began to seem like Beltre was never going to get old, we finally got signs last season that Father Time was doing its thing when his K/9 reached the 20.0 mark right on the nose which was the first time that number ever went that high. Injuries also dogged Beltre for the second season in a row as all those years manning the hot corner have taken its physical toll. If Beltre does return for one more go at it (likely with the Rangers in free agency), he will have to settle for AL-only classification given the erosion/injury concerns. Either way, though, this has been one tremendous career.

2019 PROJECTION: .275 14 HR 67 RBI 45 R 1 SB

Kyle Seager: Given that we have always had a soft spot for Seattle Mariners third baseman Kyle Seager, it was particularly tough for us to bear witness to what could only be classified as a brutal season for the veteran in 2018. At one time considered one of the more underrated hitters in fantasy baseball given the yearly 25-30 homers, 80-plus RBI, and an average that wouldn't kill you, Corey's older brother saw those numbers crater by quite a bit last season, to say the least (22-HR, 78-RBI, .221). What stood out when gazing at Seager's advanced metrics was a big spike in strikeouts as his 21.9 K/9 represented the first time ever reaching the 20.0 mark. In addition, Seager' lost patience at the dish as his terrible 6.0 BB/9 was a career-worst number in that category. So when combining the increase in K's and the dip in walks, it was easy to see why Seager's average dropped the way it did and this probably impacted the entirety of the numbers going in the wrong direction as well. With stolen bases also no longer part of the equation (just 2 steals total in 630 at-bats) and the totality of the offensive statistics declining for the third season in a row, Seager no longer qualifies as a starting third baseman for 2019 fantasy baseball.

2019 PROJECTION: .257 24 HR 76 RBI 65 R 2 SB

Miguel Sano: Injuries and staggering underperformance at the dish ruined the 2018 season for Minnesota Twins third baseman Miguel Sano and so a total reset for the coming year is in order. With Sano struggling terribly with the bat, the Twins made the decision during the summer to send him back to the minors to try and figure things out on that front. When Sano was called back up after a 28-game stint both at Single and Triple-A, a knee injury suffered in early September wound up finishing his season for good. In the end, Sano batted just .199 with 13 home runs and 41 RBI in 299 at-bats and a pathetic 38.5 K/9 showed just how much the guy was fighting his game pretty much throughout the season. While he will still be just 25 when 2019 gets underway, it is well-established that Sano is a major batting average liability due to the annual 30-plus K/9 rates and the struggles there take a bunch of the value away from the power which is always usually quite potent. Having been on record in these pages as big Sano critics in the past, we remain of the opinion to avoid him if possible in drafts this spring.

2019 PROJECTION: .239 24 HR 59 RBI 55 R 1 SB

Todd Frazier: When you get to the point in your career where you are lauded more for being an awesome teammate than your actual on-field production, you got some problems to deal with. This seems to be where we are now with New York Mets third baseman Todd Frazier whose past as a top 40-home run monster with the Cincinnati Reds is now becoming a distant memory. The fact of the matter is Frazier has not been very good the last two seasons where has managed to post a hideous .213 average in both campaigns and in terms of 2018, recorded just 18 home runs, 59 RBI, and 54 runs scored on a miserable Mets team. While Frazier is still surprisingly running a bit (9 steals) at the age of 32, injuries became a concession to age last season as he spent a lengthy stint on the DL with a left rib cage strain.

With Frazier also beginning to strike out more (K/9 up to 23.7 last season) and forever dealing with unlucky BABIP's, the outlook for 2019 suggests he is nothing more than a backup option at third base for at least the beginning of the season.

2019 PROJECTION: .224 23 HR 68 RBI 65 R 7 SB

Brandon Drury: Few players in Major League Baseball during the course of the 2018 season had a more difficult time physically than Toronto Blue Jays third baseman Brandon Drury. Two major health issues and two teams later, Drury's year was a complete washout as he got into only 26 games total where he hit just .169 with a single home run and 10 RBI. This after Drury was a much-discussed trade acquisition by the New York Yankees the previous winter with the idea he would man the third base position and possibly be an option there into the future. Those plans never came to fruition as Drury hit the DL the first week of April with severe migraine headaches which apparently were being caused by blurred vision that went back to his days in the Arizona Diamondbacks organization. The Yanks then turned to 2018 sensation Miguel Andujar to take Drury's place and the rest, as they say, is history. With Andujar showing uncanny hitting ability as a rookie, the Yanks flipped Drury to the Blue Jays where he still couldn't hit before suffering a season-ending broken hand in early August. Clearly, it is impossible to judge Drury on anything he did last season given all the health trouble and instead we need to go back to his 2016-17 campaigns with the Diamondbacks to remind ourselves what he is capable of. It was during this time when Drury hit a total of 29 home runs and batted .282 and .267 respectively. Those are decent power numbers for a guy who will still only be 26 to begin the 2019 season and who also remains in a prime hitter's park. With that said, Drury is nothing but a deep league or AL-only play when it comes to drafts this spring due to all the health concerns.

2019 PROJECTION: .266 14 HR 57 RBI 54 R 2 SB

Christian Villanueva: While it took three different organizations and 9 years of professional baseball to finally get an extended look at the major league level, San Diego Padres third baseman Christian Villanueva had his moment in the sun during the first portion of the 2018 season as he busted out of the gates to smack 8 home runs and bat .317 in the months of March/April. Likely taking advantage of opposing pitchers who didn't have much of a book on his high-strikeout tendencies, Villanueva crashed back to reality starting in May which began a three-month stretch where he failed to hit better than .206 in any of the following three months. Villanueva then suffered a fractured finger towards the end of August which wound up ending his season early as he finished with 20 home runs, 46 RBI, and a .236 batting average in 351 at-bats. An older prospect who turned 27 last June,

Villanueva has a bit of a Quad-A stench to him and in general, he is very limited in terms of any possible fantasy baseball value given the annual high strikeout rates (27.0 K/9 in 2018) resulting in some ugly batting averages. While no one doubts the above-average power, Villanueva is not guaranteed anything in terms of a possible starting gig with the Padres this season. Even in NL-only leagues, Villanueva is barely worth owning.

2019 PROJECTION: .234 19 HR 53 RBI 48 R 2 SB

THE REST

Yangervis Solarte (2B): Despite being given the opportunity to play half his games in a launching pad ballpark in Toronto's Rogers Center after years of dealing with the spacious dimensions of Petco Park in San Diego, Toronto Blue Jays third baseman Yangervis Solarte managed to put forth WORSE numbers offensively in 2018. Just 17 home runs, 54 RBI, and a .226 average in 506 at-bats (all declines compared to the previous season with the Padres) were all that Solarte was able to manage a year ago and the underwhelming performance didn't make it a lock the Blue Jays would pick up his option. While he still qualifies both at second and third base, Solarte still doesn't run (1 total steal in 2018) and his patience at the dish remains lacking (6.1 BB/9). You can do better even for your third base backup.

Evan Longoria: It likely becomes apparent you have reached a new low as a once potent MLB hitter when your name appears under "The Rest" portion of the position rankings. This is where San Francisco Giants former All-Star third baseman Evan Longoria belongs after the aging veteran hit .244 with 16 home runs and 54 RBI in 512 at-bats last season and without the name brand attached to it, those numbers would barely be worth inclusion on an NL-only roster. With Longoria's once decent plate approach going into the toilet (4.3 BB/9) and the injury bug now constantly cropping up, do yourself a favor and look for a younger backup third baseman with more upside than this waste.

Colin Moran: Serving as one of the key prospects that headed to the Pittsburgh Pirates in the Gerrit Cole trade last winter, third baseman Colin Moran did a decent job in his first extended look in the majors last season as he batted .277 with 11 home runs and 58 RBI in 465 at-bats. Be that as it may, the former 2013 first-round pick is already 26 and the previous minor league numbers were nothing that got the hype meter going. So while Moran is capable of approaching 20 home runs if he receives enough at-bats this season, there is not much else to fall back on here since there is no stolen base game to speak of and it remains a strong possibility opposing pitchers will have a better read on how to attack him this time around.

Jeimer Candelario: Early on in the 2018 fantasy baseball season, it seemed like the Detroit Tigers had a budding talent on their hands in the form of third base prospect Jeimer Candelario. While he was not included on almost all "Top Prospect" lists heading into the year, Candelario suggested he may have been somewhat overlooked as he hit 8 total home runs the first two months in with averages of .283 and .262 respectively. Alas, opposing pitchers began to go to town on some of the holes in Candelario's swing once they compiled a decent amount of intel on him and the results the rest of the way were quite ugly. In the end, Candelario's 19 home runs and 78 runs scored were decent but the .224 average and 25.8 K/9 not so much. With Candelario's overall offensive profile proving itself to be quite limited and with an expected short leash given the utter lack of prospect pedigree, this is one player you can safely look beyond in spring drafts.

Johan Camargo: Yet another prospect who contributed to the Atlanta Braves winning the NL East crown in 2018 was third baseman Johan Camargo as he contributed 19 home runs and 76 RBI in 524 at-bats while also playing very good defense. Far from the upper-level prospect Ozzie Albies or Ronald Acuna Jr. are, Camargo still proved himself a useful player to both the team and the fantasy baseball community. That usefulness in the latter is capped bit though as Camargo doesn't run (just one steal) and his .272 average centered into the mediocre range. While we don't anticipate Camargo ever contributing in the stolen base category, he does possess solid walk (9.7 BBB/9) and strikeout (20.6 K/9) metrics that hint at an average uptick. In the end, however, we are talking about just a backup in all mixed league.

Zack Cozart: The first season of the three-year deal worth $38 million that third baseman Zack Cozart signed with the Los Angeles Angels prior to the start of 2018 didn't go as planned for all involved as the veteran went down for the season in June with a torn labrum in his left shoulder which required surgery. Prior to the procedure, Cozart was not hitting much at all as he recorded just 5 home runs, 29 runs scored, and a .219 average in 253 at-bats. Now 33 and coming off a very serious surgery, you have to wonder if Cozart is even capable of contributing anything meaningful for 2019 fantasy baseball. You should not be interested in finding out.

Jung Ho Kang: It has been nothing short of a disaster the last two seasons for veteran third baseman Jung Ho Kang as the Korean import missed all of 2017 while dealing with legal trouble that put his VISA in jeopardy due to a substance abuse problem that included his THIRD DUI. While that major red flag was eventually remedied this past April, Kang never made it back to the Pirates due to a wrist injury that first cropped up while he was preparing his comeback in the minor leagues. Eventually, season-ending surgery was needed to fix the wrist and so as a result, Kang has not faced major league pitching since 2016. While Kang clearly proved himself to be of use in fantasy baseball that season when he clubbed 21 home runs, the fact he will now be 32 when 2019 comes around off such a long layoff makes him nothing but a lottery ticket late-round pick for those who are in deeper leagues.

Jedd Gyorko: Down to just eligibility at third base after years of carrying multiple positions, the flawed offensive game of the St. Louis Cardinals' Jedd Gyorko really stands out when it comes to his 2019 fantasy baseball stock. Managing just 11 home runs, 47 RBI, and a .262 average in 402 at-bats last season is not going to get it done and having turned 30 this past September, Gyorko is about as boring a player as there is in today's game.

Martin Prado: It was another lost season for Miami Marlins veteran third baseman Martin Prado in 2018 as the former batting average asset got into just 54 games due to three separate stints on the disabled list which included injuries to his hip, quad, and hamstring. Those type of wear-and-tear injuries are classic symptoms of an aging player and Prado certainly qualifies there as he will be 35 when the 2019 season gets underway. Having built a career out of being an underrated hitter during his Atlanta Brave years, Prado has now hit just .250 and .244 the last two seasons as the injuries have completely derailed his offensive game. Considering that much of Prado's fantasy baseball value was tied into .300 batting averages given his mediocre home run and stolen bases totals, the dip in that category the last two years has made him an almost useless commodity. That doesn't figure to change in 2019 as Prado turns another year older.

Matt Duffy: Boring is the key word when describing the offensive game Tampa Bay Rays third baseman Matt Duffy brings to the fantasy baseball table and this was further borne out in 2018 when the 27-year-old hit 4 home runs, stole 12 bases, and batted .294 in 560 at-bats. While Duffy brings a nice high-contact/patient approach to the dish that fits in nicely on the high-OBP Rays, his lack of impact numbers in the homer/steal categories leave him mostly for the AL-only crowd.

Pablo Sandoval (1B): Serving as a butt of all jokes for the better part of the last four seasons after signing that ridiculous five-year contract worth $90 million with the Boston Red Sox despite a reputation for not ever being in shape, San Francisco Giants third baseman Pablo Sandoval was actually semi-productive the first half of 2018 when he smacked 8 home runs and batted .250 in 204 at-bats. With the Red Sox having thrown in the towel on their gigantic Sandoval miscalculation the season prior, the Giants literally bought as low as possible here in the hopes some magic could be rekindled going back to his productive previous stint with the team from 2008-14. Unfortunately, the aging Sandoval (32 last August) is about as big a mess physically as you can get given his annual weight problems and that issue goes hand-in-hand with the dramatically declining offensive numbers the last few seasons. Thus, it was no shock when Sandoval blew out a hamstring last August that ultimately finished his season early. So as we look toward the 2019 season, it is tough to imagine the Giants giving Sandoval enough of an opportunity to even have a smidge of value in NL-only leagues and that means the veteran can be avoided altogether.

OUTFIELDERS

Draft Strategy: Whether you are in a league that plays three or five outfielders, it is imperative you make a pick here by the end of Round 3 at the latest. Ideally, you want a five-tool outfielder to serve in your top OF 1 spot and then use the other two spots for a home run hitter and a speedster respectively. Those in five-outfielder formats need to go two more deep on this strategy.

Mookie Betts: Even though Los Angeles Angels outfielder Mike Trout is the reflexive (and probably correct) pick to front all 2019 fantasy baseball drafts, a strong case can be made the Boston Red Sox' Mookie Betts is just as deserving. In what was nothing short of a fantasy baseball statistical bonanza, Betts went absolutely nuts last season as he won the AL batting crown by hitting .346; while also adding personal-bests in homers (32), runs (129), and steals (30). Add in the 80 RBI and Betts was downright phenomenal in all five of the standard ROTO categories. The real amazing here is that Betts turned just 26 this past October and so he is looking at a good 4-5 seasons of this type of monstrous production before age begins to do its thing. With Betts' advanced metrics also shinning beyond reproach (13.2 BB/9, 14.8 K.9), feel free to pick him first or second this spring.
2019 PROJECTION: .329 30 HR 95 RBI 127 R 28 SB

Mike Trout: By now we get the sense Los Angeles Angels outfielder Mike Trout is so consistently excellent that some in the fantasy baseball community are looking to draft someone else (Mookie Betts?) ahead of him for 2019. While Betts is certainly worthy of being the top pick in drafts, we side with Trout for the SIXTH season in a row as he amazingly will be just 27 this season. In 2018 the numbers were of the video game variety again as Trout batted .312 with 39 home runs, 79 RBI, and 104 runs scored; while also continuing to play Gold Glove defense. It also was nice to see Trout keep on running as he swiped 24 bases to preserve five-tool superstar status for at least one more season. Other than maybe the steals falling by the wayside as he moves closer to 30, there is nothing to suggest Trout won't be the numbers robot he always has been and so his name should be the first called out once again on draft day.
2019 PROJECTION: .308 37 HR 86 RBI 110 R 21 SB

J.D. Martinez: Despite haggling over contract terms last winter, the Boston Red Sox and outfielder J.D. Martinez were all smiles throughout the 2018 season as both team and player had a simply phenomenal year. Putting himself squarely in the AL MVP conversation with outfield mate Mookie Betts, Martinez took the mantle from the New York Yankees' Aaron Judge as the best pure slugger in the game a year ago when he slammed 43 homers, drove in 130 batters, scored 111 runs, and batted .330. Even though Martinez doesn't run (just 6 stolen bases), there was not a better four category power producer in the game last season. Still, in his prime at the age of 31, Martinez should be good to go again as a top-tier OF 1 for 2019 fantasy baseball and only some nagging injuries in his recent past serve as a minor concern. Yes, Martinez' .375 BABIP was very much into the lucky realm but the guy also has had a knack for beating the curve by a wide margin in the past (marks of .389 in 2014 and .378 in 2016) which lessens the threat of the batting average sliding. While we still prefer Mike Trout and Betts over Martinez given the stolen base ability of the first two, there is no reason the latter should not last past the end of Round 1 in drafts this spring.

2019 PROJECTION: 42 HR 126 RBI 107 R 5 SB

Bryce Harper: While shortstop Manny Machado may have something to say about it, free agent outfielder Bryce Harper is ready to set records in terms of the massive contract he is expected to ink sometime over the winter in entering the open market at just 26. Harper certainly did what he could to maximize his earnings potential in 2018 as he hit 34 homers, drove in 100 batters, and scored 103 runs for a surprisingly listless Washington Nationals team. What was also encouraging to see was Harper stealing 13 bases which were the second-highest total of his career and came just a year after compiling only 4 in 2017. It wasn't all positive however as Harper's average struggled to reach even .220 during the early summer and he needed a hot to finish to post a still ugly .249 mark. What is really shocking is that this is the second time in the last three seasons Harper has failed to hit .250. A lot of that volatility has been as a result of some rapidly fluctuating BABIP marks and in 2018 that number was slightly in the unlucky realm at .289 but also WAY down from .356 the season prior when Harper batted .319. What we do then is look at some of the advanced metrics and here it is mostly good as Harper walks at some of the highest rates in baseball which will only help a batting average but his strikeouts have trended up of late in rising to 24.3 last season. Since it is tough to get a true gauge here given all the conflicting numbers, we instead should fixate on the supreme power game and remaining speed in keeping Harper as a late first-round or even early second-round pick given the addition of some new names at the top of the overall rankings.

2019 PROJECTION: .288 35 HR 97 RBI 104 R 11 SB

Christian Yelich: Always one of the more popular outfielders in yearly fantasy baseball drafts during his Miami Marlins days due to obvious five-tool ability/potential, the hype meter almost exploded when Christian Yelich was traded to the Milwaukee Brewers last winter. Getting to escape the spacious Miami ballpark to a launching pad in Milwaukee that especially favors left-handed batters like Yelich, all of a sudden the guy was finding himself being picked in the second round of most 2018 drafts. While Yelich was very solid during the first half of the season, the numbers took on a Marlins feel in terms of being good but not great and they certainly fell short of expectations given the new locale. The second half became a whole different story however as Yelich went on a truly epic tear offensively that resulted in him taking home the NL MVP award. In one of those magical breakout seasons where it all came together, Yelich set career-high in ALL five standard ROTO categories with his 36 homers, 118 runs, 110 RBI, 22 steals, and .326 batting average. Add in ongoing terrific walk (10.4 BB/9) and strikeout (20.7 K/9) rates and Yelich came up smelling like roses everywhere. Given that Yelich is really just now entering into his prime in turning 27 last December, there is no reason he can't be in the MVP conversation for the next few seasons and thus be deserving of first-round consideration for 2019.

2019 PROJECTION: .317 34 HR 114 R 115 RBI 19 SB

Aaron Judge: If not for an errant July pitch by the Kansas City Royals' Jakob Junis that broke the wrist of New York Yankees slugging outfielder Aaron Judge, it is likely the 2017 Rookie of the Year would have been right there in the MVP conversation for the second time in two MLB campaigns. With a 25-home run, 60 RBI, .276 first-half performance that included customary high walk totals, Judge was proving to be the better slugger in a Yankees outfield that included the newly-acquired Giancarlo Stanton. Unfortunately, fate intervened with Junis' misplaced throw and the result was Judge missing all of August and most of September which put a major hurting on his counting numbers. While Judge did return for the last few games of the season, his final composite numbers of 27 homers, 67 RBI, 77 runs scored, and a .278 average was WAY down from his eye-popping rookie haul. Be that as it may, the performance metrics were pretty much in sync for Judge last season compared to 2017 and on that front, it is particularly interesting how he has posted decent enough averages (.284 and .278) despite sky-high K/9 rates (30.7 and 30.5 respectively). Drawing some of the highest walk totals on a per game basis is certainly responsible for that trend to continue and so we can't automatically assume like we did last spring the strikeout issues will result in a negative average. Instead, let's focus on the fact Judge could easily clear 40 homers and 100 RBI and even make another push to 50 and 110-plus as well. With an expected price tag that will likely fall somewhere in Round 2, Judge seems set to once again be a slightly cheaper version of J.D. Martinez with a lower average.

2019 PROJECTION: .275 44 HR 117 RBI 124 R 7 SB

Ronald Acuna Jr.: Yeah that was certainly worth the wait. When it came to 2018 fantasy baseball drafts, the level of hype surrounding top Atlanta Braves outfield prospect Ronald Acuna Jr. was beyond comparison. Considered the number 1 prospect not only for the Braves but also in ALL of baseball, Acuna Jr. possessed the type of insane power/speed five-tool ability that makes all who play fantasy baseball weak in the knees and it was under this setting where the kid became the obsession of many when it came to spring drafts. While we always preach caution in such scenarios, an exception was made for Acuna Jr. given our strong belief the talent would provide immense numbers as soon as the promotional call was made. That call would come at the end of April which then set in motion an insane rookie performance which was highlighted by 26 home runs, 16 stolen bases, and a .293 average in just 487 at-bats at the age of 20. It is beyond scary to think how good Acuna Jr. will be and we can absolutely envision a scenario where he challenges Mike Trout for top draft honors as soon as 2020. While Acuna Jr. does strike out a lot (25.3 K/9) which is surely understandable given the very young age, at the same time it is encouraging he also draws a high number of walks (9.2 BB/9). Since Acuna Jr. has the top-end speed to beat the BABIP curve on an annual basis, a string of .300 seasons should be in the offing. In addition, the power/speed game is going to be ridiculous here and 30/20 should be easily attainable if Acuna Jr. avoids the sophomore slump. The talent is really that great all the way around and if you so choose to use a late first-round pick here, we won't argue.

2019 PROJECTION: .298 34 HR 84 RBI 96 R 23 SB

Juan Soto: Maybe MLB teams should begin giving more consideration to promoting teenage prospects given how incredible both the Atlanta Braves' Ronald Acuna Jr. and the Washington Nationals' Juan Soto performed in 2018. The younger of the two outfielders at the age of 19 when first called up by the team, Soto was incredible as he hit 22 home runs, drove in 70 batters, and batted .292 in 494 at-bats. Not to be overlooked, it is almost unheard of for someone as young as Soto to come up with such an advanced plate approach like he showed last season (16.0 BB/9, 20.0 K/9) and so we could be talking about batting title material here. Then when you add in the fact Soto has tremendous bat speed and growing natural power, 30-35 home runs as soon as this season is absolutely attainable. While you can debate between Soto and Acuna Jr. about who will be the better overall player, there is no arguing that both should be gone by the end of Round 2 at the latest in 2018 drafts.

2019 PROJECTION: .308 27 HR 86 RBI 93 R 9 SB

Charlie Blackmon: It was another year of excellence from Colorado Rockies outfielder Charlie Blackmon in 2018 as the leadoff man once again helped across the board in hitting 29 homers, scoring 119 runs, collecting 70 RBI, and batting .291. Even though Blackmon's days of high-end running are finished, he still swiped 12 bags last season to at least remain a contributor there. Also, while Blackmon's power remained very impressive, it came to bear that the 37 homers he hit in 2017 belonged in the outlier bin. Aging a bit as Blackmon turns 32 in July, the guy has still fully transitioned himself from a mediocre home run hitter/potent stolen base guy to just the opposite and more of the same should be in store for 2019. One thing that does need to be mentioned though is the trend of Blackmon becoming more strikeout-prone by the year as his K/9 has gone from 15.9 in 2016 up to 19.3 last season. Other than that, Blackmon is safe to draft in Round 2.
2019 PROJECTION: .298 30 HR 78 RBI 115 R 11 SB

Starling Marte: Maybe he didn't need the juice after all! Somewhat of a radioactive fantasy baseball stock coming into the 2018 season off a PED suspension the year prior, Pittsburgh Pirates outfielder Starling Marte reaffirmed his five-tool ability which was highlighted by him hitting 19 home runs and stealing 33 bases in 576 at-bats. What is interesting is that virtually nothing from Marte's statistical profile changed last season when compared to before the PED bust and so that once again makes Marte a stable fantasy baseball commodity for 2019 as he makes our grade as a low-end OF 1. Despite still being allergic to walks last season (5.0 BB/9) which continued a career-long trend, Marte's power/speed game is incredibly fantasy baseball-friendly and maintaining a K/9 rate under 20.0 on an annual basis helps keep the average afloat as well. Having turned 30 this past October, Marte is moving closer to the age where the speed begins to leave the station but he should be good for another year or so in terms of possessing optimal power/speed ability before the latter starts to erode. Highly recommended.
2019 PROJECTION: .280 19 HR 81 RBI 86 R 29 SB

Giancarlo Stanton: Once the New York Yankees officially acquired hulking slugger Giancarlo Stanton from the Miami Marlins last winter, we admit that it was tough not to be sucked into the belief he could make a run at 70 home runs in 2018. After all, Stanton was coming off a season the year prior when he slammed 59 for the Marlins while operating in one of the biggest ballparks in the majors and since he was now headed to a launching pad in Yankee Stadium, imagining another 11 bombs being added to the ledger didn't seem so outlandish. Unfortunately, Stanton predictably had to deal with the often-overlooked "adjustment" phase in terms of handling the big-market microscope that comes with playing in New York. While he went through some pronounced swings in production on almost a week-to-week basis, the end result of 38 homers, 110 runs, and 100 RBI came in at very acceptable levels. In terms of the negatives, Stanton's batting average of .266 remained typically shaky and the positive gains he made in strikeouts in 2017 failed to stick as well (29.9 K/9). Having turned 29 last November, Stanton is past the stage of his career where any further improvement could be expected and so he figures to be a more expensive version of Khris Davis going forward.

2019 PROJECTION: .263 44 HR 123 RBI 110 R 4 SB

Andrew Benintendi: When you share a Boston Red Sox outfield with AL MVP candidates Mookie Betts and J.D. Martinez, it can be tough to stand out as youngster Andrew Benintendi likely found out in 2018. Entering into spring drafts with a ton of hype in the same mold of a Christian Yelich, Benintendi was already coming off a 20-HR/20-SB/.271 AVG. campaign the year prior that seemed to be the floor of what he was capable of achieving in 2018. Unfortunately, Benintendi went down as a bit of a disappointment as he declined in home runs with 16, slightly improved with 21 steals, and batted a solid .291. Add in 103 runs scored and 87 RBI and Benintendi certainly was a rare five-tool contributor to his 2018 fantasy baseball owners. Still just all of 24, the former 2015 first-round pick retains some massive upside for the upcoming season and it would shock no one if he were to take the numbers and push them up another level. Already possessing tremendous plate approaches in walks (10.7 BB/9) and strikeouts (16.0 K/9), the future looks very bright.

2019 PROJECTION: .298 23 HR 90 RBI 108 R 24 SB

Khris Davis: Yeah, we think it is safe to say that Oakland A's DH/outfielder Khris Davis will bat .247 this season. In what became one of the more amazing stats in recent memory, the hulking Davis managed to post a .247 average for the FOURTH straight season in 2018; a campaign that reaffirmed his status as one of the best sluggers in the game as he cracked 48 homers, scored 98 runs, and drove in 123 RBI. By now fully established as a three-category monster, Davis is very good at what he does in terms of the power but the annually ugly average needs to be covered elsewhere. As long as you are comfortable taking on the .247 average, Davis can easily anchor your power numbers once again in 2019.

2019 PROJECTION: .247 44 HR 120 RBI 95 R 1 SB

Justin Upton: What is really interesting concerning the recent fantasy baseball status of Los Angeles Angels outfielder Justin Upton is how many seem to be getting bored of the guy. Once considered a "must have" upstart who possessed some of the same type of hype currently being attached to the Atlanta Braves' Ronald Acuna Jr., Upton has now settled into being somewhat of a boring veteran at the age of 31. This is somewhat strange since Upton remains very productive as he comes off a 2018 where he hit 30 home runs, drove in 85, and swiped 8 bases in 613 at-bats. We think some of the blasé attitude regarding Upton centers on the batting average becoming a yearly issue (between .251 and .273 each of the last 6 seasons) and for an ugly strikeout-heavy approach that is directly responsible for dragging down the former. While this is a valid concern,. Upton still excels in homers, runs, and RBI; while also still contributing a bit in steals which more than help offset the mediocre average. So if Upton were to slide in 2019 drafts again this spring, it would be a good idea to scoop him up as your OF 2.

2019 PROJECTION: .259 32 HR 93 RBI 89 R 7 SB

George Springer: If you were to give truth serum to all the fantasy baseball owners of Houston Astros outfielder George Springer last season, you would come away with a majority of opinions reporting disappointment in the offensive numbers from the team's leadoff hitter. While 22 home runs, 102 runs scored, and 71 RBI went down as helpful production, all three categories represented sizable drops from his 2017 haul (34, 112, 85). Then when you add in the fact Springer's average dropped from .283 the year prior to a mediocre .265 last season, things get even shakier here. When you break it all down, Springer has made it a habit to prove quite volatile in terms of swings in his numbers from year-to-year and 2018 was no different. Now that he is flat in his prime at the age of 29, Springer is unlikely to go above his best-case scenario 2017 production. Also, Springer continued his maddening decision not to steal bases since arriving in the majors (after being a nice weapon there while coming up the minor league ladder) and that is another negative to digest. While at one time we all were in agreement Springer had the potential to reach OF 1 status, those days seem to be finished as he seems settled into the OF 2 range.

2019 PROJECTION: .273 27 HR 84 RBI 110 R 5 SB

Mitch Haniger: Serving mostly as an upside curiosity the last couple of springs, the health finally cooperated enough for Seattle Mariners outfielder Mitch Haniger to show himself to be a very good high-end OF 2 capable of contributing in all five standard ROTO categories. Having gone into the 2018 season at the magical age of 27, Haniger put up career-highs everywhere as he hit 26 homers, scored 90 runs, drove in 93, and batted a solid .285. Add in 8 stolen bases and Haniger was one of the better buys in 2018 fantasy baseball considering the very cheap spring price. Like we already noted, it really all just came down to good health as Haniger showed flashes of this kind of ability in 2017 but he would spend a chunk of the year on the DL that served to dull the momentum. With Haniger now having revealed his very impressive potential, the question is whether he can maintain those levels going into 2019. On that front things looks pretty good as both Haniger's walk (10.2 BB/9) and strikeout (21.7 K/9) rates both check out nicely and 38 doubles possibly portend to another level of power being on the way. When you take into consideration the fact West Coast players tend to come a bit cheaper in annual drafts, Haniger looks like a tremendous buy once again.

2019 PROJECTION: .280 28 HR 89 RBI 86 R 7 SB

Eddie Rosario: For some strange reason Minnesota Twins five-tool outfielder Eddie Rosario doesn't get included when talk turns to some of the top young hitting outfielders in today's fantasy baseball but he absolutely deserves full mention here as the guy has now put forth back-to-back excellent seasons from 2017-18. While Rosario did see a slight statistical decline almost across the board last season, the numbers still remain terrific as he batted .288 with 24 home runs and 8 stolen bases for the Twins. Just now getting into his prime years after turning 27 last September, Rosario just needs to work on his utter lack of patience (5.1 BB/9) in order to unlock another small level jump in production. Even if that doesn't occur, we strongly suggest you invest heavily here.

2019 PROJECTION: .290 25 HR 80 RBI 88 R 10 SB

Lorenzo Cain: Sometimes annual MVP candidates can come in non-traditional packages; with an overall excellent game overcoming the tendency for voters to succumb to the appeal of big offensive number candidates. Such a player in 2018 was Milwaukee Brewers outfielder Lorenzo Cain who not only once again played Gold Glove defense but also put forth multi-category production which was highlighted by 10 homers, 90 runs scored, 30 stolen bases, and a .308 average. Severely underrated throughout his career, Cain's advanced metrics all were superb as well as he posted 11.5 BB/9 and 15.2 K/9 rates that helped him become a constant weapon on the bases. While Cain is aging a bit as he turns 33 in April, he shows no signs of slowing down with his speed and in turn, ability to swipe bases. It is crucial though that Cain holds onto this skill since a great deal of his fantasy baseball value comes from runs and steals. Beyond the steals, Cain has been an annual batting average star, with three of his last four seasons ending up with marks over .300. With Cain also scoring a ton of runs atop a very potent Brewers lineup and remaining capable of reaching double-digits in homers, the guy should continue being a major target for all in 2019 fantasy baseball drafts. Annually one of our favorites in these pages, count this publication as aggressive Cain hounds.

2019 PROJECTION: .314 11 HR 45 RBI 98 R 28 SB

Wil Myers (3B): It was a season to forget for San Diego Padres outfielder Wil Myers in 2018 as the early-round pick amassed just 343 at-bats due to a litany of health problems. Things got off to an ugly start on that front as Myers missed two months with a severe oblique strain and then in the second half of the year went back to the DL with a foot contusion. In between all the time off, Myers showed why interest in his offensive game remains high in yearly fantasy baseball drafts as he hit 13 home runs, stole 13 bases, and posted a 39 both in the runs and RBI columns. Having arrived on the MLB scene at an early age, Myers will still only be just 28 when the 2019 season gets underway which means the prime years are still in their infancy. While the injuries in 2018 were a bit disturbing, we don't think this is a trend as Myers logged over 600 at-bats in both the two seasons prior. Now getting back to the numbers, Myers is holding his power/speed game nicely and that plays well both in the outfield and at third base where he picked up eligibility late last season. Keep in mind that Myers posted very potent 28/28 and 30/20 splits in homers/steals in 2016-17 respectively and he could be around that statistical ballpark this season if he can stay in one piece. The batting average is one place where Myers is quite a negative though as his .253 mark in 2018 was par for the course on that front. Now just a career .253 hitter overall as well, Myers' annually high strikeout rates certainly doesn't help the matter. With that said, we can accept the somewhat shoddy average if Myers continues to post his customarily impressive power/speed numbers. Since we have not reached the point where any erosion has occurred in the latter, keep drafting Myers as you did prior to 2018.

2019 PROJECTION: .255 26 HR 77 RBI 89 R 19 SB

Michael Brantley: Given that free agent outfielder Michael Brantley had been nothing but a monumental health mess the previous two years, it was no great surprise when the veteran hitter found himself in the late-round territory when it came to spring drafts. While this publication was running out of patience with Brantley and all the missed games like everyone else, we also made it a point to say that the guy remained one of the very best pure hitters in baseball. Continuing on that point, we also made sure to point out if Brantley could ever just scratch out 500 at-bats again, he could prove to be a tremendous value play. So whether Brantley was praying to the health gods or not, all the planets aligned on that front as he amassed 631 at-bats in what turned out to be a nice comeback season in 2018. Capable of hitting for average in his sleep, Brantley predictably batted .309 and still showed himself to be a power/speed asset by cracking 17 home runs and stealing 12 bases. When you add in the 89 runs scored and 76 RBI, it was an all-around impressive haul of numbers by Brantley. With all that being said, however, we still need to be cautious regarding an investment in Brantley this spring since he still carries an injury-prone label which will only grow at the age of 32. On the flip side, Brantley is almost a lock for another .300 average and a near 15/15 output in homers/steals which means if you can snag him at an OF 3 price, be sure to do so.

2019 PROJECTION: .310 15 HR 74 RBI 83 R 11 SB

Aaron Hicks: Kudos to New York Yankees GM Brian Cashman who made what has proven to be a tremendous steal of a trade with the Minnesota Twins for the team's faded outfield prospect Aaron Hicks after the 2016 season. While Hicks certainly needed some seasoning/improvement on his approach at the plate, he has now fully developed into one of the best two-way players in the game. Playing Gold Glove-caliber defense in the outfield, Hicks also set a slew of career-bests in 2018 when he slugged 27 homers, scored 90 runs, and drove in 79. Always possessing very good speed as well, Hicks's 11 stolen bases made him a swell four-category contributor who made the OF 2 grade last year. Even more promising is that, while Hicks' .246 average was quite ugly, a rough .264 BABIP had a lot to do with that number ending up in such shaky territory. Instead, focus in on Hicks' very good 15.5 BB/9 and 19.1 K/9 rates that both point to a future as a .280 or higher hitter. So once the average does uptick in 2019 with the luck likely rebounding, Hicks' impressive contributions in the other four categories will put him in the high-OF 2 range again. Even though the journey to get where we are now with Hicks has been far from smooth, the end result looks terrific.

2019 PROJECTION: .272 25 HR 77 RBI 94 R 10 SB

David Peralta: It may have taken a bit longer than we originally anticipated but years of this publication touting Arizona Diamondbacks outfielder David Peralta as a possible breakout candidate finally came through in 2018 as the 31-year-old clubbed 30 home runs, drove in 87, and batted .293. With Peralta also scoring 75 runs, he became a very good four-category contributor for the cost of maybe even just a waiver add early in the season. In going from just 14 home runs in 2017 to last year's 30, Peralta became more of a pure slugger as shown by an elevated swing plane (bumping up the fly ball rate) and through a K/9 rate that jumped to 20.2 as well. While you want some more walks here (just a 7.8 BB/9) to ensure the average remains in the .290 range, Peralta seems quite legit as a new member of the OF 2 club.

2019 PROJECTION: .286 27 HR 84 RBI 71 R 5 SB

Tommy Pham: The notion that the sequel is never as good as the original certainly applies to the last two seasons for multi-tooled outfielder Tommy Pham. After years of dealing with injuries and vision problems, Pham seemed to put all his vast athletic gifts together in 2017 when he posted a five-tool season highlighted by 23 home runs 25 stolen bases, and a .306 batting average. As often happens after such a big performance, Pham wanted to get paid and the contract faceoff he undertook against the St. Louis Cardinals dragged into the 2018 season which wasn't a help to anyone. Things got so heated between the two sides that the Cards traded Pham to the Tampa Bay Rays over the summer which put the capper on what became a disappointing season (21 homers, 15 steals, .275 average). Now turning 31 in March and still on the lookout for a new deal, Pham could be headed for more distractions which is not what you want to see. In terms of the advanced metrics, Pham's strikeouts were up a bit (24.6 K/9) but the walks remained very good (11.8 BB/9) which means a decent average is in play again. With Pham also solidifying 20-home run and 15-20 steal ability, there are still quite a bit of things that are attractive here for 2019 fantasy baseball.

2019 PROJECTION: ..278 23 HR 67 RBI 89 R 19 SB

Rhys Hoskins: After what could only be described as an epic home run explosion from Philadelphia Phillies rookie outfielder Rhys Hoskins in 2017 (18 long balls in just 212 at-bats), there was no stopping the hype train from picking up unending speed as fantasy baseball drafts got underway the following spring. While it is a fact that home runs are more plentiful than ever before, Hoskins represented the opportunity to get in on the ground floor for what many predicted would be a true monster performance in 2018. Once again though, the optimism outpaced the actual game production of Hoskins for long stretches of last season and while he still put forth an excellent tally of 34 homers, 89 runs scored, and 96 RBI; there was a sense that the guy was a bit of a letdown. The latter point gets driven home a bit more when you look at Hoskins' ugly .246 average and for the fact, it took an extra 448 at-bats to garner those additional 16 home runs. So it goes for Hoskins as we head to 2019 fantasy baseball as this is still a somewhat flawed power hitter who seems to be in the same mold of a Giancarlo Stanton with regards to combining big home run ability with a strikeout-heavy approach that could result in yearly batting averages that are not helpful. Turning just 26 in March, Hoskins has every right to approach 40 homers, 90 runs scored, and 100 RBI this season which is excellent three-category production but the threat of a shaky average mute some of last season's hype.

2019 PROJECTION: .263 39 HR 108 RBI 93 R 4 SB

A.J. Pollock: Good luck ever trying to figure out what you are going to get on a yearly basis from free agent outfielder A.J. Pollock as injuries and wildly swinging offensive numbers continue to undermine what at one time looked like a burgeoning career set for stardom. By now reflections of Pollock's huge 2015 campaign (.315. 20 homers, 39 SB) are becoming nothing but a distant outlier memory and in fact, the one thing we can say for sure about the guy is that he will spend time on the DL at some point during a given season. 2018 was no different as Pollock missed almost two months with a fractured thumb and a rough second half performance (.233, 9 homers, 4 steals) ended the year with more bad memories dogging his name. Now in terms of the composite numbers, Pollock's 21 homers, 65 runs scored, and 13 steals were not terrible but the .257 average marked the third straight season he went under .270 in that category. With regards to the latter, Pollock is going the wrong way both in walks (6.7 BB/9) and strikeouts (21.7 K/9) as he continues to lose overall plate discipline and having already turned 31 this past December, we are well beyond the point of the guy being in the developmental stage. So while there are still some useful power/speed numbers to pursue here, the unending injuries/lineup absences combining with the recent batting average trouble make Pollock a radioactive 2019 fantasy baseball outfield option.

2019 PROJECTION: .259 20 HR 69 RBI 75 R 15 SB

Odubel Herrera: It was a mixed bag season for the Philadelphia Phillies' Odubel Herrera in 2018 as the former five-tool outfielder began to let some of those categories fall by the wayside despite reaching close to the start of his prime years. With Herrera having planted himself firmly onto the fantasy baseball landscape back in 2016 when he hit 15 homers, stole 25 bases, and batted .286; visions of future 20/20 campaigns began to dance in the heads of prospective buyers as 2017 approached. A strange thing has happened since then however as Herrera all of a sudden lost interest in running (dropping to 8 and then 5 steals the last two seasons) and the batting average began to erode as well (.281 in 2017, .255 a year ago). On the flip side, Herrera grew into additional power as he set career-highs in homers (22) and RBI (71) last season. Alas, when you added in the shaky .255 average, 5 steals, and 64 runs scored, Herrera went down as a negative in three of the five standard ROTO categories which was not such a good thing. Now in digging into the numbers a bit more, a few things emerge that need to be pointed out. The first is Herrera's. 290 BABIP was way down from his customary mid-.300 range in that category (never under .345 in three previous MLB campaigns) and so it is likely we are looking at a decent average uptick this season when the luck factor goes back to the mean for the guy. Also, both Herrera's BB/9 and K/9 numbers were pretty much within normal ranges for him as well which means there is not as much volatility as the surface statistics may suggest. Now the one issue that is a clear negative is the erosion in steals and that seems to be a trend with Herrera that is not going to fix itself for the better. As a result, we need to price Herrera this spring without steals being a part of the statistical package. Overall though, there remains a decent amount of stuff to like here and with Herrera having turned just 27 this past December, another push upwards in the numbers is very possible.

2019 PROJECTION: .279 23 HR 73 RBI 65 R 7 SB

Andrew McCutchen: As he gets set to likely join his fourth team in the span of two years, former MVP outfielder Andrew McCutchen is having a tough time holding his offensive numbers at the age of 32. In a 2018 season split between the San Francisco Giants and New York Yankees, McCutchen batted a career-worst .255 with a paltry 20 home runs and 65 RBI in a massive 682 at-bats. Yes, a bunch of those plate appearances was in the spacious San Francisco ballpark but McCutchen's numbers started sliding a few seasons which is a trend that seems to be picking up speed. Speaking of speed, McCutchen's 14 stolen bases last season was his most since 2014 which is at least encouraging for his overall value but we saw the effects of age through another personal-worst 21.3 K/9. With McCutchen posting a neutral .304 BABIP last season and still drawing walks in the process (13.9 BB/9), we are getting a true reading of the type of player he has become of late. While McCutchen can still help you hold down an everyday starting spot this season, it centers mostly in the OF 3 range.

2019 PROJECTION: .262 20 HR 75 RBI 79 RBI 11 SB

Marcell Ozuna: Getting out of the spacious ballpark in Miami last winter when the St. Louis Cardinals acquired him via trade, the 2018 fantasy baseball outlook was shining brightly for power-hitting outfielder Marcell Ozuna. Coming off a 37-homer/124-RBI campaign the year before despite the challenging Miami digs, at least somewhat of a repeat was expected by Ozuna's prospective fantasy baseball owners last spring. Unfortunately, 2017 looks like an outlier campaign for Ozuna as he sank back down to just 23 homers and 88 RBI last season which, while still effective, is a clear step back from spring expectations. On the positive side, Ozuna's 17.5 K/9 last season was a career-best and while he should strive for more walks (6.1 BB/9), the average should fall somewhere in the middle of the .312 and .280 marks the last two years. Finally, with almost no speed to speak of (3 steals last season), Ozuna looks primed to settle back to OF 3 status.

2019 PROJECTION: .284 25 HR 90 RBI 74 R 2 SB

Michael Conforto: It has been nothing but volatility for New York Mets slugging outfielder Michael Conforto over the last season-plus as the very serious shoulder separation that required invasive surgery towards the end of what was a breakout 2017 campaign cast a giant cloud over his status the following spring. Original estimates were that Conforto would be out until sometime in May but the kid shocked everyone by being ready at the start of the 2018 season. Coming off 27 home runs the year prior, expectations were then re-set for Conforto to once again be the burgeoning star and potential high-end fantasy baseball outfielder his talent seemed to suggest. Well, maybe Conforto shouldn't have rushed to return the way he did because the guy was so bad during the first half (.216, 11 HR, 32 RBI), there was talk a return to the minors to work on the swing was needed. In situations like this though the talent eventually comes through and for Conforto that meant a bunch of power numbers after the All-Star Break (.273, 17 HR, 52 RBI) which re-established him as one of the best young sluggers in the game. With the shoulder injury another year behind him, Conforto can now make that run at 30 home runs and 90 RBI (he finished 2018 with 28 and 82 respectively) and get to work on the .243 average that in fairness, was dragged down a bunch trying to work the rust off from the first half of the season. Since we already know the power seems pretty set, the average remains the focus and on that front, there is optimism. The biggest plus is that Conforto draws a ton of walks (13.2 BB/9) and his strikeout rate a year ago did decline for the third season in a row (down to a still elevated 24.9 K/9). Any more incremental drop in K's will only combine with the terrific walk rate to send the average northward and so Conforto could be ready to become one of the better four category power-centric hitters in 2019 fantasy baseball.

2019 PROJECTION: .267 29 HR 86 RBI 84 R 4 SB

Ender Inciarte: Despite being overshadowed in a 2018 Atlanta Braves outfield that was fronted by hotshot rookie Ronald Acuna Jr. and steady veteran Nick Markakis; speedster Ender Inciarte more than did his part to make this unit overall one of MLB's best. Playing Gold Glove defense in the field, Inciarte is also making it a habit to supply annually underrated offensive seasons as he hit 10 homers. scored 83 runs, and stole 28 bases. Unfortunately, Inciarte being removed from the team's leadoff spot when Acuna was promoted robbed him of some additional counting numbers but we have seen a firmly established baseline that can be quite valuable going forward. While some will unfairly knock Inciarte's .265 average, that number was depressed a bit by a .293 BABIP which was quite a bit down from .329 and .333 the two seasons prior. Possessing tremendous contact skills (13.0 K/9) and enough walks to keep things honest (7.4 BB/9), Inciarte is a .300 hitter when all things are being equal. Add in the 10 homers and 25-30 steals and Inciarte remains severely underrated in yearly fantasy baseball leagues.

2019 PROJECTION: .290 11 HR 59 RBI 86 R 27 SB

Gregory Polanco: It was yet another year of unfulfilled expectations for Pittsburgh Pirates outfielder Gregory Polanco in 2018 as his first half was marked by some horrendous batting slumps and then was followed by him missing the last month of the season due to a deep knee bone bruise and a very serious shoulder dislocation that overshadowed a decent second half with the bat. Having made his debut at the age of 22 back in 2014, Polanco looked destined to be the next version of his then-teammate Andrew McCutchen in terms of possessing five-tool ability and in the process reaching a top-tier status in yearly fantasy baseball leagues. Alas, it has been nothing but a bumpy road since that time for Polanco as ongoing injuries, inconsistent offensive numbers, and a reputation for not being the hardest worker have made him one of the more volatile players to own in the game. With that said, Polanco's talent is still obvious and 2018 was a solid overall season as he hit 22 home runs, stole 12 bases, and collected 81 RBI. Polanco has established a 20-25 home run baseline to go with 10-15 steals which is certainly quite valuable in today's fantasy baseball but there are also negatives in terms of a batting average that has yet to top the .258 he hit in 2016. The average red flag is being dragged down by a putrid .218 career mark versus lefties but Polanco's .263 output against righties is certainly nothing to write home about. Digging into the numbers a bit more, Polanco is a very rare and strange case of a player who has good speed and who also draws walks (excellent 11.4 BB/9 in 2018) but who for some reason can't reach .300 in the BABIP realm. With strikeouts not overly concerning either (generally in the 20.0 range in his career), Polanco is actually doing what he should be doing in terms of his approach at the dish but the batted ball luck has simply not been there. That could certainly change when he returns in 2019 and with some good health, Polanco may finally put forth that upper-level campaign we all have waited for. While the odds say that won't happen, Polanco can yield helpful power/speed output to go with solid counting numbers in runs and RBI. Any average uptick would then be treated as a bonus. Unfortunately, Polanco's outlook as of this writing is very murky due to having surgery on his dislocated shoulder that also remedied a labrum tear. The typical recovery time from such a procedure is 7-9 months and so Polanco could return anywhere from mid-April to sometime in June. So at this point, Polanco can only be treated as a strict OF 3 given the expected time on the shelf to begin the new season but his talent alone makes him someone who could supply your team with a nice mid-season boost.

2019 PROJECTION: .263 17 HR 74 RBI 75 R 11 SB

Joey Gallo (1B): Serving as the poster boy for the all-or-nothing slugger would undoubtedly be Texas Rangers first baseman/outfielder Joey Gallo who in 2018 made it two seasons in a row reaching the 40 home run mark (41 in 577 at-bats), while at the same time going north of a 35.0 K/9 (35.9 K/9) for the same amount of occasions during the same span. With Gallo remaining a high walks guy (12.8 BB/9), he becomes a true three outcome hitter (walk, home run, or strikeout) which has severe limitations when it comes to the world of fantasy baseball. While on power alone Gallo is as good as it gets, his .209 and .206 averages the last two seasons in actuality take a great deal of shine away from the long ball contributions. So if the terrific home run totals get offset to a degree by the horrible hit to your team's cumulative batting average, Gallo is really left with a decent runs scored total (82 last season) to supply to any prospective owner since there is no speed to speak of (just 14 career steals in three-plus years in the majors). As we say every year in these pages, guys with Gallo's home run-centric/ugly batting average profiles are littered all over the late-rounds of a draft or on the waiver wire throughout the season. So it makes zero sense to spend a mid-round pick on Gallo whose impressive titanic blasts take on more perceived impact than what they are actually worth.
2019 PROJECTION: .208 38 HR 93 RBI 84 R 4 SB

Yoenis Cespedes: The New York Mets organization is already regretting the massive four-year contract extension worth $110 million they bestowed on slugging outfielder Yoenis Cespedes prior to 2017 as the Cuban is now 2-for-2 in terms of having completely injury-marred campaigns since then. After a series of leg injuries that ultimately resulted in a season-ending blown hamstring last August which kept him to just 81 games played (albeit with a solid .292 average and 17 home runs in 321 at-bats), Cespedes took part in just 38 contests last season before he needed to have surgery to fix calcifications in BOTH of his heels that require an 8-10 month recovery timetable. That puts Cespedes' availability for the start of 2019 very much in question and at the age of 32, his days as even an OF 2 appear to be over until the guy can prove he can at least somewhat stay on the field. Making matters even worse, unlike in 2017 Cespedes' bat looked very shaky last season as his K/9 spiked to a horrid 31.8 and only a lucky .333 BABIP saved his shaky .262 average from dropping even more into the garbage bin. Already having a reputation of being somewhat of a diva, Cespedes' never-ending injuries have almost completely overshadowed his actual on-the-field performance. With his start of 2019 also in doubt, Cespedes looks to be way too volatile to deal with from a fantasy baseball angle.
2019 PROJECTION: .273 19 HR 70 RBI 74 R 2 SB

Stephen Piscotty: Pretty much going along with everything else that went right for the 2018 Oakland A's, outfielder Stephen Piscotty posted a career-year for the team by hitting 27 home runs, driving in 88, and batting .267 in 605 at-bats. With Piscotty admittedly having a much less cluttered mind after unfortunately dealing with his mother's illness and eventual passing the previous year, the guy got back to the business of swinging a bat last season which he did at a very nice level almost all the way around. This is the potential that many saw in Piscotty when he first came up to the majors with the St. Louis Cardinals and in 2016 he was able to hit 22 homers with a .273 average which showed such ability was always possible. With Piscotty having achieved this in 2018, he can now settle in as a decent OF 3 power bat who just needs to draw some more walks (6.9 BB/9) to boost the shaky batting average.

2019 PROJECTION: .275 25 HR 84 RBI 83 R 4 SB

Mallex Smith: Speed, speed, and more speed is the name of the game for Tampa Bay Rays outfielder Mallex Smith as his first extended playing time in 2018 resulted in 40 stolen bases and 65 runs in 544 at-bats. With steals drying up like never before in today's game, Smith's ability to supply a high yield in that category is more valuable than you may think. Making matters more interesting here is that Smith is not a one-trick speed pony as he batted a very good .296 last season and could literally make a run at 90 runs scored if he grabs a firm hold of the leadoff spot to begin 2019. With the price likely remaining more affordable than you may think at least for one more season, Smith can serve as your clear stolen base anchor and help in average and runs as a nice bonus.

2019 PROJECTION: .293 4 HR 45 RBI 79 R 45 SB

Adam Eaton: Man, if Washington Nationals leadoff man/outfielder Adam Eaton can just find some semblance of health, we could be looking at a swell five-category contributor in the fantasy baseball world. Unfortunately, for the second season in a row Eaton missed a tremendous chunk of the year with injuries; with 2018 including ankle surgery wiping out almost his entire first half. When on the field, however, Eaton predictably produced as he batted .301 with 5 homers, 55 runs scored, and 9 stolen bases in just 370 at-bats. Despite all the injuries, there should be no doubting that Eaton is very talented and a 500 at-bat season would likely result in terrific five-category output that would include around a 15/20 ratio in homers/steals. In addition, Eaton has proven to be a batting average asset as he is a .287 career hitter and is also capable of scoring 100 runs batting leadoff if again the health cooperates. This is always a tough call here as Eaton is so frustrating to own given all the missed time but the payoff could be huge if he can stay upright. With all that said, count us among those who will take another shot here.

2019 PROJECTION: .304 14 HR 57 RBI 95 R 15 SB

Harrison Bader: When looking at St. Louis Cardinals outfield prospect Harrison Bader, the power/speed tools quickly jump out which undoubtedly grabs the immediate attention from the majority of the fantasy baseball community. Having been given an extended look by the team in 2018, Bader responded nicely by hitting 12 homers, scored 61 runs, and stole 15 bases in showcasing some intriguing multiple category abilities. Unfortunately, Bader lost the strikeout battle as his 29.3 K/9 was downright brutal and helped result in a .264 average. Think Chris Young during his early Arizona Diamondbacks days as a comparison in terms of what Bader could be in 2019 fantasy baseball and this means a run at 20/20 but also an average that will be a negative. Given the remaining upside since the kid won't turn 25 until June, Bader should be on the majority of sleeper lists for spring drafts.

2019 PROJECTION: .257 16 HR 54 RBI 74 R 19 SB

David Dahl: The lure of Colorado Rockies outfield prospect David Dahl remains strong as the multi-talented hitter took some very firm steps forward last season to help put what was an extremely disappointing 2017 campaign behind him. While Dahl spent half of the season in the minors, he took full advantage of a summer promotion to the Rockies by hitting .273 with 16 home runs and 5 steals in just 271 at-bats. The power on a per game basis was eye-opening and at the age of only 25 in April, Dahl continues to carry around some immense five-tool upside. Given the Colorado label and the power/speed game, Dahl will likely be a very popular sleeper pick in 2019 fantasy baseball drafts. While Dahl strikes out a bit too much (25.1 K/9), there is no denying the 25/15/.280 ability here if he can manage to break camp with the team. If it looks like Dahl will be able to do so, bump him up by more than a little in your 2019 outfield rankings.

2019 PROJECTION: .277 23 HR 65 RBI 63 R 10 SB

Yasiel Puig: The enigma that is Los Angeles Dodgers outfielder Yasiel Puig continued unabated in 2018 as the guy combined tremendous production when his head was on straight (23 homers, 15 steals, .267) but also missed extensive time with an oblique strain and later a hip problem. Now entering veteran status after turning 28 this past December, Puig seems to have settled into being a 25-30 home run bat to go with around 15 steals and a .260-ish average. Not the superstar numbers originally expected when Puig first arrived in the States from Cuba but still a very solid high-end OF 3 regardless.

2019 PROJECTION: .266 26 HR 77 RBI 73 R 16 SB

Matt Kemp: As he goes into the last year of his contract in 2019, Los Angeles Dodgers outfielder Matt Kemp is still swinging a decent enough bat as he batted .290 with 21 home runs and 85 RBI last season. With Kemp receiving a bunch of rest days in order to keep his aging body (he turned 34 last September) fresh, it is likely he can only match last season's numbers going forward. With the stolen base ability having d the station completely since 2015, Kemp is almost entirely dependent on homers, RBI, and average which greatly cuts down the margin for error given the age issue. Also, Kemp's .339 BABIP last season was very lucky and means the .290 average is not likely going to be repeated. When you also consider that Kemp has been very injury prone the last few years, it is obvious he should only be drafted at this stage of the game as a bench backup outfielder.

2019 PROJECTION: .284 20 HR 82 RBI 63 R 2 SB

Shin-Soo Choo: No one wants to ever own him of late but Texas Rangers outfielder Shin-Soo Choo continues to produce nicely as an OF 3 in yearly fantasy baseball leagues. Last season that included 21 home runs, 83 runs scored, and a .264 average for the team in 665 at-bats which, while far from potent, served as a nice value for someone who typically doesn't get picked until the late rounds of drafts. Choo still draws his walks (13.8 BB/9) and the strikeout rate (23.4 K/9) last season was not absurd either which indicate the veteran is not going off a statistical cliff just yet. On the flip side, Choo has become a batting average liability on the back-nine of his career as he has now batted under .264 in four of the last five seasons and the steals have almost left the station (just 6 a year ago). What is really comes down to here is that while Choo's numbers still show an OF 3 player, his expected 2019 ADP will be so much cheaper which makes investing in him one more time far from a risk.

2019 PROJECTION: .257 20 HR 67 RBI 81 R 5 SB

Corey Dickerson: For the second time in two years with the Pittsburgh Pirates, outfielder Corey Dickerson quietly did a nice job with the bat as he hit .300 with 13 home runs and 8 stolen bases in 533 at-bats. Yes, Dickerson took a nosedive in the power department after hitting 27 homers the year prior but just a tiny 15.0 K/9 rate showed he was far from being manhandled by opposing pitchers. In fact, Dickerson's home run output last season looks like it belongs in the outlier bin and so it is a smart idea to project a push back to around 20 bombs this year to go with 70-plus runs and RBI. Finally, Dickerson has now batted .282 and last year's .300 since coming to the Pirates and given the terrific contact skills, another helpful number there is likely.

2019 PROJECTION: .284 19 HR 65 RBI 78 R 5 SB

Nick Markakis: Perhaps we are past the time where veteran outfielder Nick Markakis deserves more respect with the bat then most have given him credit for. Serving as a team leader and sparkplug for the playoff-bound 2018 Atlanta Braves, Markakis had one of his best seasons ever at the age of 34 when he batted .297 with 14 homers, 78 RBI, and 93 runs scored while operating near the top of the order. Even though the totality of Markakis' numbers only yield around OF 3 value, the guy is a terrific contact hitter (11.3 K/9, 10.2 BB/9) who can post good averages and pile up the counting numbers in runs and RBI. At the very least, Markakis looks like a nice backup outfielder for another season or so who will cost very little at the draft table.

2019 PROJECTION: .288 11 HR 84 RBI 77 R 1 SB

Ian Happ: We were guilty as charged in somewhat over-hyping Chicago Cubs outfield prospect Ian Happ for 2018 fantasy baseball as it quickly became clear early on last season the kid needed some more swing refinement as the K's piled up in bunches. Happ was so bad during the first half of the season overall that he was kicked to the waiver wire by many of his original fantasy baseball owners which were somewhat understandable. As ugly as things were early on, however, the talent that made Happ the 9th overall pick in the 2015 MLB Draft eventually began to bubble to the surface as he put forth enough solid work during the second half to finish with 15 home runs, 8 steals, and a .233 average in 462 at-bats. The major red flag here centered on Happ's truly horrendous 36.1 K/9 rate which is Joey Gallo territory and make it virtually impossible at that level for him to put forth even a .250 average. Now some hope does lie in the fact Happ is a walks machine (15.2 BB/9) which is especially impressive for such a young hitter but his performance there is undermined to an extent by all of the K's. Moving into the more glamorous numbers, Happ no doubt carries with him solid power/speed ability that could be of the 25-HR/15-SB variety down the road. With Happ not turning 25 until August and with no guarantee the K's will come down this season, his overall outlook for 2019 fantasy baseball is much dimmer compared to the previous spring.

2019 PROJECTION: .248 19 HR 54 RBI 67 R 9 SB

Nomar Mazara: Now three years into his still very young MLB career, Texas Rangers outfielder Nomar Mazara has the consistency thing down pat as he has hit exactly 20 home runs in each of those campaigns. Last season those 20 homers were paired with 77 RBI, 61 runs, and a shoddy .258 average but it remains important to mention Mazara will turn only 24 this April which means some upside remains. Be that as it may, the current version of Mazara is a bit underwhelming as he took a step back both in walks (7.5 BB/9) and strikeouts (21.6 K/9) last season compared to 2017 and he has no speed to speak of with just 3 career steals. Since there are no steals to be had, it is imperative Mazara hit for average and around 25 homers to hold OF 3 value in fantasy baseball leagues but he is not quite there yet. Still, Mazara can easily reach those figures in 2019 or soon thereafter given his youth and the ballpark is certainly an attraction. So a late-round pick seems like a smart idea given the upside Mazara still brings to the table.

2019 PROJECTION: .267 21 HR 79 RBI 65 R 1 SB

Austin Meadows: Kudos to the always forward-thinking Tampa Bay Rays for securing top outfield prospect Austin Meadows from the Pittsburgh Pirates for starting pitcher Chris Archer last summer and already we are getting a glimpse of the sizable upside here as he hit 6 home runs, stole 5 bases, and batted .287 with the two teams in a cumulative 191 at-bats in 2018. Having been the ninth overall pick in the 2013 MLB Draft, Meadows always carried around some pronounced hype and it appears he is ready to make a power/speed impact during what is expected to be his first full season in the big leagues. While Meadows does need to show some more patience at the dish (5.2 BB/9), the tools are very impressive and it should not shock anyone in the least if the Rays made out on another key trade. Given the draft pedigree and upside alone, Meadows should be a prominent name on any sleeper list this spring.

2019 PROJECTION: .270 16 HR 54 RBI 65 R 10 SB

Steven Souza Jr.: The annual frustration that comes with owning talented but flawed Arizona Diamondbacks outfielder Steven Souza Jr. continued unabated in 2018 as the guy missed more than half the year with injuries and then hit just .220 with 5 homers and 6 steals in the 272 at-bats when on the field. By now it is common knowledge that Souza Jr. is one of those guys who can put up some very good power/speed numbers on yearly basis to spike the excitement meter but then, on the other hand, find a bunch of this enthusiasm fall by the wayside as the batting average hovers in the gutter due to unending strikeout issues. Keep in mind though that it was just in 2017 when Souza slammed 30 home runs and stole 16 bases but again the average was more than underwhelming at .239 which reinforces the limitations. It does stand to reason that a much better season on the health front for Souza Jr. would result in a solid uptick in numbers across the board outside of the average and OF 3 status is achievable under such a scenario.

2019 PROJECTION: .235 24 HR 75 RBI 73 R 11 SB

Jay Bruce (1B): Usually one of the more durable players in the game, the injury bug really came up and bit New York Mets outfielder Jay Bruce in 2018 as his 361 at-bats represented a career-low and helped result in underwhelming counting numbers in homers (9), RBI (37) and runs (31). Add in a brutal .223 average and about the only positive for Bruce in 2018 was that he gained first base eligibility to go with his outfield responsibilities. With all that said, it was just in 2017 when Bruce clubbed 36 home runs and drove in 101 batters and since he will turn just 32 in April, a solid rebound campaign is likely. In deeper formats, Bruce is certainly worth a buy-low look despite retaining a very boring overall label.
2019 PROJECTION: .257 27 HR 94 RBI 75 R 2 SB

Carlos Gonzalez: It looks like Carlos Gonzalez' days in Colorado with the Rockies are finished as he heads into free agency off just an all right 2018 campaign which included 16 homers, 64 RBI, and a .276 batting average. With the Rockies having a crowded outfield, CarGo didn't play as much as in years past (just 504 at-bats) but when on the field, the power and most of the advanced metrics remained steady. The problem with Gonzalez going forward as he gets set to join a new MLB organization has been the drastic road/home splits that read as follow for his career: .323/142 HR/497 RBI at home and .251/89 HR/278 RBI on the road. In addition, Gonzalez has not been a stolen base asset for years and so he has the look of a guy who will play off past achievements in likely being drafted ahead of where he should be this spring.
2019 PROJECTION: .270 15 HR 63 RBI 67 R 4 SB

Brandon Nimmo: The New York Mets look like they got themselves a keeper in high-OBP/non-stop hustling outfielder Brandon Nimmo. A slow developing 2011 first-round pick of the team, the issue with Nimmo always centered on how much power he would be able to hit but non-stop injury absences of Yoenis Cespedes helped prove the point moot during what was a nice full-season campaign by the kid in 2018. Operating mostly out of the leadoff spot due to some tremendous patience (15.0 BB/9), Nimmo managed 17 home runs, 77 runs scored, and a .263 average in 535 at-bats. A nice bonus also came in the form of 9 stolen bases as Nimmo never showed much in the way of ability on that front while coming up the minor league ladder. Given that Cespedes is not due to return to the team until sometime in the middle of July at the earliest, Nimmo will have a long leash to begin the 2019 season where he once again is the favorite to bat leadoff. Now to put Nimmo's 2018 in full perspective, it needs to be said that the guy should probably be in some sort of platoon as he hit just .234 versus lefties. Nimmo also struck out at a high 26.2 K/9 clip which means the average may not be great once again. Finally, it is just as likely Nimmo's 9 steals last season will vanish now that pitchers/catchers will be paying closer attention and so it would not be smart to project any contributions there this spring. So while Nimmo looks like a nice player who can score runs and maybe take a shot at 20 homers, he is best left for backup duty on your 2019 fantasy baseball roster.

2019 PROJECTION: .266 18 HR 55 RBI 77 R 7 SB

Ryan Braun: We should just put Milwaukee Brewers outfielder Ryan Braun on the "day-to-day" injury report now because everyone knows the aging veteran will be under such a distinction for long stretches of the upcoming 2019 season. Past steroid usage no doubt has done a number on Braun's body as he has dealt with nonstop injuries for the last three seasons and the offensive numbers have turned sharply downward as well. Now an "old" 35, Braun managed just 20 home runs, 64 RBI, and a shoddy .254 batting average last season as his walk rate of 7.6 BB/9 was at its lowest point since 2014. With opposing pitchers no longer fearing Braun, they are attacking him aggressively like never before and so look for the rising 19.0 K/9 from last season going northward in 2019 as well. While it was nice to see Braun still run enough to swipe 11 bags, that statistic is in jeopardy of completely falling off the map as well given the advancing age/ill health. In short, you are severely living in the past if you decide to go down the Braun well once again this spring and we actually suggest staying completely clear of this daily headache entirely.

2019 PROJECTION: .257 19 HR 66 RBI 55 R 8 SB

Brett Gardner: Perhaps showing the effects of age (having turned 35 last August) which is especially rough on a speed-oriented player, New York Yankees Gardner's .233 average was his worst since debuting as a rookie in 2008. In addition, Gardner went from 21 homers/23 steals in what was a resurgent 2017 campaign all the way to a 12/16 split last season as he was so bad during the second half (.209 average) that many of his owners kicked him to the curb entirely. With the Yankees once again having a crowded outfield to begin 2019 (Giancarlo Stanton, Aaron Hicks, Aaron Judge), Gardner is looking at part-time duty at best and a full-on backup gig at worst. In either scenario, we would take a total pass.

2019 PROJECTION: .240 11 HR 43 RBI 84 R 14 SB

Jackie Bradley Jr.: It can be tough being Boston Red Sox outfielder Jackie Bradley Jr. given the fact he would arguably be ranked fourth by the majority of the fantasy baseball community if one were told to place the team's players at the position in order of offensive potency. The fact of the matter is that Bradley Jr. ranks well behind Mookie Betts, Andrew Benintendi, and J.D. Martinez when it comes to yearly fantasy baseball impact but there are still some things to like here. In terms of those positives, Bradley Jr.'s 13/17 split in homers/steals last season was a decent haul in those categories; not to mention a solid 76 runs scored. The negatives center on a .234 batting average and a light 59 RBI caused by being forced to hit towards the bottom of the lineup. With regards to the average, Bradley has become a liability there since he has hit under .250 in four of his five MLB seasons and a career-worst 25.6 K/9 a year ago suggest this will continue to be an annual struggle. Well into his prime as he turns 29 in April, Bradley Jr. looks to be right on the border of being an OF 3 for 2019 fantasy baseball.

2019 PROJECTION: .239 16 HR 63 RBI 74 R 15 SB

Adam Jones: Free agency beckons for veteran outfielder Adam Jones this winter but it is expected to be far from a robust market for the fading former All-Star who is leaking numbers everywhere. One of the most durable players you will ever see, the issues with Jones now are strictly with his offensive game as he comes off a 2018 campaign that saw the power completely go off the cliff (just 15 homers in 613 at-bats); while also managing shoddy numbers in runs (54) and RBI (63) on a truly miserable Baltimore team. On the plus side, Jones managed to hold the average to a steady .281 and he even chipped in 7 steals which were his most since 2014. That all being said, Jones is an old 33 with a ton of mileage on his body and with a BB/9 that sank to a laughable 3.9 last season, opposing pitchers no longer have much to fear here. As a result, Jones' average is on borrowed time and don't count on 7 steals happening again either. Add in the vastly declining power and Jones clearly looks like old news.

2019 PROJECTION: .273 17 HR 67 RBI 58 R 5 SB

Kevin Pillar: While the fantasy baseball community has a strong tendency to obsess over those players who are gifted with the ability to both hit for power and steals bases, sometimes we get cases where such an individual slips through the cracks for one reason or another. That label would certainly apply to Toronto Blue Jays outfielder Kevin Pillar who has now posted HR/SB ratios of 16/15 and 15/14 the last two seasons despite vastly fluctuating ownership percentages during that span. The most likely reason for this is due to Pillar's inability to hit for average (.256 and .252 the last two seasons) and since that category is so easy to read even for a fantasy baseball novice, the impression is the guy is not worth your time. That would be a mistake though as Pillar has more than proven his power/speed chops and he remains entrenched in one of the better home run parks in the majors. An 18.1 K/9 last season gives hope to a possible average uptick someday but the pathetic 3.3 BB/9 serves as the major detriment there. If Pillar can somehow coax the latter number up to around 6.0, a .270 average is very possible. Then when you combine that with 15/15 ability, Pillar takes on quite an intriguing look.

2019 PROJECTION: .257 17 HR 55 RBI 68 R 14 SB

Kyle Schwarber: Despite not turning 26 until this March, the statistical dye seems to be cast for Chicago Cubs slugging outfielder Kyle Schwarber in terms of his high-end power being paired with some annually ugly batting averages. The 2018 season was no different on that front as Schwarber's 26 home runs were certainly a nice haul but the ugly .238 average took a bunch of shine off of the power numbers. Strikeouts remain a tremendous problem for Schwarber as he has yet to post a K/9 lower than last season's 27.5 but on the other hand, few players draw more walks as shown by a fantastic 15.3 BB/9. With just a bit more improvement in the K's, Schwarber could possibly reach around a .260 average but for now, grade him as the flawed overall hitter he always has been.

2019 PROJECTION: .240 28 HR 60 RBI 65 R 3 SB

Gerardo Parra: Almost from the moment the Colorado Rockies foolishly handed over a 3-year deal (plus an option) worth $27.5 million to speedy outfielder Gerardo Parra prior to the start of the 2016 season, a logjam in the team's outfield has resulted in some pretty inconsistent playing time since. In the three years since becoming a rich man, Parra has failed to post more than last year's 443 at-bats in any one of those seasons and the numbers have been quite mediocre as well. 2018 was typical of this as Parra batted a solid .284 but posted just a shoddy 6/11 split in homers/steals. With the Rockies likely picking up Parra's option for 2019, there could finally be a chance for 500 at-bats since Carlos Gonzalez is not expected to return to the team and David Dahl is still finding his way to becoming a regular. As a result, Parra looks like a very smart pick in five-outfielder formats and especially in NL-only leagues given the likelihood of a useful batting average and decent enough counting numbers if the at-bats are there. Forget the power as Parra has not reached double-digits in homers since 2014 but maybe he could scratch out 15 steals and 70 runs if all breaks right which would be a decent haul of numbers. While far from exciting, Parra should still be considered a fantasy baseball factor.

2019 PROJECTION: .288 8 HR 58 RBI 73 R 14 SB

Manuel Margot: Catching a lot of fantasy baseball sleeper attention last spring was San Diego Padres prospective leadoff hitter/outfielder Manuel Margot and this optimism was mostly centered on the fact the speedster put forth a 13/17 ratio in homers/steals in his 2017 rookie debut. Unfortunately, Margot hit a typical developmental setback last season as he was simply brutal for most of the first half of the year and then had to rally late to put together 8 home runs, 11 steals, and just a .245 average in 519 at-bats. Some perspective is needed here however as Margot's .281 BABIP was very unlucky and especially for someone with his type of speed. Also, Margot's 17.0 K/9 was terrific and high-contact skills such as this will often result in a string of decent batting averages. Finally, Margot is just 24 and so he is still a few years away from reaching his prime. Since the hype has almost completely eroded here for 2019, a tremendous buying opportunity is at hand this spring.

2019 PROJECTION: .264 11 HR 53 RBI 72 R 14 SB

Enrique Hernandez: Much in the same way that the Houston Astros utilized and benefitted from super utility man Marwin Gonzalez, the Los Angeles Dodgers received a quietly very good 2018 season of production from Enrique Hernandez. Qualifying at second base, third base, and the outfield, Hernandez posted career-high in homers (21), RBI (52), and runs scored (63) for the AL West champions and at the same time gained a foothold in the fantasy baseball realm. While it is a minor bummer that Hernandez doesn't steal bases (just 3 thefts in 2018), his shaky surface .256 average should have actually been much better due to the fact he suffered some brutal BABIP luck (.266). In addition to the pronounced BABIP issue, Hernandez put forth some very good plate approach numbers in walk (10.8 BB/9) and strikeout (16.9 K/9) rates that further suggest a decent average in 2019 could be on the way. Not turning 28 until August, Hernandez is really just getting started as a major league regular and since he presents such good versatility and underrated offensive production, the guy makes the grade as a very nice bench bat who can fill in all over the field in a pinch when needed.

2019 PROJECTION: .275 22 HR 59 RBI 73 R 4 SB

Billy Hamilton: It took a while but the fantasy baseball community likely has finally come to grips that Cincinnati Reds outfielder Billy Hamilton has been nothing short of being one of the most overrated players in the game. We sounded the alarm on Hamilton soon after his 2013 debut as the hype went bonkers given his video game-like minor league stolen base numbers and our forecast has more than come true as he is barely holding onto a starting outfield gig at this point. While Hamilton has picked up steals by the boatload in recording four straight seasons of 50-plus in that category which is no small feat, he has also been almost literally awful everywhere else. For one thing, Hamilton is lucky if he can reach 5 home runs and 30 RBI in any one season which is a huge negative in those categories. In addition, Hamilton is now just a career .245 hitter and he also struck out at a personal-worst 23.7 K/9 rate last season. With the Reds trying their best to unload Hamilton on any team who is showing a shred of interest in the speedster, it doesn't portend to good things happening here from a fantasy

baseball perspective in 2019. Also with Hamilton's steals dropping off to 34 last season, he may not even be as big a help there anymore as well.
2019 PROJECTION: .244 4 HR 28 RBI 71 R 37 SB

Josh Reddick: It was somewhat of a pretty standard season for Houston Astros outfielder Josh Reddick in 2018 as the guy spent time on the DL, posted a decent 17/7 split in homers/steals, but let his owners down by sinking to just a .242 batting average. Taking these one at a time, Reddick remains a big injury risk who almost always spends at least one stint on the DL each season and so that alone needs to be factored in as a clear negative for his 2019 draft cost. On the other hand, Reddick is still holding a solid power/speed game which is always a nice help in yearly fantasy baseball leagues. Finally, last season's average can be tossed in the "fluke" bin as Reddick's .258 BABIP was incredibly unlucky and both his terrific 10.1 BB/9 and 15.8 K/9 rates point to a hitter who is much more of a .280 guy. With an annual draft cost that goes typically into the late rounds, Reddick still has quite a bit to offer for those in deeper leagues.
2019 PROJECTION: .278 17 HR 70 RBI 65 R 8 SB

Jorge Soler: Both the post-hype sleeper and the fresh start tag applied to Kansas City Royals outfielder Jorge Soler once the 2018 season came around and it certainly looked early on that the two issues combined together to finally unleash the potential that followed the Cuban import to the majors back in 2014. For starters, a big spring training performance where Soler cracked 6 exhibition home runs carried over into March/April of the regular season when he added two more long balls with a .302 batting average. That early flurry made it appear as though things were beginning to come together for Soler who was once talked about as one of the very best hitting prospects in baseball while coming up the Chicago Cubs minor league system but alas, the fun didn't last. While Soler did crack an impressive 6 home runs in May, his average for the month slipped to .259 and he was at an even worse .194 with one homer in June when he suffered what became a season-ending fractured toe. Now with regards to 2019 fantasy baseball, there are some positive things to lean on in terms of what we saw out of Soler a year ago. Clearly, the power took off a bit as Soler hit a total of 9 home runs in 257 at-bats and he will be reaching the magical prime age of 27 when the 2019 season gets underway. On the negative side, Soler needed the fortunate assistant of a .340 BABIP to hit a modest .265 and the batting average is likely to be a problem going forward since he continues struggling with strikeouts as evidenced by his ugly 26.8 K.9 last season. So while the rebuilding Royals will give Soler every chance to find himself at the major league level at least for the start of the upcoming season, he looks

to be nothing more than a bench outfielder with perhaps one more year of possible upside remaining.
2019 PROJECTION: .254 14 HR 54 RBI 50 R 7 SB

Avisail Garcia: Chalk up another win for the outlier police when it came to the 2018 version of Chicago White Sox outfielder Avisail Garcia. After shocking everyone by putting forth a scorching .330 batting average with 18 home runs and 80 RBI in 2017, Garcia's sole purpose the following season was to prove those instantly suspicious numbers were not of the outlier variety. Well, Garcia royally failed on that front as he absolutely went into the gutter both in RBI (49) and batting average (.236); with both numbers completely overshadowing a decent 19 home runs. As a result of the step back in production, we are pretty much back to pre-2017 status for Garcia and this would have him mostly as a backup outfielder for mixed leagues this season. With Garcia also trotting around ugly walk (5.2 BB/9) and strikeout (26.5 K/9) rates a year ago, the guy looks to be a complete mess offensively heading into the spring.
2019 PROJECTION: .255 20 HR 66 RBI 56 R 4 SB

Joc Pederson: We maybe received some optimistic news from Los Angeles Dodgers faded outfield prospect Joc Pederson last season as the slugger may finally have refined his batting approach enough to where we can think about diving back in here for 2019. Prior to last season, there was almost no way you could stomach owning Pederson for long as some truly horrific strikeout problems sent both his batting average and overall fantasy baseball stock deep down into the toilet. While the power remained steady given how naturally strong Pederson is, the all-or-nothing aspect of his game blended in with dozens of other similarly-skilled hitters that took up residence on the waiver wire. With all that said though, Pederson made some firm gains in the strikeout area last season as his 19.2 K/9 was a career-best and actually went slightly above league average. Considering that Pederson's K/9 was a brutal 27.3 in 2016, you can see how well he has worked to fix this issue. With Pederson also drawing walks like he always had done previously (9.0 BB/9), it only took a very unlucky .253 BABIP from preventing his .248 average from going higher. While Pederson's big minor league stolen base numbers will never surface in the majors by the looks of it (just one steal in 2018), we can see a move towards 30 homers and a .260 average if he can hold last season's strikeout gains. This is certainly enough to put Pederson back in play as a decent bench outfielder this spring.
2019 PROJECTION: .257 28 HR 67 RBI 65 R 2 SB

Byron Buxton: Just look away all 2018 fantasy baseball owners of Minnesota Twins outfielder Byron Buxton. In fact, just skip over this paragraph entirely and go right onto the next player so you don't subject yourself again to the horrors that were Buxton's campaign last season. The carnage all began in spring training when a good number in the fantasy baseball community jumped fully back onto the Buxton bandwagon after the former 2012 number 2 overall pick put forth a very good second half performance in 2017 that finally began to reveal the extreme power/speed potential he always carried from the moment the guy turned pro. The big finish allowed Buxton to finish with a very intriguing 16 home runs and 29 stolen bases; while at the same time sending his 2018 fantasy baseball stock careening to early-round status as many had visions of even more power/speed numbers the following season. This was one peanut stand that was not on board with such a strategy as we stated in our draft guide a year ago how concerning Buxton's nasty 29.4 K/9 rate was and that until he learned to put bat to ball more consistently, he would be prone to going back to being the .230-hitting disappointment whose athleticism couldn't be put to use simply due to a lack of being able to collect hits. Well let's just say Buxton's 2018 owners would have taken .230 in the average department as what unfolded next was nothing but a complete and utter abomination. The carnage started in mid-April when Buxton was placed on the DL with a stubborn bout of migraines and then was followed by a hairline fracture in his toe suffered later in the month caused by a fouled off pitch. Unbelievably, the Twins activated Buxton in early May before the toe was completely healed and so by the end of THAT month he went right back on the DL for the third time when X-rays revealed the break was still there. Fast forward to mid-July when while on a rehab assignment, Buxton suffered a hand/wrist injury that had him starting and stopping preparations to return to the Twins which dragged on into August. Eventually, the Twins decided not to wait any longer and publicly announced Buxton would not be called up to the team even when rosters expanded in September. That put the bow on a complete disaster of a season for Buxton who in 28 games with Minnesota batted just .156 with zero home runs and 5 stolen bases. While a small sample size, Buxton also showed no progress on the contact rate front as his 29.8 K/9 remained hideous. So while it is easy to just completely throw out Buxton's 2018 season given all the injuries, the fact he is still prone to a massive strikeout rate makes him an annual fantasy baseball risk that will carry into 2019 despite the depressed draft cost. The tools will always be there as Buxton retains very good power and impressive speed but we are reaching the point where chasing the potential here is proving to not be worth the time and effort. With Buxton turning only 25 this past December serving as a glimmer of hope that the upside window is still open, the wounds of 2018 will be tough to look past when it comes to drafts this spring.

PROJECTION: .245 15 HR 65 R 57 RBI 16 SB

Brian Anderson (1B): With the Miami Marlins having literally traded away their entire 2017 outfield last winter, it was up to the team's minor league reinforcements to try and stem the statistical bleeding. Included in this group was third baseman/outfielder Brian Anderson whose impressive plate skills (19.3 K/9, 9.3 BB/9) allowed him to hit a solid .273; while also adding 11 homers and 87 runs scored. Despite being what looks to be a nice player offensively, Anderson is very limited in terms of fantasy baseball since he doesn't run (just 2 steals) and the expected helpful averages are mostly going to be empty since the power is nothing but mediocre. The dual eligibility at third base and the outfield can be a help in a bench capacity but nothing more.

2019 PROJECTION: .279 14 HR 68 RBI 89 R 2 SB

Mark Trumbo: Getting a bit up there in age as a big-bodied slugger is never a good thing when it comes to health and one only has to look at Baltimore Orioles DH/outfielder Mark Trumbo as clear evidence of this trend. Turning 33 this January, Trumbo endured nothing but injury trouble in 2017 as an early bout of knee pain in May never went away until the veteran decided to finally have season-ending surgery in August. In between all of the knee issues, Trumbo did his usual bit of striking out a bunch (24.3 K/9), hitting for a mediocre average (.261), and cracking home runs at a decent clip (17 in 358 at-bats). Given the age and increasingly poor health, a major drop in numbers could happen at any moment here but Trumbo's annual fantasy baseball draft cost is never prohibitive by any means. This means those in AL-only formats and deeper mixed leagues can grab Trumbo as a very affordable and still potent bench bat for at least one more season.

2019 PROJECTION: .263 22 HR 65 RBI 57 R 1 SB

Hunter Renfroe: The San Diego Padres have likely come to accept by now that slugging outfield prospect Hunter Renfroe "is who he is" in terms of being capable of high-end power (two straight seasons with 26 homers in less than 500 at-bats each) but also a batting average drain (.248 in 2018). Like most young pure sluggers, Renfroe loses the battle to strikeouts (24.7 K/9) but unlike let's say a Kyle Schwarber, he doesn't help offset the average hit from all those whiffs by walking a lot (just a 6.8 BB/9 a year ago). As a result, you simply can't grade Renfroe as anything but a borderline OF 3 in deeper formats or more ideally a backup if possible.

2019 PROJECTION: .245 27 HR 76 RBI 57 R 4 SB

Marwin Gonzalez (1B, 2B, SS): Supreme utility man Marwin Gonzalez is one of those classic fantasy baseball hitters who yield a major portion of their value based almost solely on qualifying for a high number of positions. In terms of Gonzalez, he will head into 2019 with eligibility at first base, second base, shortstop, and the outfield and so he serves as a tremendous bench weapon that you can plug in all over the field when needed. Gonzalez is not too shabby with the bat either as he comes off a 2018 where he hit 16 homers drove in 68 batters, and scored 61 runs. There are clear limitations though such as Gonzalez losing almost all of his previous average speed (just 2 steals last season) and his .247 average was way down from the last year's mark of .303. Still, the reason you are drafting Gonzalez is because of his massive eligibility haul and that won't change this season.
2019 PROJECTION: .255 15 HR 74 RBI 65 R 4 SB

Trey Mancini (1B): Like everything else associated with the 2018 Baltimore Orioles, first baseman/outfielder Trey Mancini was dragged down by the complete ineptitude of the team as he batted just .242 with 24 home runs and 58 RBI. While the homers were decent and matched his impressive 2017 rookie haul, Mancini needed a big finish to reach that point as he was largely silent with the bat for long stretches during the first four months of the year. In addition, Mancini's .242 average was WAY down from his .293 the year prior and only drawing walks at a 6.9 BB/9 clip certainly didn't help there. With Mancini also proving to be a bit susceptible to strikeouts (24.1 K/9), his immediate 2019 fantasy baseball outlook seems very suspect when you also consider the Orioles are going to be awful again this season. While you can certainly find a starting spot for Mancini in AL-only leagues this spring, in mixed leagues he only qualifies as an average backup hitter.
2019 PROJECTION: .267 24 HR 64 RBI 73 R 1 SB

Max Kepler: Now three full seasons into his MLB career, Minnesota Twins outfielder Max Kepler had a very strange 2018 on a number of different levels. On the surface, Kepler's personal-best 21 home runs and 80 runs scored were a solid haul but the .224 average was brutal. While Kepler's power continues to grow at a slow but steady pace, his average has been a major problem in failing to even reach .250 in any one of his three seasons. What is interesting at least when it came to last season was that Kepler's advanced metrics in walks (11.6 BB/9) and strikeouts (15.7 K/9) were both phenomenal and far from indicative of someone who would have such a ghastly average. A beyond unlucky .236 BABIP takes quite a bit of the blame for the .224 average as well and so Kepler stands a good chance of finally going above the .250 mark if the batted ball results move back toward the mean. Even if that happens though, Kepler remains very limited given the fact he has almost zero speed (just 4 steals last season) to add to the solid but not great pop.

2019 PROJECTION: .257 23 HR 64 RBI 83 R 5 SB

Shohei Ohtani: While throwing pitches will be out of the question due to undergoing Tommy John surgery last fall, the Los Angeles Angels anticipate having Shohei Ohtani available as a slugging outfielder early on in the 2019 season. As dazzling as Ohtani was while toeing the rubber before his elbow went bad a year ago, he was just as impressive with the bat as he hit .285 with 22 home runs, 61 RBI, and 10 steals in just 367 at-bats. The power was certainly as advertised but Ohtani added in 10 bonus steals which made the overall picture look that much sweeter. While the 27.8 K/9 rate was ugly, Ohtani's solid 10.1 BB/9 kept any possible average damage to a minimum. So while there are concerns about Ohtani's debut timeline coming back from the elbow surgery, he certainly makes the grade as a sizable upside OF 3 this season.

2019 PROJECTION: .275 25 HR 78 RBI 73 R 11 SB

Randal Grichuk: Serving as yet another of the endless high-end home run/shoddy batting average sluggers, Toronto Blue Jays outfielder Randal Grichuk performed his predictable game in 2018 by hitting 25 home runs in just 462 at-bats but then also supplied a terrible .245 average as he struck out a ton (26.4 K/9). By now we have seen more than enough of Grichuk to realize he is not going to change his statistical stripes much and this is likely the reason the usually conservative St. Louis Cardinals gave up on him so quickly after 2017. With guys fitting Grichuk's numbers profile littering the waiver wire, there is no need to use a draft pick here.

2019 PROJECTION: .246 24 HR 65 RBI 63 R 2 SB

Dexter Fowler: You can't blame the St. Louis Cardinals if they already have buyer's remorse for investing five years and $82.5 million in outfielder Dexter Fowler prior to the 2017 season. For a team that is annually lauded as one of the smartest organizations in the game, it was a bad misplay in giving the flawed and injury-prone Fowler such a hefty deal as we saw in a disaster of a 2018 campaign that saw him bat just .180 with 8 home runs and 5 stolen bases in 334 at-bats. Things got so bad before Fowler went down for the year with a broken foot in August that then-manager Mike Matheney made no secret of his desire to plant Fowler firmly on the bench. As far as what went wrong, it first needs to be said that speed-based players such as Fowler never age well in terms of fantasy baseball production. Never a great batting average asset to begin with, it was always of chief importance that Fowler kept stealing bases and hitting home runs for him to hold even OF 3 value. While the home runs are remaining somewhat steady, Fowler predictably is

starting to show less inclination to steal bases which is no shock since he will be 33 in March. With the batting average going into the toilet last season, Fowler's loss of a power/speed game turns him into nothing but a bench outfielder in terms of fantasy baseball usage. That being said, the Cards still have three more years of big money invested in Fowler and so they will undoubtedly hand him another starting outfield spot to begin 2019 in an effort to see if he can be somewhat salvaged. In Fowler's defense, a .210 BABIP was criminally unlucky and an excellent 11.4 BB/9 indicate a batting average jump back up to around .265 is almost guaranteed. Still, with the steals going by the wayside and injuries continuing to cloud the outlook, Fowler again is nothing but a backup outfielder at best.
2019 PROJECTION: .262 14 HR 59 RBI 65 R 7 SB

Jesse Winker: With the Cincinnati Reds undertaking a roster rebuild heading into 2018, the team was liberal in giving some of their younger players a chance to show they could stick as a major league regular going forward. One such player who benefitted from this setup was the Reds' 2012 first-round pick Jesse Winker who locked down a starting outfield spot in spring training and then proceeded to post some very intriguing numbers the first four months of the season. We said just the first four months only due to the fact Winker suffered a late July right shoulder subluxation that required season-ending surgery but the kid clearly did more than enough to be a factor in terms of 2019 fantasy baseball. Operating out of the leadoff spot for a majority of his games, Winker showed off terrific plate skills in terms of drawing walks (14.7 BB/9), keeping his strikeout downs (13.8 K/9), and also getting on base (.405 OBP). While he didn't run at all (zero steals), Winker's 7 home runs and .299 average in 334 at-bats at the age of 24 solidify his standing as an OF 3 with remaining upside. With Winker still not carrying much attention in the fantasy baseball world, he could turn out to be a terrific bargain as a late-round pick this spring.
2019 PROJECTION: .304 11 HR 57 RBI 65 R 1 SB

Teoscar Hernandez: The full-season debut for Toronto Blue Jays outfield prospect Teoscar Hernandez had some nice moments in 2018 but the slugger got exposed as the year went on as the strikeouts began to pile up. In the end, Hernandez finished as a typically flawed home run hitter in pairing 22 home runs with a .239 average; with the latter seriously being dragged down by a terrible 31.2 K/9 rate. As we have said multiple times in these pages, guys with Hernandez' hitting profile are a dime a dozen and so he really only carries bench value in mixed fantasy baseball leagues this spring.
2019 PROJECTION: .242 20 HR 55 RBI 62 R 4 SB

THE REST

Kevin Kiermaier: Once again it was a combination of never-ending injuries and another ugly batting average that doomed the 2018 fantasy baseball prospects of Tampa Bay Rays outfielder Kevin Kiermaier. As far as the injuries were concerned, Kiermaier now has made it three straight seasons of failing to reach 500 at-bats; with an April torn thumb ligament costing him two months and then a fractured foot caused by an HBP forced an early finish. The unfortunate thing is that despite all the health trouble, Kiermaier has some talent as he is capable of hitting homers and also stealing bases. Over the last three seasons, Kiermaier has posted HR/SB ratios of 12/21, 15/16, and 7/10 which is more impressive when you consider all the injury absences. If Kiermaier can somehow just scratch out 500 at-bats, we could be looking at a 20/20 run but for now, the guy can only be graded as a bench outfielder at best in deeper mixed leagues this spring.

Domingo Santana: Perhaps unfairly lost in the shuffle that was the crowded Milwaukee Brewers outfield in 2018 was multi-category contributor Domingo Santana who actually spent time back in the minor leagues despite hitting 30 home runs, swiping 15 bases, and batting .278 in what was a terrific breakout campaign the year prior. Alas, the arrivals of Lorenzo Cain and Christian Yelich last winter pushed Santana out of the picture but the obvious talent remains very intriguing here as we look towards 2019. The crowding problem remains however as Ryan Braun is expected to hold his leftfield spot to at least begin the year but we all know how brittle the former "MVP" has become which at least lends hope Santana can find his way to enough at-bats to make an impact. While Santana really needs to get the strikeouts under control (29.3 and 33.8 the last two seasons), the power/speed game makes him a guy you all should monitor this spring. If a trade were to send Santana to a team that would then utilize him as a starter, bump him up significantly on your cheat sheets.

Leonys Martin: While there is no denying the fact that Cleveland Indians outfielder Leonys Martin failed to come through as a highly touted five-tool prospect when making his way through the Texas Rangers organization, it is also worth noting that the guy has produced enough decent numbers when healthy since that time. As an example of the latter, 2018 served as another typical Martin season (especially now that he has reached his 30's) in that he smacked 11 home runs, stole 7 bases, and batted .255 in a year split between the Detroit Tigers and Cleveland Indians. Unfortunately, Martin contracted a serious bacterial infection in early August that resulted in him missing the rest of the season. Be that as it may, Martin has proven he can be a quiet 15/15 guy with an average that won't kill you so he could easily attain decent backup outfielder status for 2019 fantasy baseball in a power-packed Indians lineup.

Chris Owings: For the second straight season, Arizona Diamondbacks infielder/outfielder Chris Owings missed half the year with serious injuries; with 2018 resulting in just 309 at-bats where he hit .206 with 4 home runs and 11 steals. While we can throw out the average due to Owings suffering the effects of a very unlucky .265 BABIP, overlooking the big injury factor is not as easy. The real shame of it all is that Owings has proven himself to be both a home run hitter and a stolen base weapon which always plays well in fantasy baseball but the high volatility factor makes him nothing but a late-round speculative pick.

Lewis Brinson: The main return piece sent to the Miami Marlins from the Milwaukee Brewers in the Christian Yelich deal last winter, so far the early returns on outfield prospect Lewis Brinson are not very good. Evoking strong comparisons to the Minnesota Twins' Byron Buxton, Brinson's tremendous natural tools in power and speed are being completely derailed by the kid's simple inability to hit (.199 average and 29.6 K/9 last season). As we have all seen from Buxton the last few seasons, those tools mean nothing if you can't get on base or drive the baseball consistently and this is what Brinson is now facing as we move towards 2019. While the 11 home runs in 406 at-bats were decent, Brinson hardly showed much interest in running by picking up just 2 steals. If the steals are not there and the average remains in the garbage zone, Brinson all of a sudden has almost zero value to speak of. So while the tools and upside keep him relevant as a monitor candidate early on this season, anything more would be a reach.

Franchy Cordero: The future seems bright in the San Diego Padres outfield as prospect Franchy Cordero has paired with Franmil Reyes to given the team two young bats who hint at some very solid upside. While Reyes was more of a power hitter out of the gate in 2018, Cordero blended his game by hitting 7 home runs, stealing 5 bases, and batting .237 in 154 at-bats last season. Like with his teammate though, Cordero struggles with strikeouts (35.7 K/9 in 2018) and that needs to be rectified in a major way. On the more optimistic side of things, Cordero's 9.1 BB/9 was very good for a young hitter and in 2017 at Triple-A he had posted a 17/15 split in homers/steals to show multi-category promise. In deeper formats, this means Cordero can be taken with one of your last picks in the draft but anything more shallow means the waiver wire to begin the season.

Scott Schebler: While a decent player on the surface, Cincinnati Reds outfielder Scott Schebler gets lost in the massive amount of flawed home run hitters in today's game and that will likely result in him being an afterthought when it comes to 2019 drafts. Just one year after opening a slew of eyes by cracking 30 home runs for the team, Schebler jogged back down to only 17 last season as opposing pitchers no doubt had a more refined plan of attack on his swing. Also, Schebler's .255 average last season was well-earned as his .301 BABIP was almost right on the neutral number of .300 and so he won't be a help in that area either. Add in single-digit stolen base ability and Schebler is really just for the NL-only crowd.

Nick Williams: Even though the jury is still out on how much of an impact hitter Philadelphia Phillies outfield prospect Nick Williams will develop into, his current version of numbers have at the very least earned a bench spot for 2018 fantasy baseball. With 17 homers, 50 RBI, and a .256 average in 448 at-bats last season show, Williams is still quite a ways away from graduating into possible starting status but the fact he is just 25 means a few years of upside remain. Unfortunately, Williams doesn't run (just 3 steals in 2018) which would make this somewhat boring player look a bit more intriguing.

Michael Taylor: While he still can't hit a lick (under a .235 average in four of five MLB seasons), Washington Nationals outfielder Michael Taylor does some decent damage when on base as he racked up 24 steals in just 385 at-bats in 2018. Always serving as somewhat of a yearly fantasy baseball tease, Taylor failed to build off a very intriguing 19-home run/17-steal/.271 average the year prior as an insane strikeout rate continues to threaten his status as a major league regular. Last season Taylor's K/9 of 30.1 made him 5-for-5 in having a plus-30.0 mark in that category and the batting average will remain a huge problem until this is even somewhat remedied. Turning 28 in March, Taylor is likely running out of time to convince the Nats or another MLB team that he can be a starting outfielder and all the power/speed potential in the world will mean squat if the hits can't be picked up consistently.

Franmil Reyes: The San Diego Padres have to be pumped up about the progress of slugging outfield prospect Franmil Reyes who was hardly overmatched against MLB pitching during a 2018 debut that saw him smack 16 home runs in just 285 at-bats. Obviously, Reyes looks like an instant power/home run asset for yearly fantasy baseball leagues but now we wait to see what happens with the other statistical categories. Digging in on that front, Reyes struggled with strikeouts like most other young sluggers last season in posting an ugly 28.1 K/9 but a very lucky .345 BABIP helped prevent the .280 average from going into the gutter. Certainly, Reyes has some work to do with the K's in order to maximize his full potential but at the age of just 23 to begin the 2019 season, there is some sizable upside here that makes the kid a must add to your spring sleeper list. While there could be some growing pains that set Reyes back a bit this season, the talent is also there for him to hit 25 home runs.

Delino DeShields: It still is not happening yet when it comes to Texas Rangers running dervish outfielder Delino DeShields with regards to proving himself to be an everyday player, as a .216 average in 393 at-bats last season showed. So far it is all steals and nothing else for DeShields as he did swipe 20 bags a year ago but obviously, we need to see more from the guy before we take him seriously again as a possible pickup. There is some optimism to be found in DeShields' nice 10.9 BB/9 and decent enough 21.1 K/9 last season but he must bat above .260 to make the utter lack of power/RBI contributions worth the add. Until we see such progress, you can avoid DeShields this time around.

Daniel Palka: It took outfield prospect Daniel Palka making it to his third MLB organization before finally getting a chance in the majors and that came in 2018 when the slugger opened some eyes by slamming 27 home runs and driving in 67 batters in just 449 at-bats for the Chicago White Sox. As one would predict for a rookie hitter who predominantly swings for the fences, Palka's strikeout rate was ghastly (34.1 K/9) and that led to an unhelpful .240 average. With Palka not drawing much in the way of walks (6.7 BB/9), we can easily see the strong limitations here. Overall, Palka is pretty much a one-trick home run pony and he should be avoided in all but AL-only leagues.

Alex Gordon: With the Kansas City Royals stuck with enduring one more year on the ridiculous $72 million pact they signed outfielder Alex Gordon to prior to the 2016 season, the team will likely have no choice but to hand an undeserving starting spot to the guy this spring. Having now hit .220, .208, and .245 the last three seasons, Gordon is as big a batting average drain as there currently is in the majors. In Gordon's defense though, he did actually post a decent 13/12 ratio in homers/steals last season but that is just putting lipstick on the statistical pig. Even in very deep mixed leagues, you want to do your best to steer clear of this mess.

Mark Canha: If you were a member of the 2018 Oakland A's batting lineup, you hit home runs at a decent clip and this included outfielder Mark Canha who supplied 17 in 411 at-bats for the AL Wild Card winners. While Canha has flashed some decent ability since debuting with the team back in 2015, 20 home runs and around 65 RBI would be a best-case scenario here which doesn't move the interest needle much in the fantasy baseball world.

Also with Canha having never hit over .254 in any of his four MLB campaigns and possessing nothing in the way of speed, he just barely makes the cut as an AL-only hitter.

Lonnie Chisenhall: While elbow and shoulder ailments are as bad as it gets for a pitcher, a severe calf injury is right at the top of the list for a hitter as they often involve very long stints on the DL as Cleveland Indians outfielder Lonnie Chisenhall could attest to. After all, it was a Grade 3 calf strain that knocked Chisenhall out for what would turn out to be the remainder of the season when he went down at the beginning of July. Limited to just 29 total games where he hit .321 with 1 home run in 95 at-bats, Chisenhall is well off the fantasy baseball radar as we look toward the approaching 2019 season. A former 2008 first-round pick by the team who never has reached the heights expected given the lofty draft position, Chisenhall has been decent enough to hit .286 or better each of the last three seasons but with just moderate power. Having turned 30 last October, we are past the point where any expected improvement from Chisenhall is unlikely which makes him just AL or NL-only material depending where he ends up as a free agent.

Denard Span: Veteran outfielder Denard Span kept on trucking' in 2018 as he once again grabbed hold of some leadoff duties and proceeded to hit 11 home runs, steal 9 bases, and bat .261 for the Seattle Mariners. As of this writing, the Mariners have not yet decided whether they would pick up Span's option for 2019 but either way, we are looking at a guy who will be 35 in February and with no guarantee of everyday at-bats this season. While Span still draws walks (10.2 BB/9) and keeps the K's to a minimum (15.8 K/9), you really don't want to invest in aging speed-oriented players such as this.

Clint Frazier: The prized return to the New York Yankees from the Cleveland Indians in the Andrew Miller deal back in the summer of 2016, top power-hitting outfield prospect Clint Frazier had a season to forget a year ago. Having seen a possible starting outfield spot fall by the wayside when the Yankees acquired Giancarlo Stanton from the Miami Marlins last winter, Frazier predictably was sent to the minors to begin the season and that began a series of promotions and demotions with little in the way of hitting (.265, zero home runs in 41 at-bats) before a concussion suffered on July 19th at Triple-A ultimately finished his year for good after a series of setbacks. While Frazier turned just 24 last September, his stock has taken a bit of a hit in the Yankee organization as he was involved in multiple trade rumors throughout last season and into the winter. While the power has always been Frazier's calling card, he has also struggled with strikeouts during his stints with the Yankees since being acquired as shown by K/9 rates over 30.0 both in 2017 and 2018. By the time you read this Frazier could very well be with a new organization but failing that, the Yankees could also give him another long look in spring training which means he would carry some sleeper upside as a late-round pick. Either way, Frazier doesn't seem as much of a "must get" guy as he was just a few seasons prior.

Bradley Zimmer: While the fantasy baseball community knew there was some major strikeout/batting average risk at hand, upside still attached itself to Cleveland Indians outfield prospect Bradley Zimmer entering into the 2018 season as the team's 2014 first-round pick helped earn at least a moderate sleeper tag in spring drafts after smacking 8 home runs and stealing 18 bases in his 332 at-bat debut the year prior. Unfortunately, Zimmer's 2017 sky-high 29.8 K/9 rate (which led to a shoddy .241 average) became even WORSE last season as that number ballooned to an unfathomable 38.6 (dropping the average further into the toilet at .226). With just 2 home runs and 4 steals in 114 at-bats, Zimmer was a monumental bust before he went down for the remainder of the season and likely a decent portion of 2019 as well due to needing labrum surgery in his shoulder. Given the fact that Zimmer's contact rate is truly hideous and that he is trying to recover from serious surgery, you should really just put him out of your fantasy baseball plans until 2020.

Gorkys Hernandez: Whenever an MLB hitter posts a power/speed ratio of 15/8 like veteran San Francisco Giants outfielder Gorkys Hernandez put forth in 2018, attention automatically gets drawn from the fantasy baseball community. Alas, this focus should be short-lived as Hernandez is already 31 and never had hinted at such ability previously which calls into question the staying power of such numbers. While in NL-only leagues you can throw a dart to see if Hernandez can post a similar power/steal output this season, avoid such a plan everywhere else.

Kole Calhoun: Having started sliding statistically in 2017, the bottom completely fell out for Los Angeles Angels outfielder Kole Calhoun last season as he batted a horrendous .208 with 19 home runs and 6 steals in 552 at-bats. While a terribly unlucky .241 BABIP caused the average to go quite a bit lower than it should have gone, Calhoun has now batted under .260 in three of his five MLB seasons and the modest 6 steals he had a year ago represented a career-high which further solidifies how shaky his fantasy baseball status currently is. Signed through 2019 (with an option in '20). the playing time should be there for Calhoun to at least begin the new season but his overall mediocre offensive game makes him worthy of just AL-only consideration.

Charlie Culberson (SS, 3B): Already onto his fourth MLB team as he turns 30 in April, Atlanta Braves shortstop/outfielder Charlie Culberson looks to be a better real-life player than a fantasy baseball one. Just 12 home runs, 4 steals, and a .270 average was the haul Culberson put forth offensively in 2018 as a part-timer on the team and he is expected to take on similar responsibilities in 2019 as well. That means he should be left to the wire even in most NL-only leagues.

Travis Jankowski: With stolen bases having plummeted around the game the last few seasons, speed specialists such as San Diego Padres outfielder Travis Jankowski take on a bit more value in the fantasy baseball world. While Jankowski does little else of note as he hit .259 with just 4 home runs last season, the 24 steals in just 387 at-bats at least keep him somewhat relevant for those who need a speed infusion on their rosters. Be that as it may, Jankowski doesn't currently have a path to everyday playing time on the 2019 Padres and so on that aspect alone, you should try to find your bench steals weapon elsewhere.

Eric Thames (1B): Outside of the insane April blockbuster performance that made Milwaukee Brewers first baseman/outfielder Eric Thames the toast of the fantasy baseball town upon returning from playing in Korea in 2017, the slugger's performance since then has been nothing of underwhelming. Once again struggling with a massive strikeout problem that plagued him his first go-round in the majors before heading East, Thames batted just .219 with 16 home runs and 37 RBI in 278 at-bats last season. A 34.9 K/9 was simply ridiculous and while Thames has some tremendous natural power, he is looking like an all-or-nothing home run guy for 2019 fantasy baseball.

Jacoby Ellsbury: Already having a reputation for being one of the most injury-prone players in all of baseball, New York Yankees outfielder Jacoby Ellsbury took things to a whole new level on that front in 2018 as he missed the entire season due to a litany of ailments that went a mile long. The carnage began in spring training when Ellsbury came down with an oblique strain that led to him beginning the year on the DL and it ended with the veteran needing surgery on his hip to fix a torn labrum in August. While the six-month recovery time needed for the hip surgery should have Ellsbury ready for Opening Day, he is slated to be nothing but a fourth outfielder with a massive contract in 2019. In other words, avoid this annual mess and instead, ponder how on earth Yankee GM Brian Cashman could have been so foolish in handing this guy such an obscene deal in the first place.

Steven Duggar: After losing a spring training battle versus veteran Austin

Jackson to be the team's starting centerfielder to begin the 2018 season, San Francisco Giants outfield prospect Steven Duggar bided his time at Triple-A (where he batted .272 with 4 homers and 11 steals) before eventually being called up in July to serve as the short end of a platoon with Gorkys Hernandez. Originally a sixth-round pick of the Giants in 2015, Duggar possesses some interesting power/stolen base potential but he also has some glaring weaknesses in terms of contact rate (28.9 K/9 both at Triple-A and in 41 games at the major league level last season) and issues versus righties (.222 in 99 San Francisco at-bats). A labrum tear that required season-ending surgery last August robbed us of getting a longer look at Duggar's potential but he should be in line to challenge for the centerfield job again this spring training. Given the expected batting average struggles and the clear problems facing righties (which is obviously the pitching fraternity you want your hitters to succeed against given they make up the majority of hurlers in the game), Duggar is worth drafting just in NL-only or very deep mixed leagues.

Jarrod Dyson: While Rajai Davis has generally gotten the most pop in the fantasy baseball community as a guy who annually keeps himself relevant almost solely through the stolen base, veteran outfielder Jarrod Dyson has gone along the same career path as his counterpart but with much less fanfare. Up until an injury-marred 2018, Dyson put forth a streak of six straight seasons with 25 or more steals despite mostly being a fourth outfielder during that span. As noted, Dyson couldn't extend that run to seven straight last season due to suffering a serious groin injury at the start of July that eventually led to surgery in September after a series of failed rehab assignments. Prior to suffering the injury, Dyson perhaps signaled his days as a major leaguer may be numbered as he batted a horrid .189 and mostly got his 16 stolen bases as a bench player. Despite such a rough campaign, Dyson has one more year to go on his deal with the Arizona Diamondbacks and so he could reprise his fourth outfielder designation for another go-round. Even if that were to happen, the odds are long that Dyson will ever be able to hit enough to find 20 steals again.

Juan Lagares: Still under contract for at least one more season, the New York Mets are hoping to get something out of their investment in outfielder Juan Lagares for 2019. To this point it has been nothing but serious injuries for Lagares; with the latest being a torn ligament in one of his toes of all things that led to season-ending surgery last May. The real shame of it all was that Lagares was hitting a scorching .339 to go with his standard Gold Glove defense in centerfield before the latest health disaster struck but at least the tools are still there for him to possibly contribute again this season. On the latter front, Lagares could benefit from the likely absence of Yoenis

Cespedes at the start of the year and the possible move of Jay Bruce to first base to stake to his claim to more consistent time in center. Turning a still young 30 in March, Lagares should at the very least be on the NL-only radar given his solid speed and bat but the massive injury threat makes him of very little use in mixed leagues.

Mac Williamson: While nobody would ever doubt that grip-it-and-rip-it San Francisco Giants outfielder Mac Williamson certainly can smack the baseball a country mile, there is also a warranted debate about whether he can hit enough to stick in the major leagues. Already having turned 28 last July, Williamson caught some early attention when he hit a home run in three of his first five games with the Giants after being called up at the end of April but that flash represented the clear high point of his season as there would be only one more long ball the rest of the way. Making matter worse was the fact an April concussion wound up plaguing Williamson off-and-on into the summer and the Giants were ultimately forced to shut him down in early August as the symptoms wouldn't go away. As a result, it is tough to gauge what would have happened in terms of Williamson's numbers if he hadn't suffered the concussion but one thing we can say for certain is that the batting average (.213 last season) would not have been pretty given the strikeout tendencies. Even though Williamson does draw walks (10.5 BB/9), he gives off a Christian Villanueva aroma as a borderline QUAD-A guy who should not be drafted anywhere.

Derek Fisher: So far Houston Astros outfield prospect Derek Fisher is 0-for-2 in terms of his failure to impress team brass with the bat and carve out a role for himself at the major league level when given the chance to do so. In 2017 it was Fisher batting just .212 with 5 home runs in 166 at-bats and last season things got worse as those numbers sank to .165/4 homers in another 86 plate appearances. The biggest issue has been the strikeouts which were completely obscene for Fisher during those stints (32.5 and 48.8 K/9's respectively) and considering how deep the Houston farm system goes, there is a chance the lefty slugger will be left behind if he doesn't start producing soon. While no one doubts Fisher's ability to hit the long ball, the fact he is already 25 and seemingly unable to get a handle on the strikeouts at the major league level give one the sense we could be looking at a QUAD-A guy.

Adam Duvall: After hitting a very impressive 33 and 31 home runs as a power revelation both in 2016 and 2017, the bottom completely fell out for Cincinnati Reds outfielder Adam Duvall last season. With his K/9 creeping up to a scary 27.4, Duvall managed just a .195 average and all of 15 home runs as the Reds began sending him to the bench for more than a few games during the second half of the season. Already established as a limited offensive player who gained almost all his fantasy baseball value through the home run, Duvall now looks like nothing better than the endless flawed power bats flooding all waiver wires in today's game.

Adam Engel: Despite not showing much skill in the way of actually picking up a bunch of hits, there is no debating the fact Chicago White Sox outfield prospect Adam Engel has some very potent speed capable of picking up steals at a decent clip. Engel began to reveal this ability last season as he accrued 16 steals in just 463 at-bats for the team but they came with a shoddy .235 batting average. While Engel did also add 6 home runs, he is likely slated for a bench role on the team this season in mostly working as a late-inning running weapon. Under that setup, Engel would have almost no fantasy baseball value to speak of.

Jacoby Jones: Taking things to the extreme in terms of posting some solid power/speed numbers but with a truly horrendous batting average, we present to you the 2018 version of Detroit Tigers outfielder Jacoby Jones. With 11 home runs and 13 stolen bases in just 467 at-bats, Jones certainly showed off some intriguing fantasy baseball tools. Unfortunately, the .207 batting average and pathetic 30.4 K/9 rate almost completely stopped the conversation cold on Jones' potential fantasy baseball impact. As a result, Jones is another case of a player who is way too flawed to overlook the negatives.

Tony Kemp: After he hit 10 home runs, stole 24 bases, and batted .329 at Triple-A in 2017, Houston Astros utility man Tony Kemp put himself onto the radar of the fantasy baseball community. 2018 would see Kemp receive a decent look by the team due to injuries to Jose Altuve and George Springer and the result was 6 homers, 9 steals, and a .263 average in 295 at-bats. Clearly, there are some helpful tools that Kemp possesses and in particular his ability to hit homers and steal bases make him a name to store away if injuries open up some more playing time again this season. Until that happens though, Kemp can stay on the wire.

Greg Allen: Some new stolen base specialists revealed themselves during the course of the 2018 fantasy baseball season and one of them worked in Cleveland in the form of Indians outfield prospect Greg Allen. Possessing track meet speed, Allen has put up some big stolen base totals while coming up the minor league ladder and he showed off this skill in picking up 21 bags during a 291 at-bat stint with the team last season. This is a one-trick pony all the way through as Allen batted just .257 and he has just single-digit home run power as well. A healthy Indians outfield to begin the season likely means Allen will either be slated for backup duty or even begin the year in the minors but an opportunity to grab more consistent time would make him a must add on the steals aspect alone.

Jason Heyward: The poster boy for irresponsible MLB spending, Chicago Cubs outfielder Jason Heyward remains the butt of all jokes as he was once again pretty miserable in terms of the offensive game. While no one can take away what a tremendous defender Heyward is, there is almost no fantasy baseball appeal left here as he hit just .270 with 8 home runs and 1 steal in 489 at-bats last season. With the steals now falling completely by the wayside and the power never coming anywhere near the levels he showed when first arriving on the MLB scene, Heyward should be completely avoided.

Cameron Maybin: The tour around the majors for veteran outfielder Cameron Maybin continued in 2018 as he added both the Miami Marlins and Seattle Mariners to the ever-growing ledger of MLB teams he has played for. Having already classified himself as an overall disappointment after being picked 10th in the 2005 MLB Draft, Maybin's career-long batting average struggles continued in 2018 as he batted .249 with 4 home runs and 10 stolen bases in 384 at-bats. A free agent as of press time, Maybin is likely out of chances to be a starting outfielder to begin the 2019 season and the potential we once chased has almost completely vanished.

Tyler O'Neill: Even though Harrison Bader received much of the attention, the St. Louis Cardinals have a second promising outfield prospect in the form of slugger Tyler O'Neill. The power is the name of the game here as O'Neill slammed 26 home runs at Triple-A before adding 9 more during a 61-game stint with the team last season. O'Neill also has a bit of speed to his game and 10 stolen bases could be in the offing if the at-bats are there. On the flip side, O'Neill's 40.1 K/9 in his 142 at-bats with the Cardinals last season was pathetic and he was lucky to bat .254 with such a mark. Since O'Neill also doesn't draw walks (just 4.9 BB/9 in 2018), we are looking at a guy who needs a bunch of work before we can even consider an investment.

Dustin Fowler: Fully recovered from the gruesome broken leg he suffered during his major league debut a year earlier, Oakland A's outfielder Dustin Fowler began the overdue process of showing what he could do for the team by hitting 6 home runs, stealing 6 bases, and batting an ugly .224. The average can be excused somewhat since Fowler was a rookie but there is no denying the fact he needs to vastly improve on a pathetic 3.9 BB/9 rate to help boost the former number. Still just 24 and with some interesting power/speed performances in the minor leagues in the books, Fowler is not the worst way to spend a very late-round pick.

Ben Gamel: Representing the empty batting average class of hitter, Seattle Mariners outfielder Ben Gamel drove that point further home in 2018 when he batted .272 with 1 home run and 7 steals in 293 at-bats. Relegated mostly to backup duty last season, Gamel only gains a tiny sliver of attraction if injuries open up some more playing time. Until that happens, Gamel should not be drafted.

Hunter Pence: While we were as big a fan of the guy as anyone, it is beyond time to retire veteran outfielder Hunter Pence's name with regards to fantasy baseball as he enters into free agency prior to turning 36 in April. Injuries have almost completely derailed Pence the last few years and 2018 was beyond rough as he hit just .226 with 4 home runs and 5 steals in 248 at-bats. Once one of the more quietly effective five-tool players in the game, Pence is now nothing but waiver fodder.

Carlos Gomez: Even though he is still only going to be 33 when the 2019 season gets underway, veteran outfielder and former first-round fantasy baseball star Carlos Gomez could be out of chances to stick with a major league team. That's what happens when you bat .208 with just 9 home runs and 12 steals in 408 at-bats last season and also strike out at a 25.2 K/9 clip. It is ride off into the sunset time here.

Chad Pinder (2B): With 15 and 13 home runs the last two seasons, Oakland A's infielder/outfielder Chad Pinder has shown some skill with the long ball in terms of any possible fantasy baseball usage. That is pretty much where it ends though in talking up any further impact as Pinder has hit just .247 collectively in three MLB campaigns and he also has just 2 steals total during the same span. In other words, leave Pinder on the wire.

Billy McKinney: Having gotten away from the logjam among the New York Yankees outfield through a midyear trade to the Toronto Blue Jays last season, prospect Billy McKinney showed promise by hitting 6 home runs, stealing a base, and batting .252 in a 132 at-bat cup of coffee stint with the team. That performance may very well have given McKinney the inside track to a starting job to begin the 2019 season but even under such a scenario, we are looking at just an AL-only option at best. With McKinney having struggled to hit for average at multiple minor league stops and possessing pretty much nothing in the way of speed, there is not much here for a prospective owner to hang their hat on.

Aaron Altherr: It was a beyond rough go of it for Philadelphia Phillies outfielder Aaron Altherr in 2018 due to missing more than half the year with injuries and even spent time back in the minors as he batted just .181 with 8 home runs and 3 stolen bases. This just one year after Altherr went .272/19/5 in those respective categories which show at least some intriguing upside. Unfortunately, Altherr has to prove himself all over again this spring to the Phillies and even if he grabs a starting spot, there is not enough in the way of numbers yet to recommend a play.

UTILITY

Nelson Cruz: Now turning 39 this July, aging DH Nelson Cruz is still holding steady with his power game as he comes off a 2018 campaign that included 37 home runs and 97 RBI with the Seattle Mariners. That being said, Cruz is finally showing signs of aging as the home run total declined for the third straight season, he battled some injuries during the year, and his isolated power slipped a bit. Given how great Cruz has been since becoming somewhat of a late-blooming slugger, we have to anticipate some more erosion in 2019 as we would anyone approaching 40. What is encouraging last season was that Cruz was able to maintain both his K/9 (20.6) and BB/9 (9.3) rates which shows the bat speed is holding steady. Given the plethora of power available throughout the game though, you might want to start looking for a younger option to fill your home run count. Finally, it should be noted that Cruz no longer carries outfield eligibility at least to begin the new season.
2019 PROJECTION: .267 35 HR 91 RBI 75 R 1 SB

Evan Gattis: Heading into the 2018 fantasy baseball season, we spoke about the very good value being presented by Houston Astros catcher/DH Evan Gattis as he was set to play every day at the latter spot in the order and in the process remain capable of big power. That is exactly what would take place as Gattis slammed 25 home runs and drove in 78 while holding down the daily DH spot which was a nice added bonus in terms of counting statistics but the rest of the numbers package was lacking. Unfortunately, Gattis also loses catcher eligibility to begin the 2019 season and that all of a sudden makes him just a flawed slugger like we see out of countless guys across the majors. In addition, the Astros declined a qualifying offer on Gattis last October which puts him into a free agent market that may not be overly interested in a limited/aging slugger. Overall, until Gattis reclaims catcher eligibility, he will be nothing but a bench UTIL-only bat given the ugly average (.226 in 2018) negative that always goes in conjunction with just the power game.

2019 PROJECTION: .234 23 HR 74 RBI 45 R 1 SB

Kendrys Morales: With one more year left on his deal, Toronto Blue Jays DH Kendrys Morales will likely be in the realm of his 2018 numbers (.249, 21 homers, 57 RBI) that make him just a backup UTIL bat in deeper mixed fantasy baseball leagues this season. Getting a bit up there as he begins 2019 at the age of 35, Morales is pretty much a home run/RBI asset and not much else as he qualifies just in the UTIL spot to begin the year. While Morales can get very hot at times with the home run swing, he is barely holding on to relevancy as an aging veteran.

2019 PROJECTION: .254 22 HR 65 RBI 57 R 1 SB

STARTING PITCHERS

Draft Strategy: High incidence of injury and very good depth once again makes it a bad idea to draft a starting pitcher with an early round pick this spring. While we all would love to have a Max Scherzer or a Chris Sale, you can easily put a very solid five-man rotation together through a series of mid-round picks that can begin as early as Round 5 if you wish. In the meantime, stock up on the more durable and effective hitters before beginning to address this volatile spot.

Max Scherzer: Even though he is approaching the mid-30's and has an insane amount of innings under his belt, Washington Nationals ace Max Scherzer retained the mantle as the best pitcher in baseball for at least another season. In a 2018 campaign that saw him register a career-best K/9 of 12.24, Scherzer once again went nuclear with his numbers in posting a 2.43 ERA, .0.91 WHIP, and a .187 BAA. The topper though was Scherzer hitting the hallowed 300-K mark on the button and the fact he achieved this in just 220.2 innings further solidified his status as the best strikeout artist in the game. While it is just mildly concerning that Scherzer will turn 35 in July, his stuff remains as good as ever and so far is showing zero slippage as the BB/9 (2.08) and HR/9 (0.94) were all within career norms. We began saying a few seasons ago that it was Scherzer and not the injury-prone Clayton Kershaw who should be graded as the top pitcher in yearly fantasy baseball leagues and that opinion has been nothing but validated since.
2019 PROJECTION: 20-8 2.57 ERA 0.98 WHIP 279 K

Jacob DeGrom: Despite only posting a record of 10-9 due mainly to a comical lack of run support, the Cy Young Award couldn't be denied to New York Mets ace Jacob DeGrom who set all sorts of MLB records on the way toward what can only be described as a spectacular season all the way

around. The surface numbers were downright silly as DeGrom's 1.70 ERA, 0.91 WHIP, and 269 strikeouts in 217 innings showed and along the way the righty also reaffirmed his status as one of the most dominant fantasy baseball aces in the game. Then there was the slew of records as DeGrom became the first pitcher since 1900 to record at least 260 K's, 50 walks or fewer, 10 home runs allowed or fewer, and a sub-2.00 ERA. Want more? How about setting the all-time MLB record with 24 straight quality starts to end the season; plus pitching 29 outings with three or fewer earned runs. Getting back to the numbers, DeGrom has now cemented his status as a 200-K star with strikeout totals of 239 and 269 the last two season; not to mention the fact both his walks (1.91 BB/9) and home runs allowed (0.41 HR/9) in 2019 were as good as it gets. While we can do nothing about the lack of wins outside of hoping Met hitters give even a modicum of support for DeGrom next season, the fact of the matter is that at the age of 30 he is here to stay for a while as a supreme fantasy baseball ace who is deserving of being in the draft tier of Chris Sale, Max Scherzer, and Corey Kluber.
2019 PROJECTION: 14-8 2.34 ERA 0.98 WHIP 255 K

Chris Sale: Firmly headed toward another Cy Young Award as he ended the first half of the season with a dominant 2.23 ERA, 0.90 WHIP, and a truly silly 188 K's in 129 IP; Boston Red Sox ace Chris Sale saw his second half almost completely derailed due to two separate DL stints caused by shoulder woes. This marked the second straight season where Sale found trouble either on the health or declining performance front (September of 2017) which may be an indication that years of heavy usage could now be negatively impacting his ability to pitch an entire year at optimum efficiency. Sale's 158 innings pitched last season were his lowest ever since becoming a committed starter in 2012 but there is also no denying those frames were truly dominant as usual (2.11 ERA, 0.86 WHIP, and career-best 13.50 K/9 rate). With Sale's career-best 0.63 HR/9 last season working in top-notch conjunction with ongoing splendid control (1.94), his status as a top-five fantasy baseball ace survives into the 2019 season. Given that Sale's average fastball velocity of 95.4 last season was also among the highest of his career, we can concretely make the argument there has been no drop-off in terms of raw stuff and that really the only concern we have for 2019 is the threat of another injury.
2019 PROJECTION: 17-10 2.84 ERA 0.95 WHIP 245 K

Justin Verlander: Some athletes are just physical freaks of nature and Houston Astros ace starter Justin Verlander certainly is a charter member of this group as he continues to roll out Cy Young-caliber seasons into his mid-30's and undertaking insane workloads that few other pitchers can approach. 2018 was no different as Verlander won 16 games, registered dominant ratios (2.52 ERA, career-best 0.90 WHIP), and struck out 290 batters (another personal-best 12.20 K/9) in 214 innings at the age of 35. Simply put, there may not be a better workhorse pitcher in the modern era as Verlander has now pitched over 200 innings in 11 of the last 12 seasons and the fact he remains a top-tier ace in all phases as he turns 36 in February is astounding. While one would have to think Verlander will eventually have to pay the piper for such insane workloads, he could be the pitching version (and clean version?) of former Boston Red Sox DH David Ortiz who was still hitting like he was in his prime all the way to retirement. With yet another career-best walk rate (1.56 BB/9) last season, the fact Verlander is still introducing new heights of performance this late in his career makes him truly one of the best starters to ever play the game. Given all that we have discussed, there is almost no way you can't have Verlander graded as anything but a top fantasy baseball ace once again this season.

2019 PROJECTION: 17-7 2.63 ERA 0.97 WHIP 255 K

Gerrit Cole: No one would blame fans of the Pittsburgh Pirates or even members of the team's front office if they had ongoing sleepless nights during the course of the 2018 season as they watched their former pitcher and now current Houston Astro Gerrit Cole undertake what could only be described as a massively dominant campaign in every sense of the word. Whether it was the 2.88 ERA, the 1.03 WHIP, the 15-5 record, or the ridiculous 276 strikeouts in just 200.1 IP (12.40 K/9); Cole left those connected to his former organization wondering why the guy didn't produce such results when he was wearing a Pirates uniform. That is a valid question as Cole served as mostly a frustrating enigma during his five seasons with the Pirates in often struggling with injuries and underwhelming numbers (outside of his very good 2015). Be that as it may, Cole became the rare pitcher to better his statistics across the board moving from the NL to the AL and rare cooperating health probably had a lot to do with it. Getting back to the production, you could surely wonder if Cole's 2018 belongs in the outlier bin as he never has come anywhere close to such insane strikeout numbers before (previous K/9 high of 9.00 in 2014) and his ERA's the two years prior to last season came out to just 3.88 and 4.26 which helped set in motion the trade to the Astros. As a result, it is a good idea not to pay top dollar for Cole this season given his checkered injury history and the outlier effect but the guy also can easily go right back into Cy Young contention on an Astros team that will supply him many chances for wins. We always suggest steering clear of paying for career years however and Cole is certainly in this grouping for 2019 fantasy baseball.

2019 PROJECTION: 17-8 3.24 ERA 1.09 WHIP 239 K

Blake Snell: You got to be kidding me! Even though the fantasy baseball community was in general agreement about the very intriguing future potential of hard-throwing Tampa Bay Rays pitching prospect Blake Snell, even the guy's mother could not have foreseen the utterly insane numbers put forth by the lefty as he rightfully captured the American League Cy Young Award. Having put forth a 4.04 ERA and 8.28 K/9 the year prior that tempered immediate expectations, Snell sailed past those previous digits by a mile last season with a 1.89/11.01 respectively. The fact Snell was able to post an ERA under 2.00 in the American League was already beyond impressive but also accomplishing that while operating in the always brutal AL East added validity to talk it was one of the best pitched seasons in MLB history. As they say, the numbers don't lie and with Snell keeping the ball in the park (0.80 HR/9) and showcasing big velocity (average fastball of 96.5), it would be the understatement of the century in saying he has already reached fantasy baseball ace status. About the only concerns we have here are a bit of a poor walk rate (BB/9 of 3.19) and that really his numbers have nowhere to go but down from here. Yes, there was quite a lucky BABIP of .241 that helped push that ERA down past where it should have gone but both Snell's FIP (2.95) and XFIP (3.16) were excellent. Given the 221 strikeouts in just 180.2 frames, we feel confident in forecasting Snell for another top 5-10 starting pitching output this season.
2019 PROJECTION: 16-5 3.21 ERA 1.07 WHIP 225 K

Aaron Nola: Yeah we nailed this one. It was only a few short years ago where we screamed to the rafters regarding our strong recommendation to fully buy into burgeoning Philadelphia Phillies pitching prospect Aaron Nola but a rough 2016 (4.78 ERA) earned us quite a bit of scorn from the fantasy baseball community. Undeterred, we went right back to the well in recommending Nola for 2017 and the rest, as they say, is history as the righty has been a top-tier starter since. After a very good 3.54 ERA in 2017, Nola put himself squarely into the NL Cy Young conversation last season with an even better 2.37 mark. When you also take into account Nola won 17 games, registered a WHIP of 0.97, and reached the 200-K level for the first time in his career with 224 in 212.1 innings; the guy was able to stand with almost any other starter in 2018 fantasy baseball. Still, just 25 as we get set to begin the 2019 season, Nola has fully graduated to SP 1 status and the fact he will come cheaper than the Max Scherzers, Chris Sales, and Corey Klubers of the world make him that much more attractive. When you look at the fact Nola also possesses top-notch control (2.46 BB/9) and keeps the ball in the park (0.72 HR/9), you can see there is little debate about him being one of the best starters in the game. So while there were a few bumps along the developmental road, Nola is now a fully graduated ace in all formats this season.

2019 PROJECTION: 16-7 2.73 ERA 0.99 WHIP 219 K

Noah Syndergaard: Always right at the top of potential Tommy John victims prior to every season, New York Mets nuclear-armed starter Noah Syndergaard survived another year without having to undergo the dreaded procedure. Be that as it may, Syndergaard still dealt with injury/illness as he spent two separate stints on the DL for a strained index finger and foot-and-mouth disease. The strained index finger cost "Thor" seven weeks and was primarily the reason he was only able to throw a total of 154.1 innings where he still pitched very well (3.03 ERA, 1.21 WHIP, 155 K). Still, Syndergaard's fantasy baseball owners were let down even beyond the injuries due to the fact his K/9 sank from 10.09 in 2017 to a lowered 9.04 a year ago. That issue is really just a minor quibble though as Syndergaard's average of 98.1 on his fastball was the best in baseball and is a very good sign moving forward that the strikeouts will remain immense. Really it all comes down to health for Syndergaard and on that front, he is as risky as it gets considering the annually high draft cost. Just like with Stephen Strasburg, you almost go into an ownership of Syndergaard expecting at least one DL stint but the hope is that it will be on the shorter end regarding time missed. If Syndergaard can scratch out 180 innings, there is no doubt he will be a top five or so starter but this one could go either way.
2019 PROJECTION: 14-10 2.88 ERA 1.11 WHIP 194 K

Luis Severino: Prior to the start of the 2018 fantasy baseball season, we talked extensively about how New York Yankees ace starter Luis Severino represented a decent-sized risk for those willing to pay the early-round price tag on the ascending power arm. It was understandable the allure of Severino given that he was coming off a spectacular 2017 campaign that saw him log a 2.98 ERA, 1.04 WHIP, and a monstrous 230 strikeouts in just 191.1 IP. While you will get no argument from us about how overpowering Severino is, we did share our concern about how the big increase in innings the righty threw that year compared to 2016 (a jump of more than 60 total) could lead to fatigue and then some depressed numbers/injuries in 2018. Well early on last season it looked like we overreacted to such a worry as Severino was arguably the best pitcher in baseball during that time as he put up a 2.31 ERA, 1.01 WHIP, and struck out 144 batters in 128.1 IP but then the second half arrived which is when the troubles began. Almost as soon as the All-Star Game festivities were finished, Severino went into a complete tailspin that saw him struggle mightily for almost all of July and August. While Severino did recover to post a decent September, his composite second-half 5.57 ERA, 1.43 WHIP, and 76 K in 63 IP were the classic signs of a fatigued pitcher. While clearly a tale of two halves, Severino still managed a very good final season ERA of 3.39 and he crossed the 200-K and 10.00-plus K/9 rates for the second season in a row (220, 10.35 respectively) to cement his status as one of the best strikeout arms in baseball. As far as the second half fade, it was nice to see Severino not come down with an injury and being able to push through the struggles and complete the season should have him more capable of holding up over the six-month grind in 2019. With both control (2.16 BB/9) and home run (0.89 HR/9) rates that remain excellent, Severino should absolutely be kept in the SP 1 range for drafts this spring.

2019 PROJECTION: 19-7 3.15 ERA 1.10 WHIP 227 K

Corey Kluber: Already with two AL Cy Young Awards in the bag, Cleveland Indians ace starter Corey Kluber kept trucking along with another spectacular season in 2018 that could have netted a third trophy. For the third time in the last five seasons, Kluber went under a 3.00 ERA with a 2.89 mark and he also extended to five his streak of 200-plus strikeout campaigns with 222 in 215 innings. Known as one of the most durable pitchers in all of baseball (five straight 200-plus inning seasons), Kluber is starting to show some signs of aging when you look at the advanced metrics. While the surface numbers were terrific, Kluber's average fastball velocity last season was down to 92.4 which marked the fourth straight year that number declined (down from 94.6 in 2014). The fact he will turn 33 in April and has all those massive workhorse seasons under his belt could very well mean Kluber is beginning to enter into a decline phase no matter how slight that may be currently. Increased age also brings a heightened risk of injury and the possibility of a late-season fade like we are now seeing out of Jon Lester. Of course, Kluber certainly helps himself by remaining excellent both with his control (1.42 BB/9) and the home run rate (1.05 HR/9) is not horrific either. So while we will sound just a slight age-related alarm here so that you are aware of all the possibilities in 2019, Kluber looks safe to draft as your SP 1 for at least another season or two.

2019 PROJECTION: 19-7 3.08 ERA 1.04 WHIP 227 K

Trevor Bauer: It has become an annual tradition in these pages each spring to wonder if THIS was finally the year Trevor Bauer would put it all together and become the monster ace pitcher his overpowering but wild stuff always hinted at being. We were finally able to put that line of thinking to bed in 2018 however as Bauer reaching the magical age of 27 (when both hitters and pitchers seem to make their biggest jump in production) resulted in him absolutely dominating the opposition as the strikeouts piled up by the boatload. The numbers were quite staggering as Bauer's season resulted in a Chris Sale-like campaign that included a 2.21 ERA, 1.09 WHIP, .208 BAA, and an insane 221 strikeouts in only 175.1 IP. Alas, Bauer suffered a stress fracture in his right tibia in mid-August that pretty much ended his regular season in its tracks (save for 8 innings in late September in prepping for the playoffs). As tough a literal break as that was, Bauer's work when on the mound was downright ridiculous and we have no hesitation in saying he has firmly reached ace-status when it comes to 2019 fantasy baseball. While we always knew Bauer was a true strikeout artist, ill control and a propensity for giving up home runs always held him back (having never posted an ERA under 4.00 in going back to his 2012 debut with the Arizona Diamondbacks). Well that is no longer a concern as Bauer's 0.46 HR/9 was as good as any pitcher in baseball last season and while his 2.93 BB/9 is not exactly glowing, it still represents clear progress for Bauer who was previously in the mid-to-high-3.00 range in that category. Since Bauer was already one of the toughest pitchers to get a hit off of in baseball, the improvements in the home run and walk rates helped thrust him right to ace territory. More of the same should be in play for 2019 and if the health cooperates, Bauer could win the CY Young and lead the majors in strikeouts.

2019 PROJECTION: 18-7 2.57 ERA 1.10 WHIP 277 K

Clayton Kershaw: A few seasons ago we took a ton of heat for our opinion that Los Angeles Dodgers ace and multiple Cy Young Award winner Clayton Kershaw had firmly fallen behind the Washington Nationals' Max Scherzer given the fact the lefty was so much less dependable on the health front and also due to a velocity decline that was not talked about as much as it should have been. Well as we head towards the 2019 fantasy baseball season, we think Kershaw has fallen behind even more ace-level starters such as Chris Sale, Jacob DeGrom, and Corey Kluber to name a few as he comes off a third straight season with a sizable amount of time spent on the DL. Kershaw would miss almost all of May and most of June with a back injury and that joins previous hip issues which have elicited talk that all those seasons of very heavy usage at a young age earlier in his career are now taking a physical toll. In addition to the ill health, we have clear number concerns as well despite Kershaw putting up another terrific ERA (2.73) and WHIP (1.04) last season. What needs to be noted is that the ERA was Kershaw's highest since 2010 and the WHIP his worst since 2012. Both those numbers have also been on a three-season rise as well as both trends are becoming quite solidified. Even more worrisome is the continued declining velocity and this is something that is a major threat for Kershaw and his numbers going forward. After averaging 94.3 on his fastball back in 2015, Kershaw has now dipped down to just a 91.4 mark a year ago and that in turn has led to elevated HR/9 marks each of the last two seasons as opposing hitters are not having as much trouble making good contact anymore with the heater. These are all intertwined issues impacting Kershaw as he turns 31 in March but you get the sense he is an old 31. The numbers certainly back this notion up and that is why we advise extreme caution here considering the annual fantasy baseball price tag figures to remain very high. This is an obviously declining stock that needs to be handled with care and if it were up to us, we would absolutely look past Kershaw in all drafts this season and go with a more stable ace if you choose to spend a high pick on a pitcher.

2019 PROJECTION: 16-5 2.84 ERA 1.10 WHIP 174 K

Madison Bumgarner: In 2017 it was a foolish dirt bike accident that caused a shoulder tear which kept him out for two months. Last season it was a broken pinkie finger suffered as a result of being hit by a comebacker. Hopefully, for those planning on investing in San Francisco Giants ace Madison Bumgarner for 2019 fantasy baseball, things will go a lot more smoothly for the lefty on the health front. Before we go into what we anticipate for Bumgarner this season, it is imperative we take a closer look at the shoulder accident from 2017 in order to see just how much that devastating injury has had on his stuff. As we have always pointed out, a shoulder injury for a pitcher is so much worse than a bum elbow given the fact the former has a long history of eroding both velocity and the crispness of the overall stuff. Thus it is interesting to note that Bumgarner's velocity drop beginning in 2016 has not corrected itself since and in actuality have slipped a bit more. Back in 2015, Bumgarner's average fastball velocity was 93.0 and last season that number was down to just 91.4. On a related front, the drop in velocity has adversely affected Bumgarner's strikeout ability in a drastic way; going from a K/9 of 9.97 in 2016 all the way down to just an average 7.57. That is certainly no coincidence and this is a crucial thing to digest in accepting the reality Bumgarner's stuff no longer looks like ace-level and that his days of 200 strikeouts are likely gone for good. Even beyond the velocity/K's, Bumgarner's previously splendid control fell by the wayside last season as his BB/9 jumped up to a shaky 3.06 and it is possible he is now looking to change his approach (with resulting less location success) given the realization he is not able to collect the high amount of strikeouts as he once did. Finally, Bumgarner's 3.26 surface ERA last season looked good on paper but a lucky .274 BABIP covered for some sketchy FIP (3.99) and XFIP (4.32) marks. If it sounds like this is a lot of bad news, that's just due to the clear evidence Bumgarner is a shell of his former ace-level self and he should certainly be treated that way at the draft table this spring. Remember we are not paying for past results but instead need to focus on future potential. On the Bumgarner front, this is looking murkier than ever before.

2019 PROJECTION: 14-11 3.48 ERA 1.22 WHIP 153 K

Patrick Corbin: As the initial March/April start of the 2018 fantasy baseball season unfolded, many who failed to take advantage of the very affordable price tag of Arizona Diamondbacks starting pitcher Patrick Corbin the previous spring had to wonder how they missed the boat on the power lefty. It was not an overstatement if you were to argue that Corbin was the most dominant pitcher in baseball early on in the season as he came out of the gates posting a 2.25 ERA, .169 BAA, and 55 K's in 40 innings in March/April. While Corbin predictably was not able to keep up such a lofty standard, his end result numbers were still terrific (3.15 ERA, 1.05 WHIP, .217 BAA, 246 K in 200 IP) and he even got some down-the-ballot Cy Young votes as well. While Corbin's 11.07 K/9 was by far the best mark of his career, it is also not a total shock since the guy's stuff has some of the most wicked movement in all of baseball. With an average fastball velocity of just 91.0 last season that still was able to garner so many K's, it speaks to just how good Corbin's stuff really is. Now in terms of the rest of the 2018 statistical package, both Corbin's HR/9 (0.68) and BB/9 (2.16) were as good as it gets and so you really can see just how he literally gives almost no edge to opposing batters and this also speaks to him being quite a stable investment based solely on the numbers for the upcoming season. About the only concern we have here is Corbin's checkered injury history which includes a Tommy John elbow surgery and while he did stay relatively healthy in 2018, there were some fluctuations during the year in terms of velocity which is at least somewhat worrisome. Be that as it may, Corbin is not going to cost ace-level draft dollars this spring and even at an SP 2 price we are willing to take a chance here on a guy with top-shelf stuff who at the age of 29 remains firmly in his prime.
2019 PROJECTION: 15-7 3.19 ERA 1.04 WHIP 248 K

Stephen Strasburg: Another year and another season derailed by injury and disappointing numbers for Washington Nationals pitcher Stephen Strasburg. Given all the historical volatility, we can pretty much dig up any blurb we wrote on Strasburg the last five years or so and generally the information would be the same in terms of the guy possessing ace-level stuff but also a complete inability to ever make it through a given season without at least one stint on the DL. So those who ultimately decide to draft Strasburg each spring do so knowing he will be sidelined at some point but then go through the mental exercise hoping that maybe his absence will be on the short end of things this time around. 2018 was not such a season as Strasburg was limited to just 130 total innings due to neck and shoulder trouble that required multiple DL stints and then when on the mound, was not very good in logging a 3.74 ERA. For a guy who was once advertised as being a can't miss ace who would challenge for multiple CY Young's, Strasburg has only once in the last seven seasons finished with an ERA under 3.00 and the home runs are starting to go out at an increasing rate (a career-worst 1.25 HR/9 a year ago) as well. So even though Strasburg remains a terrific strikeout artist (156 in those 130 innings), the guy is as frustrating a player as there is to own in yearly fantasy baseball leagues and we for one are not going to willingly travel down this injury-filled road yet again.

2019 PROJECTION: 14-9 3.54 ERA 1.15 WHIP 188 K

Charlie Morton: In a Houston Astros rotation that also included past Cy Young Award winners and future contenders Justin Verlander, Dallas Keuchel, and Gerrit Cole; it looked like through the first two months of the 2018 season that veteran righty Charlie Morton was most deserving of the AL version of the trophy. Having already established his story as a mid-career renaissance guy who altered his approach to unlocking some hidden velocity, Morton was almost unhittable the first two months of the season when he registered ERA's of 1.72 and 2.90 respectively. Then there were the strikeouts as Morton punched out 85 batters in 67.2 innings during that span as his fantasy baseball owners were basking in their extreme fortune considering the mid-round price tag earlier that spring. It was at this point though where we pointed out Morton's career-long tendency of giving up home runs and walking an above-average amount of batters would conspire to somewhat interrupt all of the fun and then there was the matter of the fortunate BABIP's that helped fuel the statistical explosion the first two months of the season as well. Despite another month of very good pitching, Morton did, in fact, make a firm about-face after the All-Star Break as the home runs began to fly out more frequently and then there was the evident fatigue as his 34-year-old arm began to leak velocity which caused the hit rate to jump. The unfortunate topper was Morton coming down with two separate bouts of shoulder trouble that almost completely derailed his September when fantasy baseball leagues were decided and this added a very negative finish to the regular season. As tough as these concluding weeks were, Morton still posted a second straight terrific season for the Astros in setting career-bests in ERA (3.13), WHIP (1.16), BAA (.211), and strikeouts (201). That is an absolute bountiful of extremely positive numbers for Morton and no doubt they will help earn him a hefty payday in free agency. With all that said, Morton turned 35 last November and the shoulder trouble that flared at the end of last season and that could be an early warning sign he may not physically be able to handle a full six-month pitching grind anymore. Not to be overlooked was Morton's ongoing struggles with control as his 3.45 BB/9 last season was more than ugly. Finally, the Astros not extending a qualifying offer to Morton last October could serve as a telling sign they are not bullish on his future impact as well. So, in essence, we have to tread very carefully with Morton when it comes

to 2019 fantasy baseball drafts given all those red flags no matter the new location.
2019 PROJECTION: 14-10 3.48 ERA 1.17 WHIP 186 K

Zack Greinke: When reports began to surface early in spring training that Arizona Diamondbacks starter Zack Greinke was barely reaching the low-80's with his fastball, alarms began to go off all around his stock in terms of spring drafts. The fact Greinke was aging at 34 and with a long history of 200-inning seasons under his belt, made it sensible he was possibly headed to some pronounced arsenal erosion. In the end, though the velocity issue was a whole bunch of nothing as the righty's 3.21 season ERA was just .01 higher than his 2017 comeback campaign and a 1.08 WHIP and 199 K's in 207.2 was pretty darn good as well. Now in terms of the velocity, it is true 2018 marked the third straight season Greinke has seen a decrease in that category and the dip to just a 90.0 average fastball is getting awfully close to the Danger Zone for a pitcher. Keep in mind that even prior to the velocity decrease beginning in 2016, Greinke was a guy who always gave up a lot of home runs. The latter will only become more of a problem with the additional velocity he loses going forward and anyone who has owned Masahiro Tanaka the last two seasons can attest to how frustrating such a pitcher can be. Now in getting back to the 2018 numbers, Grienke's 8.62 K/9 and 1.86 BB/9 were both very solid but the 1.21 HR/9 and lucky .272 BABIP (adjusted FIP ERA of 3.70) failed to impress. As we always suggest in cases of a "name brand" player who is looking at a possible decline in numbers given the ravages of age, getting off the ride a year early as opposed to a year late is the way to go.
2019 PROJECTION: 14-10 3.59 ERA 1.10 WHIP 190 K

Walker Buehler: Already with a sterling reputation for developing high-end pitching prospects, the Los Angeles Dodgers unveiled a true gem in 2018 when 2015 first-round pick Walker Buehler proceeded to go out and perform like an overnight fantasy baseball ace. Unleashing a hellacious fastball that came in on average at 96.7, Buehler registered a sparkling 2.62 ERA, 0.96 WHIP, .191 BAA, and 151 strikeouts in 137.1 innings. What really puts Buehler right at the top of the class of the next great young starter's in today's game is not just the extreme velocity of his fastball but also the insane amount of movement he generates on all his pitches. Since Buehler also keeps the ball in the park (0.79 HR/9) and his control checks out nicely (2.42 BB/9), opposing hitters don't have much of a chance against this Noah Syndergaard clone. While there is always risk investing in young/hard-throwing arms given the high incidence of Tommy John, on talent alone Buehler already is as good as any pitcher in all of baseball.
2019 PROJECTION: 15-7 2.84 ERA 1.04 WHIP 197 K

David Price: No one could blame pricey Boston Red Sox lefty starter David Price if he desired to completely flush the 2017 season out of his memory forever given the fact he survived a few Tommy John scares and also off-the-field battles with team front office members and alumni. Considering all the turmoil and the exorbitant $217 million dollar contract, Price was not exactly in good graces with the always rough Boston fans as well. As almost always happens in situations such as this, all it took was for Price to pitch at a high level again to push all those negatives aside and he did just that in a 2018 campaign that saw him register a 3.58 ERA, 1.14 WHIP, and collect 177 K in 176 innings pitched. While Price did receive some batted ball luck through a .274 BABIP (adjusted FIP ERA of 4.01 and XFIP of 3.95), his 9.05 K/9 and 2.56 BB/9 were all within previous career norms. A 1.28 HR/9 was quite elevated but that number was also in outlier territory for Price who generally has been around 1.00 in that category in the past. Despite the notion Price is once again trustworthy off such a solid season, we still are quite leery here for a number of reasons. The first is that Price's past with forearm trouble is a major threat that could crop up at any moment. Also, Price is now an old 33 given the very high workloads throughout his career. Add in the always tough AL East environment and we side with taking a pass here unless you can get Price at a steep discount. **2019 PROJECTION: 15-7 3.54 ER 1.15 WHIP 175 K**

German Marquez: Somewhere former Colorado Rockies ace pitcher Ubaldo Jimenez is nodding his head in admiration over what 23-year-old righty German Marquez was able to accomplish on the mound in 2018 despite calling the launching pad that is Coors Field home. Having hinted at above-average ability the year prior when Marquez posted a 4.39 ERA in 162 innings for the team, the fireballer took things to another level and then some in 2019 as he broke Jimenez' team record for strikeouts in a season by punching out 221 batters in 191 innings. While Marquez' surface 3.76 ERA and 1.20 WHIP were quite good considering the home ballpark environment, it needs to be mentioned that his second-half performance (2.55 ERA, 0.97 WHIP, and insane 11.72 K/9) helped clinch many fantasy baseball league championships for those who had an ownership stake in the kid. Adding to the excitement here is that Marquez' 3.76 ERA should have been even LOWER due to the fact his .311 BABIP was a bit on the unlucky side and when adjusted, revealed more impressive FIP (3.33) and XFIP (3.11) marks. Turning just 24 in February, Marquez is on the fast track to upper-level fantasy baseball pitching status but he has to show more sustainability than Jimenez who quickly flamed out after his initial flurry with the Rockies. Marquez should be up to the task given the fact his control is already so much better than anything Jimenez showed during his time in the majors (BB/9 rates of 2.72 and 2.59 the last two seasons) and an average fastball velocity of 95.7 should ensure a string of 200-K/10.00-plus K/9 rates will flow freely. Yes, the Coors Field concern always gives one pause when it comes to investing in Colorado pitchers but trust us when we say Marquez is the real deal.

2019 PROJECTION: 15-8 3.57 ERA 1.19 WHIP 234 K

Mike Foltynewicz: Get used to spelling this last name as Atlanta Braves righty Mike Foltynewicz just got done making opposing hitters look downright foolish for almost the entire 2018 season. Having previously carried a reputation for being a very talented but also very wild prospect (2010 first-round pick by the Houston Astros), Foltynewicz' early MLB results were not overly pretty as both walks and home runs became major issues. With ERA's of 5.71, 4.31, and 4.79 during his first three partial seasons with the Braves, Foltynewicz was virtually ignored in fantasy baseball drafts last spring as it was tough to still see any upside here going forward. Well the proverbial light bulb went off and in blinding fashion last season as Folty rode an overpowering career-best 96.8 average fastball velocity to punch out 202 batters in just 183 innings; while also using the heater to help register ace-like ratios of a 2.85 ERA, 1.08 WHIP, and insane .198 BAA. With Foltynewicz establishing himself as one of the toughest pitchers to get a hit off of in all of baseball, it is imperative he continues working on the free passes which remained an issue (3.34 BB/9) during the monster season. Also while there were clearly a ton of well-earned positives, Foltynewicz' .251 BABIP was well into the lucky territory. Even that became somewhat of a positive though as Folty's adjusted FIP (3.38) and XFIP (3.77) ERA's were still more than decent. Now even though it is likely Foltynewicz will see his surface ERA jump up a bit due to the BABIP factor alone, his ability to strike out batters and keep the hits to the minimum should still allow him to hold a lot of the 2018 gains. Count us as being sold.

2019 PROJECTION: 14-9 3.33 ERA 1.10 WHIP 214

Masahiro Tanaka: For the second season in a row, New York Yankees hurler Masahiro Tanaka combined sometimes brilliant ace-level pitching with a ridiculous amount of surrendered home runs that ruined a good number of outings on just a few pitches. As a result, Tanaka can be an extremely volatile guy to own in fantasy baseball given the fact that any individual outing can go from great to awful due to the annual home run problems and this can be beyond stressful for his owners. Now in terms of the 2018 season, Tanaka's first half was a mess as he posted a 4.54 ERA and gave up 18 of the 25 home runs he would yield during the course of the year. What is crazy is that despite the homers, Tanaka was actually pitching very well as opposing hitters batted just .229 against him during the first half but the ratios were ugly based almost solely on the long ball damage. Once Tanaka got that issue under control during the second half with just the 7 homers given up, his ERA during that span became an excellent 2.85 despite a BAA going UP to .248. In the end, Tanaka's composite 3.75 ERA was well down from the 4.74 he achieved the year prior and his 9.17 K/9 was the second season in a row going over the 9.00 mark despite still pitching with a partially torn UCL. What is interesting is that you don't hear much anymore about Tanaka's UCL tear given that he has now gone three full seasons pitching with the injury without succumbing to Tommy John but the threat does remain that any one pitch can end his season in its tracks. That being said, Tanaka seems locked in as a strong SP 2 whose control remains excellent (2.02 BB/9) and who is really just held back by the home runs. Unfortunately, it is simply impossible to predict when Tanaka's gopher ball problems will rear its ugly head and so he will certainly once again test his owners' patience throughout the course of 2019.

2019 PROJECTION: 15-7 3.39 ERA 1.15 WHIP 163 K

Jose Berrios: Last spring on our website, we tabbed Minnesota Twins top pitching prospect Jose Berrios as our "Darkhorse AL Cy Young" winner as this peanut stand was admittedly seduced by the wicked stuff the righty brought to the table and also for the fact the previous underlying metrics hinted at such a sizable leap in development. Early on in the course of the 2018 season it certainly looked like Berrios was going to make us look clairvoyant as he went into the All-Star Break with a solid 3.68 ERA, a terrific .212 BAA, and 127 K's in 127.1 IP. What we failed to consider in making Berrios our possible off-the-radar Cy Young pick was the fatigue factor that almost always serves as the impetus for a second-half fade by a young hurler going through his first full year as a major league starter and that is where things went off the rails here a bit. With almost all of Berrios' advanced metrics heading in the wrong direction, his second-half run was a clear step or two down from the first as shown by a much shakier 4.15 ERA, .235 BAA, but a still impressive 75 K in 65 IP. In the end, though, the totality of Berrios' season was still very impressive as he cemented his reputation for being a strikeout asset (202 K's in 192.1 IP for a 9.45 K/9) and the ratios were not too shabby either (composite 3.84 ERA and 1.14 WHIP). Now there was some help on the BABIP front (.270) which helped mask an ugly 1.17 HR/9 and a bit of a shaky 2.85 BB/9 but the bottom line is that Berrios is right there as one of the brighter future pitching stars of the game and he should be treated as such for 2019 fantasy baseball. This is a guy who is talented enough to reach ace status as soon as this season and the best part is that you may be able to grab him for as cheap as an SP 3 price.

We suggest you bid aggressively here as maybe our Cy Young prediction on Berrios was a just year too early.

2019 PROJECTION: 16-8 3.35 ERA 1.11 WHIP 217 K

Jon Lester: Turning 35 in January and with a ridiculous amount of innings already under his belt, Chicago Cubs All-Star lefty Jon Lester keeps on trucking along in posting another very good season in 2018. With an ERA of 3.32 and 18 wins for a Cubs team that went right back to the postseason, Lester did his part to show he is not done yet being a front-of-the-rotation guy. This is where we pump the brakes on all the positive talk however as Lester did reveal some negative signs last season that perhaps do hint at some age-related giveback in numbers that could portend to more trouble ahead. As we noted in our draft guide a year ago, aging pitchers with very heavy previous career workloads often have big first-half performances that are then followed by second-half struggles as their bodies are not as capable of handling a six-month season at optimal efficiency. Lester went along with this prediction as his dominant first half 2.58 ERA was followed by a rough 4.50 second half that saw the velocity decrease as the season went on. Then there was the fact Lester's .290 BABIP was a bit on the lucky side and when adjusted, resulted in FIP (4.39) and XFIP (4.43) marks that were quite ugly. Even more concerning is Lester's average fastball velocity dipping for the third season in a row down to a very shaky 91.5 and a decrease from 180 strikeouts in 2017 to just 149 a year ago is a sign that maybe he is losing impact there as well. With a WHIP that has cemented itself in the high 1.30 range the last two seasons, Lester is leaking some statistical air everywhere and that threatens his standing as even an SP 2 for 2019 fantasy baseball. As we always note, it is a good idea to try and do your best to move away from name brand veterans a year early instead of a year too late like we suggest doing with Lester this season.

2019 PROJECTION: 14-8 3.75 ERA 1.31 WHIP 157 K

Mike Clevinger: After coming up and posting surprisingly decent numbers as a late MLB arrival at the age of 26 in 2017 (3.11 ERA, 10.13 K/9), the task at hand for Cleveland Indians righthander Mike Clevinger was to prove that performance was no fluke the following season. Well, we would say Clevinger more than fulfilled that directive as he was so good in 2018 (3.02 ERA, .222 BAA, 207 K) that he even caught some low-scale Cy Young praise. While we were among those who were skeptical of Clevinger's 2017 out-of-the-blue performance, there should no longer be any doubt that the guy has cemented a top SP 3 classification going forward this season in fantasy baseball. The strikeout ability is what really stands out with Clevinger who is now a member of the 200-K club and whose K/9 of 9.32 more than validated the 10.13 mark from the year prior. Even more intriguing is the fact that Clevinger made sizable inroads with his control last season (going from a 4.44 BB/9 in 2017 down to 3.02 a year ago) and the 0.95 HR/9 rate has not been a big hindrance for him yet either. Despite being an older prospect who took some extra time making it to the majors, Clevinger seems like a safe fantasy baseball commodity from where we stand.

2019 PROJECTION: 14-10 3.08 ERA 1.19 WHIP 204 K

Chris Archer: While Pittsburgh Pirates hard-throwing righty Chris Archer has been a recommended play in these pages during the recent past, we went in the opposite direction last spring by jumping ship from his stock for a number of reasons. Despite nobody with a brain disputing the very potent strikeout ability of Archer, the fact he was still struggling to add a third pitch to his repertoire made him more hittable than one would think given the high-end power stuff. These issues revealed themselves in Archer making it three seasons in a row in 2018 where his ERA finished above 4.00 (4.31) but only had an injury absence preventing him from making it four years in a row with 200-plus strikeouts. When you get conflicting trends in terms of strikeouts and ERA, this usually has to do with poor control, home run tendencies, or both. Archer qualified on both ends last season (2.97 BB/9, 1.15 HR/9) and the homers, in particular, have been a frustrating problem that serves to ruin an otherwise excellent given start due to one or two misplaced pitches up in the zone. Having turned 30 last September, we have reached the point with Archer where what you see is what you get and this qualifies him for top-end SP 3 status through the strength of what can be very effective strikeout totals which will only get an added boost pitching a full season in the National League.

2019 PROJECTION: 12-12 4.105 ERA 1.25 WHIP 227 K

Zach Wheeler: Clear evidence that the phrase "it is not how you start but how you finish" undoubtedly would have New York Mets righty starter Zack Wheeler as a spokesman when it came to the 2018 fantasy baseball season. Having seen his once potent prospect status fade to the point where the Mets sent him to the minors to begin the year, it seemed like Wheeler was never going to be able to get past his annual struggles with ill control and injuries negatively impacting his numbers. While the Mets quickly brought Wheeler back up in mid-April, his first half was nothing but a mess as he sat with an ugly 4.44 ERA, 1.34 WHIP, and just a 3-6 record. It was at that point where the proverbial light bulb went on for Wheeler and shine brightly it did as he embarked on one of the most dominant second-half performances of recent memory from a guy who was not already an established star. The numbers were simply staggering as Wheeler went 9-1 after the break; while also posting a 1.68 ERA, 0.81 WHIP, and a ridiculous

.174 BAA before he was shut down early in mid-September due to workload concerns. So what exactly did Wheeler figure out in order to transform himself from a guy barely hanging on as a major league regular to one of the more dominant arms in the game from one half to the next? While there were a few factors at play, the real key centered on Wheeler finally being able to harness his high-90's fastball which then removed the option of opposing hitters allowing the guy to defeat himself with walks and also curbing the ill location resulting in hard contact. Nowhere was this improvement seen in clearer terms than Wheeler's BB/9 which went from a nasty 3.35 in the first half of the season all the way down to a Cliff Lee-like 1.80 after the break. As noted earlier, the better control Wheeler showed on the mound in the second half was directly tied into a sharply decreasing hit rate as shown by .170 BAA and the home runs began to dry up as well. So clearly this was the version of Wheeler the Mets always envisioned when they acquired him from the San Francisco Giants in the Carlos Beltran deal years ago but now the onus is on him being able to repeat the 2018 post-All Star Break gains. For a guy who fought control so much in the past, this is a legitimate concern as the outlier police are blaring their sirens regarding Wheeler's second-half performance but at the same time, it is entirely possible having stable health for the first time in his MLB career was all that was needed for the potential to come to the forefront. With many in the fantasy baseball community likely holding some doubt about Wheeler's ability to continue his ascension into 2019, the spring draft cost may be cheaper than one would think which will only help those who are interested in going back down this road again. When you break it all down, Wheeler is a "line in the sand" guy who you either believe has made the jump to upper-level status or instead subscribe to the notion he will go back to being an inconsistent/injury-prone frustration. When it comes to this peanut stand, we advise doing your best to secure Wheeler as your SP 4 as anything requiring a higher draft cost will increase the amount of hurt to your roster if things take a bad turn.

2019 PROJECTION: 14-10 3.73 ERA 1.14 WHIP 186 K

Jameson Taillon: Having beaten back cancer and rampant injuries since first reaching the majors in 2016, it was nice to see Pittsburgh Pirates starting pitcher Jameson Taillon take a firm step forward in his development in 2018 as he posted a 3.20 ERA, 1.18 WHIP, and struck out 179 batters in 191 innings (8.43 K/9). Not to be overlooked in those swell numbers were the innings tally as Taillon finally found consistent health for the first time as a major leaguer and we are now beginning to see all the potential that was burgeoning here after the Pirates made him the second overall pick in the 2010 draft. Still quite young as he turned 27 this past November, Taillon stands a great chance of being a firm SP 2 if he takes another small leap forward this season. The only thing preventing Taillon from reaching ace status is a strikeout rate that falls short of the majority of SP 1's in fantasy baseball but there is still a bunch to like here in terms of control (2.17 BB/9) and a home run rate that is not obscene (0.94 HR/9). Given the neutral .298 BABIP last season, Taillon is lacking in any sort of numbers volatility and so he should be trusted almost fully in 2019 drafts.

2019 PROJECTION: 14-9 3.43 ERA 1.17 WHIP 186 K

Yu Darvish: It looks like we can add Yu Darvish to the growing list of top-shelf Japanese pitching talent who flamed out under a hail of injuries after just a few seasons in the States. Having quickly grabbed the mantle of fantasy baseball ace when he arrived with the Texas Rangers back in 2012 through a power pitching approach that included some of the best strikeout ability in the game, the cracks began to show in 2015 spring training when Darvish was forced to undergo Tommy John elbow surgery. While he did make it back in the middle of 2016 with his fastball intact and the strikeouts continuing to pile up at a very high rate (which helped overcome a more pronounced home run tendency), Darvish's health continued to betray him from that point forward. With the home runs doing more damage to Darvish's ERA compared to prior to the surgery (3.06 in 2014 right before the Tommy John; 3.41 in 2016 and 3.86 in 2017 afterward), what we saw last season was nothing short of a complete abomination. Fresh off signing as a free agent with the Chicago Cubs for a massive six-years and $126 million, Darvish first hit the DL in early May with the flu and then went back in the middle of the month due to right triceps tendinitis. Since Darvish dealt with the same bout of right triceps tendinitis prior to his Tommy John in 2015, the Cubs moved very cautiously with their new investment from that point forward. Despite the added care the team gave him, Darvish bottomed out in August when he exited a rehab start and soon was ruled out for the remainder of the season due both a stress reaction on the tip of his right elbow which led to a debridement surgery in September and a right triceps strain. So what did the Cubs receive for all that money bestowed to Darvish in Year 1 of his new deal? Try 8 starts, a 4.95 ERA, and 1.43 WHIP which if you removed the name brand would be a haul that would relegate any pitcher who put up this slop to be left to rot on the waiver wire. With all that said, Darvish should be 100 percent ready for 2019 spring training but it needs to be emphasized the guy appears to be a clear shell of his former ace self both in terms of statistics and obviously health. Diving into the numbers a bit, Darvish still has his potent fastball as we noted earlier since he averaged a very impressive 94.8 mph on the pitch in 2018. That velocity kept Darvish as a top K/9 guy (11.03) but everywhere else there was major trouble such as in control (4.73 BB/9) and again with the home runs (1.58 HR/9). With Darvish only tossing 40 frames last season, we can toss the walk rate and somewhat the ERA into the mulligan bin. The home runs are another story though as this has become a pronounced issue since the Tommy John surgery and calling Wrigley Field home will certainly not help on that front. Then we have the utter hellacious health that alone makes Darvish completely unreliable even as a buy low SP 3. Your best bet here is to simply avoid this annual ball of stress and look for some better stability somewhere else.

2019 PROJECTION: 11-6 3.78 ERA 1.29 WHIP 173 K

Kyle Hendricks: With his 2016 monster campaign (2.13 ERA, 16 wins) belonging firmly in the outlier bin, Chicago Cubs starter Kyle Hendricks remains a very solid SP 3 option in yearly fantasy baseball leagues. Already being put in line to win a high amount of games as the Cubs continue to operate as one of the better teams in baseball, Hendricks' workmanlike 3.44 ERA, 1.15 WHIP, and .242 BAA yielded another profit for his owners given the depressed 2018 draft price. Now you won't find much in the way of strikeouts here since Hendricks' average fastball velocity has never even reached 90 in five previous MLB seasons and so 2018's 7.28 K/9 will be in the range of what we can expect going forward which is not overly exciting. However Hendricks is very durable, is still in his early prime years (he will be 28 for the 2019 season), and the fantastic control (1.99 BB/9) decreases the amount of volatility. Thus when you put together your SP 3 tiers, Hendricks should be listed prominently.

2019 PROJECTION: 15-8 3.54 ERA 1.17 WHIP 163 K

Miles Mikolas: Just like Colby Lewis before him, previous MLB washout Miles Mikolas found new pitching life in Japan where he excelled for three seasons before agreeing to come back to the States through a two-year deal worth $15.5 million from the St. Louis Cardinals last winter. Boy did that bit of foresight pay off for the Cards in a crazy good way as Mikolas started the year hot and never let up as he put forth a spectacular 2.83 ERA, 1.07 WHIP, and picked up 18 victories for the near-wild card winners. Even Mikolas' most ardent supporters couldn't have foreseen such a tremendous output and now the question is whether he can sustain this level of production going into the 2019 season. On that front, there are some concerns and the first thing that stands out was Mikolas' lucky .279 BABIP that resulted in higher FIP (3.28) and XFIP (3.67) ERA's. Now those are still very good marks which show Mikolas was legitimately tough for opposing hitters to handle and that does speak well for future performance. That said, Mikolas's margin for error with a neutral BABIP is not very significant given his well below-average 6.55 K/9. That is simply a very bad number for any pitcher but operating in the NL at least makes it not as concerning as opposed to being in the DH league. So while the BABIP luck

and lack of K's call into question Mikolas' ability to reprise his 2018 statistical output, the guy has a knack for not beating himself through the strength of top-notch control (1.30) and a splendid home run rate (HR/9 of 0.72). Those two numbers are tremendous and they do more than offset troubles with BABIP and strikeouts. What we are saying, in conclusion, is that while we do think Mikolas' ERA will rise above the 3.00 mark, he is still very capable of being a top SP 3 this season given the other skills.
2019 PROJECTION: 16-7 3.43 ERA 1.09 WHIP 154 K

Kyle Freeland: Move over German Marquez because you got some company in terms of 2018 Colorado Rockies pitching revelations. While Marquez got a major dose of deserved praise for his massive strikeout rates and second-half dominance, it was the team's 2014 first-round pick (8th overall) Kyle Freeland who had the more dominant season from start-to-finish. A bit of a rough start to the year soon morphed into something so much more as Freeland won 17 games for the playoff-bound Rockies; while also posting an ace-like 2.85 ERA despite the challenges of Coors Field. Freeland was so good that his name began to pop up on NL Cy Young Award campaigns as well and at the age of just 25, more bright days seem to be ahead. This is where we like to interject though as there were some issues regarding Freeland's 2018 season that may not be as they appear. For one thing, Freeland's .285 BABIP was on the lucky side which means his surface 2.85 ERA was not as impressive as one may be led to believe. When that ERA was adjusted, it came out to FIP (3.67) and XFIP (4.22) marks that were not as pretty to look at. In addition, Freeland has a much smaller margin for error with his approach, given the fact his 7.70 K/9 a year ago was the definition of average. So it stands to reason that since Freeland is not able to extricate himself from potential trouble with the strikeout as much as a Marquez can, the ERA will likely rise by more than a bit if the BABIP moves closer to the mean which is anticipated. Finally, Freeland's control was not overly great last season (3.11 BB/9) and that adds another layer of concern. So when you tally everything up, Freeland looks quite shaky from this vantage point going into 2019 fantasy baseball. While we applaud the terrific 2018, we also warn that Freeland figures to cost more than he should in spring drafts given the underlying concerns. Unless you can snag him as maybe an SP 4 (unlikely), then we would take a firm pass.
2019 PROJECTION: 16-8 3.48 ERA 1.27 WHIP 167 K

Dallas Keuchel: It has become quite the challenge trying to nail down projections on Houston Astros former Cy Young-winning pitcher Dallas Keuchel as his numbers have been all over the map the last few seasons. While his 2018 campaign was decent as Keuchel logged a useful 3.74 ERA and threw 204.2 innings, there are were quite a few negatives that have

called into question his fantasy baseball standing going forward. The first big red flag centered on Keuchel's terrible 6.73 K/9 rate which was down almost a complete strikeout from his 7.72 mark the year prior. While Keuchel's fastball velocity was right in line with previous career norms, the movement was not as sharp as it had been from 2015-17. The loss of above-average strikeouts wound turn out to be a sizable hit to Keuchel's fantasy baseball value since the ERA was good but not great and the 1.31 WHIP was also in shaky territory. On the positive side, Keuchel's control (2.55 BB/9) and home run rates (0.79) were impressive and this means he should remain firmly in the SP 3 realm. Add in the fact that Keuchel should win a bunch of games on another strong Houston team this season and he appears to be quite a safe investment despite some shaky advanced numbers.
2019 PROJECTION: 16-8 3.67 ERA 1.27 WHIP 155 K

Sean Newcomb: It was another season of positive development for Atlanta Braves pitching prospect Sean Newcomb in 2018 as the lefty had sizable stretches where he showed the ability to be an ace starter one day. In terms of the positives, Newcomb produced some impressive strikeout games which helped him post an above-average K/9 of 8.76 and his composite 3.91 ERA, 1.33 WHIP, and especially a very good .224 BAA were all improvements from 2017. With that said, Newcomb is still a bit rough around the edges as control remains a big problem (4.41 BB/9) and the home runs need to come down a bit as well (0.99 HR/9) since he calls a power-leaning ballpark home. It also needs to be mentioned that Newcomb's .274 BABIP was well into the lucky zone and so when his 3.91 ERA was adjusted; it came out to much more shaky FIP (4.13) and XFIP (4.33) marks that dull the hype somewhat. Still, just 25 when the 2019 season gets underway, Newcomb remains on an upward trajectory in terms of his development. At the same time, Newcomb must start getting the walks under control or else his overall progress will be stunted.
2019 PROJECTION: 14-10 3.84 ERA 1.30 WHIP 167 K

Robbie Ray: Heading into the 2018 fantasy baseball season, we sounded the alarms somewhat on Arizona Diamondbacks hard-throwing lefty Robbie Ray after his monstrous 2017 campaign (2.89 ERA, .215 BAA, 12.01 K/9 resulting in 218 strikeouts) sent the former 2012 first-rounders stock soaring last spring. While we had no qualms with Ray's nuclear fastball piling up the K's, there were some very concerning red flags which were buried underneath the surface numbers in 2017. For one thing, Ray's .267 BABIP was very lucky and resulted in much higher FIP (3.72) and XFIP (3.49) ERA's. Additionally, Ray's control was terrible (3.94 BB/9) and he also gave up too many home runs (1.28 HR/9). Combine all those potential landmine issues together and it was a miracle Ray was able to post such a lofty 2.89 ERA that season. So with all those red flags serving as a backdrop, it was no shock from this peanut stand when Ray struggled mightily to begin the season. While he did turn things around after the All-Star Break, Ray's composite 3.93 ERA and near neutral .292 BABIP went right along in conjunction with what his advanced rates suggested should have occurred in 2017. While Ray's fantasy baseball owners were unlikely to be satisfied with the statistical haul last season, it needs to be accepted that this is pretty much who he is as a flawed power arm whose choppy control remains miserable (5.09 BB/9). Add in continued struggles with the long ball (1.38 HR/9) and all the Ray strikeouts (12.01 K/9) shouldn't cloud his actual SP 3 skill set.

2019 PROJECTION: 14-10 3.84 ERA 1.29 WHIP 195 K

Jack Flaherty: Even though Miles Mikolas received a well-deserved high allotment of the pitching attention for the St. Louis Cardinals in 2018, the development of top pitching prospect Jack Flaherty should not be overlooked as well. Despite only being 22-years-old when summoned from the minors early on in the season, Flaherty seemed right at home as a major league hurler in 2018 as he registered a splendid 3.34 ERA, 1.11 WHIP, and staggering .198 BAA in 151 IP. Possessing wicked movement on his off-speed stuff and an average fastball near-94.0, Flaherty became a big strikeout weapon as well in punching out 182 batters in just 151 IP (10.85 K/9). With all that said, Flaherty also benefited from some generous BABIP luck (.257) and that helped mask some control (3.52 BB/9) and home run (1.19 HR/9) struggles. Given the high walk and home run rates, it is likely we are going to see Flaherty's ERA rise to the mid-to-high 3.00 range if the BABIP luck moves toward the mean. Given all the strikeouts that are also part of the statistical equation, that is fine as long as you price that into whatever cost you are willing to pay for the guy in spring drafts. Still a bit off the fantasy baseball radar given all the talk about Mikolas last season, it may be in the realm of possibility to snag Flaherty at an SP 4 rate which would be a major win for those who smartly try to grab an ownership stake.

2019 PROJECTION: 15-9 3.53 ERA 1.12 WHIP 189 K

Rick Porcello: It was another solid but boring fantasy baseball performance for Boston Red Sox veteran starter Rick Porcello in 2018 as he once again saw his ERA come in over the 4.00 mark at 4.28 but still was able to claim 17 wins and 190 strikeouts. Despite annual ratios that often finish in shaky territory, Porcello's extreme durability allows him to pile up strikeouts (three straight seasons of either 189 or 190 whiffs) and the wins keep flowing at a high rate (50 total during this same span) given the boost from a dominant Red Sox lineup. So while you always want to try and avoid pitchers who operate in the brutal AL East, Porcello has proven to be as dependable an SP 3 as you can get.

2019 PROJECTION: 18-8 4.07 ERA 1.17 WHIP 192 K

Eduardo Rodriguez: If only Boston Red Sox pitching prospect Eduardo Rodriguez' health would cooperate, we could then get a more firm grip on what kind of an impact starter he can be for fantasy baseball purposes. While we have now gotten four straight partial seasons out of the hard-throwing Rodriguez, constant health trouble has capped some very intriguing potential here to leave the lefty as an ongoing statistical mystery. What we can already surmise though is that Rodriguez has a knack for missing bats and he did his best major league work on this front a year ago by posting a career-best 10.13 K/9 rate (146 K's in 129.2 IP) and the 3.82 ERA was not too shabby either. Be that as it may, Rodriguez' control is still ugly (3.12 BB/9) but in his defense, that number has incrementally dropped each of the last three seasons. So as we look towards 2019, the hope is that Rodriguez can finally give us 180 innings which could then turn into 15 wins and around 200 K's easy. That potential makes Rodriguez a smart late-round pick as many in the fantasy baseball community have already moved away from the guy given all the stops and starts so far. Count us among the throng of experts who say to give this another chance as the ability is still too potent to ignore.

2019 PROJECTION: 14-10 3.77 ERA 1.24 WHIP 177 K

Luis Castillo: If one were to poll the original Luis Castillo fantasy baseball owners in 2018, the general consensus reaction to the experience would undoubtedly be a negative one. Having entered into the season as one of the more sought after sleepers on the heels of a very impressive 2017 debut (3.12 ERA, 9.87 K/9, 1.22 WHIP), predictions that Castillo was the next big power arm were being floated around the fantasy baseball community. As so often happens when the hype gets out of hand, things went in the wrong direction for Castillo early on in the season as he was battered unmercifully to the tune of an unfathomable 5.49 ERA, 1.38 WHIP, and an 8.36 K/9). Pretty much everything went wrong for Castillo during this span and it was easy to see that the kid was completely shell-shocked and lacking zero confidence. It also was at this point where many Castillo fantasy baseball owners jumped ship in sending him to their league's waiver wire en masse which was understandable considering how brutal the numbers were. However, the Reds deserve credit for sticking with Castillo through the struggles and pretty soon their patience was rewarded when the righty went on a second-half tear in logging a 2.44 ERA, 0.96 WHIP, and 9.36 K/9 rate. As a result of that run, many original Castillo owners were left seething even more than they were before as they watched an opposing league member snatch him up and gain the benefit of those tremendous numbers. So in terms of the totality of the season, it is easy to see that Castillo worked through a sophomore slump and figured things out on the fly in terms of how to adjust back against hitters who gained a book on his approach the previous winter. While it is foolish to compare the two halves of 2018 in projecting Castillo for next season, we can draw some conclusions that are bankable. The most potent would be Castillo's propensity for collecting strikeouts which have always been a part of the statistical equation here and has resulted in 263 K's in 259 career major league innings. Also not to be overlooked is the fact Castillo's BABIP of .282 was in the unlucky territory last season and so his composite 4.30 ERA should have been lower. With the walks also checking out nicely (2.60 BB/9), Castillo only has to work on keeping his very high home run rate (1.49 HR/9) in check in order for him to achieve optimum efficiency. So what we have here is a fantasy baseball stock that will be much quieter this spring then it was compared to a year prior but that just means the payoff can be more potent given the fact Castillo still retains the vast upside that made us all chase him in the first place.

2019 PROJECTION: 12-11 3.77 ERA 1.24 WHIP 179 K

Andrew Heaney: As a former 9th overall pick in the 2012 MLB Draft, Los Angeles Angels lefty starter Andrew Heaney has been a name that's drawn late-round upside interest when it comes to fantasy baseball drafts the last few seasons. Count this peanut stand as a Heaney apologist since we have always talked up the very intriguing combination of above-average strikeout ability and impeccable control in holding to the belief he could be a nice fantasy baseball asset if only the health would cooperate (having previously undergone Tommy John surgery). While things didn't exactly end well in 2018, chalk up the season as one of progress for Heaney as he at times looked like an upper-level power arm whose 9.00 K/9 rate, 4.15 ERA, and excellent 2.25 BB/9 portend to another jump in performance going forward. With his 180 innings representing by far a career-high, it is no shock Heaney's solid first half (3.78 ERA, 1.16 WHIP) was followed by a much shakier second half (4.64 ERA, 1.25 WHIP) likely due to fatigue. Perhaps most significant is that Heaney generally stayed healthy and is just entering into his prime at the age of 27 which means SP 3 status is within the realm of possibility. Given the West Coast screen and the feeling by many in the fantasy baseball community that Heaney is a bit of old news, you are likely only going to have to pay an SP 5 price this spring which is a major win for those who smartly bring the guy aboard.

2019 PROJECTION: 14-11 3.74 ERA 1.19 WHIP, 185 K

Zack Godley: Well at least we now know 2017 was an outlier. Having been hit very hard during previous MLB stints, Arizona Diamondbacks starter Zack Godley shocked the fantasy baseball community that year when he showcased some newfound velocity and used this fresh weapon to help record a 3.37 ERA, 1.14 WHIP, and a 9.58 K/9. Just like that Godley was a new darling among the fantasy baseball fraternity and it showed the following spring amid high expectations for the 2018 season. Whether it was opposing hitters adjusting to the new Godley approach, some bad batted ball luck, or a combination of both; the bottom line was that the righty's season was very ugly as shown by a 4.74 ERA and 1.45 WHIP. While Godley did maintain the velocity and strikeout rates from the previous season (9.23 K/9), everything else went into the gutter as he was widely cut loose by many of his owners in early summer. So when one began to search for the reason for the massive dip in numbers, a good place to start was an undoubtedly bit of bad luck on the batted ball (.324) that when adjusted, resulted in much more useful FIP (3.82) and XFIP (3.96) ERA's. However, Godley did have to take the hit on a big increase in walks as his BB/9 rate went from 3.08 in 2017 to a very ugly 4.09 a year ago. Besides those two issues, everything else checked out well for Godley when comparing 2018 to his breakout the previous season. With all that said, it is probably a good idea to project Godley right in between those two campaigns and this would bring forth about an SP 4 type of pitcher. Even through all the struggles last season Godley still won 15 games and another run at that number on a good Diamondbacks team in 2019 is likely. When you add the solid strikeout rate and the decent chance of an improved ERA, there are some clear things to work with here.

2019 PROJECTION: 14-8 3.93 ERA 1.16 WHIP 185 K

Michael Wacha: Volatility and St. Louis Cardinals starting pitcher Michael Wacha go hand-in-hand and this notion remained the storyline in 2018 as the righty combined decent on-the-mound results (3.20 ERA, 1.23 WHIP) with persistent injury trouble. A strained oblique during a late June start became a season-ender when Wacha suffered a setback with the injury while rehabbing in August and his 84.1 inning haul marked the third year in a row the veteran failed to reach even 170 frames. It also needs to be remembered that a bout of shoulder trouble in 2014 seemingly robbed Wacha of some of his strikeout ability; with his 2013 rookie K/9 of 9.05 never coming close to being repeated since (just once in the four following seasons that number went above a modest 8.00 in that category). Now in terms of just last season's results, Wacha's surface 3.20 ERA was very good but he also received generous BABIP help (.249) which when adjusted; resulted in more shaky FIP (4.21) and XFIP (4.12) ERA's. When you factor in that Wacha's ugly 3.84 BB/9 was a career-worst, you get the sense the guy was not anywhere near as good last season as the surface numbers would indicate. On the positive side, Wacha turned just 27 last July and remains on a Cardinals team that always provides good opportunities to collect wins. With that being said, Wacha overall looks like nothing more than a firm SP 4 option.

2019 PROJECTION: 12-7 3.88 ERA 1.25 WHIP 143 K

Ross Stripling: Well this was certainly a nice surprise. Almost completely off the fantasy baseball radar heading into the 2018 season, oft-injured Los Angeles Dodgers pitcher Ross Stripling being moved into the team's rotation out of spring training made barely a ripple as drafts finished up. That would change rather quickly when Stripling exploded out of the gates while pitching like an ace in every sense of the word and pretty soon we were looking at a guy who was sitting with a 2.08 ERA, 1.08 WHIP, and 108 K's in 95.1 innings at the All-Star Break. Perhaps we should have seen this coming as Stripling recorded decent ERA's of 3.96 and 3.75 during his first two partial seasons in the majors but still the righty took a quantum leap in production across the board in spectacular fashion. Ultimately though it became a clear tale of two halves as Stripling saw the injury bug resurface after the All-Star Break as he hit the DL with a back injury and that likely contributed to him pitching terribly (6.41 ERA) during that span. So where does Stripling go from here and where does his true ability lie? While a tough question to answer concretely, what we can do is examine the advanced metrics to get a read on Stripling's skills and on that front, there are mostly positives. Whether it is his excellent control (1.62 BB/9) or strikeout ability (10.03 K/90; Stripling checks a lot of boxes with regards to projecting him as a possible front-of-the-rotation arm for 2019. Even when looking at Stripling's composite 3.02 ERA, his XFIP of 2.99 was even lower given the fact a .322 BABIP was a bit into the unlucky territory. While Stripling does have a clear home run problem (1.33 HR/9), a ground ball rate of 45.4 that is well above his fly ball mark of 32.6 means we should probably not be overly concerned here. The biggest overall negative with Stripling is really an inability to stay healthy and there are valid concerns about whether or not his body can physically hold up to pitching a full season. The Dodgers placing Stripling in the bullpen in 2017 and even for a small stretch of last season show they are aware of this issue and so that needs to be factored into any draft cost this spring. The ability is certainly not up for debate but we grade Stripling more as an SP 3 given the injury threat.

2019 PROJECTION: 12-7 3.38 ERA 1.17 WHIP 157 K

Joey Lucchesi: While these have been lean times of late for the San Diego Padres, their fan base should at least feel pretty excited about the development of top pitching prospect Joey Lucchesi who dazzled at times during his 2018 debut in racking up 145 strikeouts in just 130 innings (10.04 K/9), while also posting a 4.08 ERA that only became inflated due to a rough ending to the season. A former 2016 fourth-round pick by the team, Lucchesi doesn't throw overly hard (average fastball just under 92) but a very funky windup that is tough for opposing hitters to pick up and some terrific movement on his pitches help to generate a high number of swings and misses. With a season of development now under his belt, we can expect another jump in production for Lucchesi in 2019 which makes him an excellent middle-to-late round upside pick.

2019 PROJECTION: 11-5 3.85 ERA 1.27 WHIP 163 K

Hyun-Jin Ryu: It has been a string of never-ending injuries for Los Angeles Dodgers Korean lefty Hyun-Jin Ryu since he first came over to the States in 2013 and 2018 was no different as he was only able to toss 82.1 innings due to a strained groin that kept him out from May until mid-August. Clearly, there are no issues about talent however as Ryu was dominant in those 82.1 innings to the tune of a 1.97 ERA, 1.01 WHIP, and 89 strikeouts. The skills of Ryu have never really been in doubt as he has generally pitched well on the rare occasions he is on the mound but the health setbacks have almost completely derailed him almost every season. A free agent as of this writing, Ryu will surely find a home somewhere this winter (and maybe even re-up with the Dodgers) and the above-average ability puts him squarely into the sizable upside SP 5 realm. If Ryu could ever just scratch out 130-150 innings, you could be looking at a massive fantasy baseball value play but until we see it, we can only suggest using a late-round pick here.

2019 PROJECTION: 8-4 3.34 ERA 1.09 WHIP 137 K

Rich Hill: The always fun story of ageless Los Angeles Dodgers lefty starter Rich Hill put forth another very good chapter in 2018 as he was once again a strikeout machine (143 K's in 125.2 IP), while also logging very helpful ratios to the tune of a 3.87 ERA and 1.11 WHIP. By now it is well known how Hill engineered one of the greatest late-career explosions of all-time as 2018 marked the fourth season in a row he posted an ace-like K/9 in double-digits and he has yet to pitch to an ERA over 4.00 since his 2015 comeback. Be that as it may, Hill does show his age in terms of poor health and anyone who invests in the guy has to accept they will only get around 120-130 innings given the rampant DL stints. With one more year to go on his contract with the Dodgers, Hill once again makes the grade as a very strong SP 4/5 but on stuff/results alone on a per start basis, his numbers actually approach SP 3 status.

2019 PROJECTION: 10-6 3.79 ERA 1.15 WHIP 154 K

Jose Quintana: The consensus thinking when projecting Chicago Cubs lefty starter Jose Quintana for the 2018 fantasy baseball season was that he was slated for a very good campaign based in large part through the opportunity to operate fully in the National League after years of putting up very underrated numbers in the American League with the cross-town White Sox. Unfortunately, Quintana didn't get the memo as he was hammered for large stretches of the season (4 of 6 months with an ERA over 4.00) that caused many of his fantasy baseball owners to contemplate throwing in the towel on him. Those who did stick it out received just an average ERA (4.03), WHIP (1.32), and strikeout rate (8.16). All of those numbers were drastic declines from the previous season split between the White Sox and Cubs and as a result, Quintana's 2019 fantasy baseball stock is looking quite a bit murky. Quintana has now posted back-to-back seasons with an ERA over 4.00 and his 9.78 K/9 in 2107 that helped fuel a lot of the hype last spring now looks like a big outlier. Also when you add in just a mediocre average fastball velocity (91.8) and a walk rate that trended in the wrong direction last season (3.51 BB/9), Quintana seems like someone you should grade just as an SP 4 this spring.
2019 PROJECTION: 14-9 4.07 ERA 1.24 WHIP 173 K

Kevin Gausman: Long a guy who served as a perennial spring fantasy baseball sleeper who would then ultimately disappoint in some very ugly ways, former 2014 4th overall pick Kevin Gausman finally showed some consistently good results as the righty starter finished with a 3.92 ERA. The impetus to the mini-breakthrough was a merciful trade from the Baltimore Orioles to the Atlanta Braves at the July 31 deadline and so moving away from the brutal AL East to the much less intense NL East was just what the statistical doctor ordered for Gausman. Further solidifying the varying levels of difficulty operating in both leagues, Gausman went from an ugly 4.43 ERA/1.38 WHIP the first four months of the season down to just 2.87/1.14 which made the righty a smart add down the stretch. In looking at the totality of Gausman's numbers, his .299 BABIP was right in the neutral zone which means he earned his ratios and there were also some nice gains made in the control area (2.45 BB/9) which was another encouraging sign. The bottom line here though is that being able to throw a full season of starts in the National League will certainly benefit Gausman and it should also allow him to move back into the 8.00-range in K/9 after dipping to just 7.25 a year ago. While this peanut stand has never been a fan of Gausman at any stage, we saw enough good things in his Braves stint last season to recommend him as an SP 5 in drafts this spring.
2019 PROJECTION: 12-10 3.78 ERA 1.27 WHIP 175 K

J.A. Happ: Making a slight twist to a very famous song about the city of New York, if you can make it in the AL East as a starting pitcher, you can make it anywhere. Such a label belongs squarely on veteran starter J.A. Happ who pitched well both last season with the Toronto Blue Jays and then later with the New York Yankees in posting a 3.65 ERA, 1.13 WHIP, and career-best 9.78 K/9. Those were certainly terrific numbers to take into free agency and even though he turned 36 this past October, Happ still appears to be at the top of his game. A bit of a mid-career bloomer after a string of high ERA's during his first few major league seasons, Happ's off-speed stuff has terrific movement to help pick a decent number of K's and continually keep opposing hitters off balance. Even though Happ continues to struggle with the long ball (1.37 HR/9), he helps offset that red flag through terrific control (2.58 BB/9). So no matter where he ends up this winter (especially any destination is the NL), Happ looks to be a firm SP 3 for at least another season or so.

2019 PROJECTION: 15-7 3.48 ERA 1.15 WHIP 188 K

Carlos Martinez: Having gone on record in these pages last spring describing how we felt St. Louis Cardinals ace pitcher Carlos Martinez was quite overrated due to career-long control and health problems, we were forced to eat crow early on as the righty was terrific the first two months with ERA's of 1.43 and 2.19 respectively. Alas, Martinez hit a wall in June (6.75 ERA) and then made good on our health concerns when he hit the DL THREE times with oblique and then shoulder trouble. The latter has been a problem for a few years now and we don't need to remind you about how shoulder injuries can be about the worst kind of injury for a pitcher. Perhaps indicating their concern regarding the ailment, the Cardinals then decided to have Martinez spend the last 1.5 months of 2018 in the bullpen where he filled the closer role that caused so much trouble during the course of the season. Given his terrific fastball, it was no shock Martinez looked like a natural closer as he nailed down 5 saves and perhaps gave the team a reason to keep him there in 2019. While that is very unlikely given Martinez' success as a starter in the past, it is something to keep in mind if you make an investment here. With an average fastball velocity of 95.6 a year ago, Martinez can easily get back to the 200-K level but health and control (4.55 BB/9) remain tremendous red flags. Given both all of the volatility and uncertainty revolving around Martinez this season, he may be too much of a headache for you to deal with.

2019 PROJECTION: 11-8 3.45 ERA 1.29 WHIP 185 K

Jake Arrieta: One guy we had zero interest in owning last spring and who we included prominently in our "BUST" list in these pages at that time was Philadelphia Phillies starter Jake Arrieta. We spoke at length then about how Arrieta's very ugly injury history and a sizable drop in average fastball velocity (from 95.1 in 2013 all the way down to 92.9 a year ago) portended to very bad things being ahead for him in 2018 fantasy baseball. While in fairness Arrieta had some good stretches during the course of the season, his overall 3.96 ERA, 1.29 WHIP, and 138 K in 172.2 IP was nothing to write home about. The severe drop in strikeouts stands out the most as Arrieta's 7.19 K/9 was way down from his high point of 9.28 in 2013 and even a notable decrease from 8.71 last season. With strikeouts no longer part of the statistical equation, right there alone Arrieta loses quite a bit of his fantasy baseball appeal. Then when you add in the fact he had a lucky .287 BABIP last season that came out to much higher FIP (4.25) and XFIP (4.08) ERA' and a HR/9 of 1.09 that is also more elevated than one would like, you wind up with a very negative overall picture here. This was no shock to us as we warned you about the Arrieta risk ahead of time and another year of decline with statistical dips and injuries marring things in 2019 stand a very good chance of happening. As a result, you can safely avoid Arrieta in most fantasy baseball leagues this season.

2019 PROJECTION: 12-7 3.86 ERA 1.28 WHIP 149 K

Steven Matz: So that is what a relatively healthy season for New York Mets lefty starter Steven Matz looks like. Annually one of the most injury-prone pitchers in all of baseball (having only once tossed more than 100 innings in three previous seasons), Matz' 154 frames a year ago translated well enough to a 3.97 ERA and 8.88 K/9. Unfortunately, Matz still has not come close to realizing the hype that was attached to his name when he first arrived back in 2015 and an average fastball velocity that has dipped from 96.1 that year down to just 93.5 last season is a big reason why. Simply put, Matz doesn't carry the same type of flash he once did and that makes his ugly control (3.39 BB/9) stand out even more. Given the utter unlikelihood Matz can stay just moderately healthy two seasons in a row, it becomes clear he is not someone you want to chase in 2019 fantasy baseball drafts.

2019 PROJECTION: 10-12 4.15 ERA 1.26 WHIP 158 K

Cole Hamels: If you ever had any doubts about the effects on a pitcher's ERA/WHIP/K Rate when comparing operating in the NL or the AL, you only have to look at the splits of Chicago Cubs pitcher Cole Hamels in 2018 after he threw both for the Texas Rangers and the Chicago Cubs after coming over to the latter during a summer trade. During the first four months with the Rangers, Hamels looked completely shot as a major league pitcher as evidenced by a nasty 4.72 ERA, 1.37 WHIP, and .258 BAA. Surprisingly the Cubs thought Hamels had something left to give for their playoff push and their faith was more than rewarded as the former All-Star overnight looked like a top-line starter again in registering a 2.36 ERA, 1.10

WHIP, and .226 BAA. Once again the stark differences' in Hamels' numbers bore out how much tougher it is to pitch in the American League and so it is a big plus that the team picked up his 2019 option. Since Hamels will now operate a full season in the National League for the first time since his Philadelphia Phillies days, SP 3 numbers are possible.

2019 PROJECTION: 10-9 3.86 ERA 1.27 WHIP 183 K

Anibal Sanchez: Aging like a fine wine, the Atlanta Braves had to be pumped about the tremendous season put forth by veteran starter Anibal Sanchez in 2018 as the righty more than did his part helping the team reach the postseason. Registering a 2.83 ERA that was his lowest since 2013 and a career-best 1.08 WHIP, Sanchez packed a ton of value into his 136.2 innings. Still showing the terrific pitch movement that made him such a big prospect with the Florida Marlins back in the day, Sanchez put up a nice 8.89 K/9 that was even more impressive when you look at the fact his average fastball velocity was just 91.0. As always during a Sanchez season, however, ill health led to extensive time on the DL but since his annual draft cost is never anything more than that a very late-round pick at this late stage of his career, you won't be able to find many more better SP 5's.

2019 PROJECTION: 10-7 3.57 ERA 1.11 WHIP 144 K

Alex Wood: While his reputation for getting injured is much-discussed, not nearly enough attention gets paid to how underrated a starting pitcher the Los Angeles Dodgers' Alex Wood has been since reaching the majors back in 2013 with the Atlanta Braves. Now with 6 seasons in the big leagues under his belt, Wood has yet to post an ERA at or above 4.00 and three times that number went below 3.50. Add in some solid-to-very-good strikeout rates during that span and there is certainly a lot to like from a fantasy baseball perspective. Unfortunately, Wood can't ever seem to avoid injuries and last season was no different as he pitched just 151.2 innings where he recorded a 3.68 ERA, 1.21 WHIP, and 8.01 K/9. While the ratios were solid, Wood's K/9 decreased for the third straight season which is troubling and could be an indication ill health is starting to take somewhat of a bite out of his stuff. Given that his average fastball velocity dropped to just 90.8 last season validates this concern somewhat as well. It is possible the grind of a six-month season of starting doesn't agree with Wood physically and that has to be factored into any decision to draft the guy this spring. A free agent as of this writing, Wood still has enough talent to make the SP 4 grade but he is more of a sketchy stock than he was just a year ago.

2019 PROJECTION: 11-8 3.57 ERA 1.22 WHIP 158 K

Julio Teheran: The enigma that is Atlanta Braves righty Julio Teheran continued onward in 2018 as he pitched to a 3.94 ERA, 1.17 WHIP, and collected 162 K's in 175.2 innings. While the overall surface numbers were decent, Teheran was extremely volatile in terms of wild swings in pitching results from literally one start to the next and this type of fantasy baseball ownership is not for the faint of heart. What is also frustrating about Teheran is that his stuff has terrific movement but at the same time, a dip to just an average fastball velocity of 90.4 last season (down sharply from 92.0 the year prior) which is troubling considering he is still just going to be 28 by the start of 2019. We can see the issues that such an erosion in velocity can cause for Teheran as his HR/9 rate was simply brutal last season in spiking to 1.40 and we don't need to tell you this is a really bad thing considering the power-leaning dimension of the Braves' ballpark. Even beyond that pronounced struggle, Teheran continues to walk too many batters (two straight seasons with a BB/9 over 3.40) and his .281 BABIP reveals that the surface 3.94 ERA should have gone even higher. So when you look at the totality of Teheran for 2019 fantasy baseball, there are just too many potential landmines here to make him worth the stress of not knowing how any one start will go.

2019 PROJECTION: 10-10 4.04 ERA 1.20 WHIP 165 K

Mike Minor: After resurrecting his once-promising career filled with serious injuries by coming back and pitching very well out of the bullpen for the Kansas City Royals in 2017 (2.55 ERA, 10.20 K/9), it certainly appeared as though Mike Minor would become the latest failed-starter-turned-shutdown-reliever as he entered into free agency that winter. In a surprise move, however, Minor signed a three-year deal worth $28 million with the Texas Rangers to once again work as a starting pitcher. In terms of fantasy baseball, the transaction pretty much cooled all interest in Minor given the severe offensive-leanings of the Texas ballpark and for the fact, the righty could never before stay healthy while undertaking the high workloads of being in a rotation. Early on it looked like the concern was warranted as Minor was hit hard throughout the course of the first half of the season to the tune of a terrible 4.89 ERA and this despite receiving a slightly lucky BABIP of .289. Those who did the crazy in sticking with Minor though got rewarded as he went on a tear in the second half which helped him to 12 total wins, a decent 4.18 ERA, and a very good 1.12 WHIP. Showing flashes of the young gun that looked like a future pitching star during his early days with the Atlanta Braves, Minor has retained the top-notch control (2.18 BB/9) which is an absolute necessity to pitch in the American League. Now let's get to the not so glowing stuff of which there are a few red flags items worth mentioning. The first is that Minor's .259 BABIP was well into lucky territory and so he didn't really pitch as well as the surface ERA shows as evidenced by much higher FIP (4.42) and XFIP (4.52) rates. Then there is the fact Minor as a fly ball pitcher is a very bad match for pitching in

Texas and so the ugly 1.43 HR/9 rate was predictable. Add in just an average K/9 of 7.57 and Minor all of a sudden looks so much less appealing in terms of prospective 2019 fantasy baseball ownership. Considering Minor is already one of the more injury-prone pitchers in the game, the negatives that reveal themselves in his advanced rates and the brutal home ballpark make it an easy call to avoid him as anything but an SP 5 this season.

2019 PROJECTION: 14-10 4.33 ERA 1.15 WHIP 137 K

Jhoulys Chacin: Feel free to label journeyman starter Jhoulys Chacin as the new Kyle Lohse in terms of the guy having a knack for posting useful ratios while at the same time winning a decent amount of games. In 2018 the Milwaukee Brewers were the beneficiaries of this habit by Chacin as the righty won 15 games while also logging a 3.50 ERA and 1.16 WHIP in 192.2 innings pitched. While Chacin was a sizable positive for anyone who owned him during the course of the 2018 fantasy baseball season, he got by with a bit of positive luck as shown by a fortunate .250 BABIP. Given all the good batted ball luck Chacin received, it was no shock that his adjusted FIP (4.03) and XFIP (4.47) moved towards the shaky range. Making Chacin's surface numbers flukier was the fact career-long tendencies of giving up a high number of walks continued (his 3.32 BB/9 became the fifth straight season with a mark in that category over 3.00) and the strikeouts were nothing to write home about either (7.29 K/9). Given that Chacin has one more year left on his deal with the Brewers, he should be in line for a high number of wins again on a team expected to be in contention but there is no guarantee the ratios will be helpful if the BABIP luck moves toward the mean.

2019 PROJECTION: 14-9 3.84 ERA 1.23 WHIP 155 K

Trevor Williams: Every season in fantasy baseball we get cases where the BABIP gods worked overtime to help a seemingly average starting pitcher go on to post excellent surface numbers which then set the stage for disappointment going into the following campaign. One of the more pronounced members of at least the former grouping in 2017 was Pittsburgh Pirates righty Trevor Williams who broke out of the gates with a big March/April (2.29 ERA) and then never really let up on his way to a composite 3.11 ERA, 1.18 WHIP, and a total of 14 wins. When you also look at the fact Williams' monster last month of the season (when he put forth a 2.20 ERA) allowed him to finish on a high note, you can see there certainly are a bunch of good vibes surrounding his name going into spring drafts. Well, allow us to throw some extremely cold water on what Williams accomplished last season as there were some major red flags that likely will cause chaos in the upcoming 2019 season for his fantasy baseball owners.

For one thing, Williams' .261 BABIP was extremely lucky and so both his FIP (3.86) and XFIP (4.54) ERA's were much less appealing. Even more troubling was Williams' awful 6.64 K/9 which is a huge fantasy baseball negative and is especially bad for anyone in innings-capped leagues. With Williams unable to consistently extricate himself from trouble with the strikeout, the expected move back to the mean with his BABIP in 2019 will lead to a sharp rise in ERA/WHIP. Add in a 2.90 BB/9 that was not overly great and Williams has more issues than Reader's Digest which makes him one to avoid for the upcoming fantasy baseball season.

2019 PROJECTION: 12-11 3.84 ERA 1.20 WHIP 135 K

Joe Musgrove: After coming over as a key piece in the Gerrit Cole trade last winter, the Pittsburgh Pirates had high expectations for starting pitcher Joe Musgrove to fill an innings void as a youthful addition to the team's rotation for 2018. While Musgrove did show flashes of being an effective starter when on the mound (4.06 ERA, 1.18 WHIP, .240 BAA), constant health trouble capped any potential impact as the righty was only able to throw 115.1 innings. Musgrove didn't make the greatest first impression as an early bout of shoulder soreness in spring training kept him on the DL to open the season all the way through the end of May. Add in a second DL stint at the beginning of July for a finger infection and a late September shutdown after suffering from a pelvic stress reaction and Musgrove seemed to touch all of the health-related bases during the course of the 2018 season. Now in getting back to the actual numbers, Musgrove was decent but only in an SP 4/5 sense given the fact he doesn't miss as many bats as you would like from a prospective fantasy baseball hurler (7.80 K/9) and there are some home run concerns as well (0.94 HR/9). On the positive side, Musgrove possesses top-notch control (1.79 BB/9) and some slight bad BABIP luck revealed he actually pitched better than his surface 4.06 ERA. Having much more value for those in NL-only formats, Musgrove is on the SP 4/5 bubble when it comes to 2019 fantasy baseball investment.

2019 PROJECTION: 12-8 3.86 ERA 1.17 WHIP 149 K

Nick Pivetta: It looked like early on in the 2018 fantasy baseball season that the Philadelphia Phillies had a burgeoning power pitching star on their hands in the form of righty Nick Pivetta as the former 2013 fourth-round pick roared out of the gates with ERA's of 3.27 and 3.24 during the first two months as the strikeouts piled up. Alas, Pivetta couldn't keep up the good work as he was absolutely hammered the last four months of the year with ERA's over 4.50 in three of them and that would shake any type of confidence the fantasy baseball community had developed in him. In addition, a composite 4.77 ERA and 1.30 WHIP were pretty ghastly and they helped overshadow Pivetta's very impressive 10.32 K/9 rate. Let it be known though that as ugly as Pivetta's surface ratios were, his .326 BABIP was quite unlucky and bears itself out in much lower ERA's in FIP (3.79) and XFIP (3.43). The latter serves as at least a bright spot for Pivetta in looking ahead to 2019 when you also combine those adjusted ERA's with the excellent K/9 and an average fastball velocity of 95.0. Clearly, Pivetta has some power pitching chops and a decent enough 2.80 BB/9 at least offsets somewhat the ugly 1.32 HR/9. If Pivetta can make inroads with the homers, his ability to approach 200 K's could make him an interesting SP 5 late-round grab if you can look past last season's surface ratios.

2019 PROJECTION: 11-8 4.15 ERA 1.28 WHIP 194 K

Shane Bieber: While he may not be able to sing as good as Justin, Cleveland Indians pitching prospect Shane Bieber looks like he has a bright future as a fantasy baseball power arm. Promoted by the team last summer, Bieber's surface 4.55 ERA and 1.33 WHIP were nothing to write home about but the righty also opened eyes by punching out 118 batters in 114.2 innings. With an average fastball velocity of 93.3 and knee-bending off-speed stuff, Bieber has a vast ceiling that could yield some intriguing sleeper numbers in 2019. Also possessing excellent control (1.81) and adjusted FIP (3.23) and XFIP (3.30) ERA's that were better than his surface 4.55 mark last season, Bieber is one to put down on your late-round sleeper list.

2019 PROJECTION: 12-8 3.63 ERA 1.28 WHIP 159 K

Marcus Stroman: If any pitcher was given a chance to completely erase the 2018 MLB season, Toronto Blue Jays righty Marcus Stroman would surely have jumped at the opportunity. No stranger to injury with a Tommy John surgery already under his belt, Stroman opened up the season as arguably the single worst pitcher in the game as a truly hideous April (8.88 ERA) was followed by an equally ghastly May (5.25). A shoulder injury during the latter month that landed him on the DL served as almost a reprieve from the torture for Stroman and his fantasy baseball owners and he came back in June looking much more like his one-time intriguing self from years prior. Unfortunately, the on-the-mound beatings returned in August and also yet another injury as Stroman began battling a stubborn blister that wouldn't let up until he was shut down for good in mid-September. In the end, Stroman's 5.54 ERA and 1.48 WHIP were as bad as it gets and he has earned radioactive status among the fantasy baseball community heading into 2019. Things were so bad last season that you almost feel the need to give Stroman a complete mulligan but it also needs to be said he simply did not pitch well one bit in between all the injuries. What really is worrisome here is that Stroman's very checkered injury history has taken a bite out of his once-potent stuff and we can perhaps see proof of this in a sinking K/9 rate that has gone from 7.65 in 2014 all the way down to a horrid 6.77 a year ago. Now on the positive side, Stroman did have some tough BABIP luck (.326) last season and when adjusted, his FIP (3.91) and XFIP (3.84) ERA's were actually pretty decent. With Stroman also keeping the baseball in the park despite the shoulder and blister trouble (0.79 HR/9) adding a bit more optimism, a case can possibly be made to buy very low here at an SP 5 sticker price in the hopes the still young (turning only 28 in May) hurler can be salvaged. Count us as among the fraternity that will take a pass as Stroman still operates in a launching pad park in Toronto and he simply can't be depended on given the never-ending health issues.

2019 PROJECTION: 8-9 4.10 ERA 1.27 WHIP 153 K

Sean Manaea: It was a tale of two halves for Oakland A's starter Sean Manaea in 2018 as he opened up the first month of the season with arguably one of the most impressive outings of the year when he no-hit the Boston Red Sox with 10 strikeouts and that splendid performance helped fuel him to a composite 3.42 ERA and .212 BAA prior to the All-Star Break. The second half would be nothing but frustration for Manaea however as his ERA during that span shot up to 4.14 and the BAA was not so hot either at an ugly .284. The bottom then completely fell out in August when Manaea hit the DL with a left shoulder impingement and that ailment ultimately led to season-ending surgery in early September where a much more serious torn labrum was discovered. A labrum surgery is right up there with Tommy John in terms of being a complete disaster for a pitcher and the early reports are that Manaea will miss at the very least the first half of 2019 and possibly even the entire season which pretty much destroys any possible fantasy baseball value. With that said, as far as the overall numbers were concerned, Manaea actually had a really nice season in 2018 as he logged an ERA of 3.59 and a WHIP of 1.08 which played well for his fantasy baseball owners. However, if you were to dig deeper on the numbers, you would see that Manaea really didn't pitch as well as his surface ratios suggested. For one thing, Manaea's .247 BABIP was well into the "lucky" range and when adjusted, his FIP (4.26) and XFIP (4.33) ERA's were quite shaky. In addition, Manaea didn't miss a lot of bats (his no-hitter notwithstanding) as shown by a very poor 6.05 K/9. With Manaea not having the ability to extricate himself from trouble via the strikeout, he could see a lot more trouble in 2019 if his BABIP luck goes back toward the mean as expected. Add in an elevated 1.18 HR/9 and Manaea was looking like a sizable regression candidate prior to going under the knife. Unfortunately, the labrum procedure will make Manaea almost a complete non-factor for 2019 fantasy baseball.

2019 PROJECTION: 14-10 3.85 ERA 1.17 WHIP 155 K

Nathan Eovaldi: The return from Tommy John surgery for hard-throwing pitcher Nathan Eovaldi was a good one as he logged a 3.81 ERA, 1.13 WHIP, and 8.19 K/9 in a year split between the Tampa Bay Rays and Boston Red Sox. Despite the challenges of the AL East and a past that was filled to the brim with some truly horrendous pitching even though he possessed an average fastball velocity that was as good as any starter in baseball, Eovaldi at least changed the narrative a bit last season on his so-far disappointing career. By now it is old news how Eovaldi's massive velocity never translated into strikeouts due to the fastball habitually coming in straight but he got more bend on the pitch than ever before in 2018 which accounted for the uptick in K rate. Add in some career-best control (1.62 BB/9) and Eovaldi at least is back on the fantasy baseball radar for 2019. Even though there were clear positives in his return last season, we have been fooled too many times in the past to totally trust Eovaldi as more than an SP 5. If he does take another step forward this season, we are not paying much to find out if this does take place

2019 PROJECTION: 9-10 3.67 ERA 1.28 WHIP 145 K

Michael Fulmer: Now three years into his MLB career, it is pretty safe to say that Detroit Tigers starter Michael Fulmer will forever be coming up short in terms of matching the eye-opening performance he put forth as a rookie in 2016. After logging a very impressive 3.06 ERA in 159 innings that season, it appeared Fulmer was set to be among the next generation of big-time pitching talents who was already knocking on the door of upper-tier status. Well, we were not among the optimists as that very next spring this publication included Fulmer on our "BUST" list in these pages given the red flags that were underneath the hood of the righthander's debut performance. With Fulmer having benefitted from very good BABIP luck (.268) that season and also showing just average strikeout ability (7.47 K/9), we sounded the alarms here and noted that he was simply not as good a pitcher as the surface numbers would indicate. Fast forward to present day and our outlook on Fulmer was nothing if not almost completely accurate as the guy has become nothing but an injury and performance-marred mess. 2018, in particular, was beyond rough as Fulmer's 4.69 ERA, 1.31 WHIP, and .252 BAA revealed and that doesn't even include the injuries that once again cropped up. In terms of the injuries last season, Fulmer missed a month with a strained oblique during the summer and then went out for good in mid-September due to a torn right meniscus that needed to be surgically fixed. Through all of these ailments, Fulmer pitched horribly as the walks crept up to career-worst levels (3.13 BB/9) and home runs were a tremendous problem (1.29 HR/9) which threatened to ruin any one of his starts. Add in the continued mediocrity of Fulmer's K/9 rate (7.48) and the guy had more warts last season than frogs in a swamp. With regards to the totality of his

season, there is really nothing positive at all to say about Fulmer which is all the more reason you should not even give a glance here during spring drafts.
2019 PROJECTION: 8-11 4.35 ERA 1.28 WHIP 123 K

C.C. Sabathia: The back-end renaissance of ageless New York Yankees lefty starter C.C. Sabathia's career added another impressive chapter in 2018 as the 38-year-old made it three seasons in a row with an ERA under 4.00 with a 3.65 mark; not to mention a full strikeout uptick in K/9 rate (8.24) and a record of 9-7 in 153 innings. By now it is old news regarding how Sabathia successfully reinvented himself on the fly after he seemed completely washed up with ERA's of 5.28 and 4.73 from 2014-15. Knowing he could no longer rely on a fastball whose average velocity had sunk to around 90 mph, Sabathia perfected his off-speed stuff with very impressive results. With that said, Sabathia continues to deal with a chronic bone-on-bone issue in his knee which required another DL stint in 2018 and that ailment could flare up at any moment to derail any given season. The fantasy baseball community is pretty aware of the Sabathia health volatility, however, and so while he will be a free agent this winter, count on the Yankees bringing him back for another year which will keep the possibility of a decent number of wins in play. Despite now being a firm SP 5 in mixed fantasy baseball leagues, Sabathia can still be a help to those who take him out another spin.
2019 PROJECTION: 10-7 3.88 ERA 1.28 WHIP 143 K

Ivan Nova: Talk about being Mr. Consistency. Pittsburgh Pirates veteran starter Ivan Nova has now registered ERA's of 4.17, 4.14, and 4.16 the last three seasons; while also striking out between 114 and 131 batters. Turning 32 in January and with one more year left on his deal with the Pirates, it seems pretty easy to project where Nova's numbers will be headed in 2019. A solid innings eater who makes the most of his limited arsenal, Nova is much more valuable in NL-only formats due to the fact his K/9 rate is quite a bit below average in hovering in the low-6.00 range.
2019 PROJECTION: 12-14 4.16 ERA 1.29 WHIP 137 K

Mike Soroka: After the Atlanta Braves went through years of miserable play at the major league level while stockpiling early round draft picks prior to opening Sun Trust Park in 2017, the team began introducing some of that top-shelf minor league talent during the course of the 2018 season. Included in this grouping was 2017 first-round pick Mike Soroka as the righty starter turned a 2.00 ERA/10.33 K/9 in 27.0 Triple-A innings to begin the season into a May promotion to the Braves at the very young age of 21. Despite only being a small sample size of 25.2 innings, Soroka was not overwhelmed in the least as he showed off a nice four-pitch arsenal (fastball, change, slider, curve) that kept MLB hitters off balance enough to record a tidy 3.51 ERA. Of course, the reason Soroka was only able to throw those 25.2 innings with the Braves was due to the fact a June bout of right shoulder inflammation spiraled into him being shut down completely in August as caution ruled the day here. That extra caution could turn out to be a very good thing for Soroka who will presumably head to 2019 spring training with the inside track to a Braves rotation spot and full health. With all that said, Soroka still should be treated as nothing more than an SP 5 with upside in terms of fantasy baseball given his youth and some remaining questions about how high the ceiling will go. While we already touched on the vast arsenal of pitches Soroka has, he is not a major strikeout guy given the fact his fastball mostly sits in the 93-94 range. That lessens the margin of error for Soroka as an MLB hurler and makes him a bit more risky in terms of possible fantasy baseball investment. Add in the rough home park and Soroka should stay in the late round draft picture this spring.

2019 PROJECTION: 9-5 3.94 ERA 1.34 WHIP 144 K

Freddy Peralta: If you owned any shares in Milwaukee Brewers pitching prospect Freddy Peralta during his MLB debut last season, it was certainly a roller coaster experience given the extreme positives and negatives that went into the kid's 78.1 innings with the club. Advertised as a massive strikeout prospect, Peralta didn't disappoint on that front as he punched out 96 batters in those 78.1 innings (good for a tremendous 11.03 K/9) and the composite 4.25 ERA was not awful either. Now in terms of the bad news, Peralta was your classic young power pitcher who collected all of those K's but who also walked the ballpark with a 4.60 BB/9. What does need to be mentioned here is that despite all the free passes, Peralta had a very good 1.14 WHIP which speaks to how tough it was to get a hit off the guy. So if Peralta can just curb the walks just a bit as he continues to develop, he could really take off in a major way given all of the anticipated strikeouts. With Peralta not turning 23 until June, the upside is crazy here and so a late-round pick absolutely needs to be saved for this burgeoning talent.

2019 PROJECTION: 9-5 3.56 ERA 1.34 WHIP 154 K

Kenta Maeda: While he still has 5 more years left on his contract, the Los Angeles Dodgers seem unsure of what role pitcher Kenta Maeda will have for the team going forward after he worked both in the rotation and the bullpen in 2018. In terms of his performance as a starter last season, Maeda got off to a very good start by pitching to a 3.12 ERA and a phenomenal 11.22 K/9 prior to the All-Star Break but things began to spiral in an ugly July and a truly hideous August that saw him moved to the bullpen. In the end, Maeda's 3.81 ERA was an improvement from the disappointing 4.22 the year prior and the biggest surprise was that he has developed into a tremendous strikeout guy since coming over to the States (career-high 10.99 K/9 last season). On the flip side, Maeda's control has gotten progressively worse in his three MLB seasons (up to a 3.09 BB/9 in 2018) and his overall poor pitch efficiency in 2018 resulted in exiting a high number of starts prematurely. Considering how much money the Dodgers still owe Maeda, it is likely they will give him another shot to be a member of the rotation in spring training and clearly the overall talent remains very intriguing. So what we would suggest here is to monitor the spring performances and then get ready to strike if Maeda does, in fact, earn another starting nod.

2019 PROJECTION: 14-10 3.78 ERA 1.17 WHIP 175 K

Aaron Sanchez: Never before have we seen a once-promising career become almost completely derailed due to finger injuries but that is exactly what has been taking place the last two seasons for Toronto Blue Jays righty starter Aaron Sanchez. In 2017 it was three separate stints on the DL due to ongoing blister problems and last season it was Sanchez suffering a bizarre right index finger contusion caused by a suitcase of all things that kept him out for two months during the summer. The finger injury resulted in Sanchez undergoing surgery at the end of September but he is expected to be ready to go for spring training. Then when Sanchez was actually on the mound, he pitched poorly in recording ugly ERA's of 4.25 and 4.89 the last two seasons. While he is still young at just 26-years-old, Sanchez is a bad fit in the AL East given the fact he has terrible control (4.97 BB/9) and also is just an average strikeout pitcher (7.37 K.9). A pitcher may be able to skirt by having only one of those above red flags but when you possess BOTH and also can't stay healthy, there is nothing else that needs to be said in terms of you needing to avoid such a player in fantasy baseball drafts.

2019 PROJECTION: 7-9 4.28 ERA 1.38 WHIP 127 K

Tyler Skaggs: Having put a 2015 Tommy John surgery in the rearview mirror, Los Angeles Angels lefty Tyler Skaggs got back toward trying to get his career back on track in 2018. While he did miss extensive time with injuries once again, Skaggs was decent when on the mound as he logged a 4.02 ERA and 9.26 K/9. While Skaggs allowed a high number of base runners (1.33 WHIP), he also dealt with a rough .328 BABIP that when adjusted, came out to FIP (3.63) and XFIP (3.79) ERA's that went lower than his actual surface mark. Still just 27, Skaggs has a bit of upside remaining but overall he looks like just a standard SP 5 from this viewpoint.

2019 PROJECTION: 9-12 3.95 ERA 1.29 WHIP 153 K

Luke Weaver: Boy that was tough to watch. Amid extremely high expectations going into the 2018 season, there is no other way to say that St. Louis Cardinals pitching prospect Luke Weaver did a complete face plant in every phase for his disgusted fantasy baseball owners. Looking nothing like the future star the year prior when he pitched to a 3.88 ERA and 10.74 K/9, Weaver was so bad that he was demoted back to the minors during the summer and then was sent to the bullpen after struggling again upon returning to the team a few weeks later. In the end, Weaver's burned fantasy baseball owners received a 4.95 ERA, 1.50 WHIP, and a mediocre 7.99 K/9 for their troubles and the reset button surely needs to be applied here. Now in taking apart the carnage, it is obvious opposing hitters came up with an approach to dealing with Weaver between the end of 2017 and the start of 2018. With Weaver showing no ability to adjust back, the hits and runs began to pile up in a very ugly way. Struggling badly both with his control (3.56 BB/9) and the home run ball (1.25 HR/9); Weaver was nothing but a liability for the duration he was on the mound last season. The question now is whether or not Weaver can be salvaged for 2019 fantasy baseball and on that front; you have to think the Cardinals will come up with some sort of plan to re-discover the 2017 form. Remember that Weaver was a 2014 first-round pick for a reason and his average fastball velocity of 94.3 last season was quite impressive. So the tools are in place for Weaver to make a mini-comeback in 2019 but we are only willing to invest an SP 5 price to find out due to how ugly last season was.

2019 PROJECTION: 9-7 3.95 ERA 1.28 WHIP 145 K

Dereck Rodriguez: Despite being an older prospect at the age of 26, the San Francisco Giants had to be ecstatic over the debut performance of righthander Dereck Rodriguez in 2018. Already having good MLB bloodlines as the son of Hall of Fame catcher Ivan Rodriguez, Dereck showed his pitching chops by logging a 2.81 ERA, 1.13 WHIP, and picking up 6 wins in 118.1 frames. While those numbers were very impressive for a rookie pitcher, they are not as exciting when looked at through the prism of fantasy baseball for a number of reasons. The first is that Rodriguez is in no way a strikeout pitcher as shown by his below-average 6.77 K/9 last season. The second issue is that Rodriguez' .257 BABIP was very lucky and when adjusted, came out to much higher FIP (3.74) and XFIP (4.56) marks that perhaps are a better indication of what type a pitcher he really is. Having already locked up a rotation spot to begin 2019, it will be interesting to see how much major league hitters adjust to Rodriguez' soft-tossing approach (average fastball velocity of 92.1). Count us as leaning on the side of those who think there will be trouble ahead.

2019 PROJECTION: 10-9 3.95 ERA 1.29 WHIP 128 K

Trevor Cahill: While clearly a journeyman pitcher, veteran righty Trevor Cahill successfully transitioned back to being in a major league rotation beginning in 2017 after years of serving as a bullpen arm due to failing previously as a starter. What is interesting is Cahill picked up some additional velocity as a starter the second time around due to an adjusted release point and this, in turn, elicited a spike in strikeouts. The result of this total transformation led to a very good 3.76 ERA and 1.19 WHIP in 110 innings a year ago for the Oakland A's. While Cahill did lose some strikeouts last season compared to 2017 (his K/9 going from 9.32 to 8.18 during that span), his puny 0.65 HR/9 rate went a long way toward the decent ERA. Despite some rough control (3.35 BB/9), Cahill seems like a good SP 5 bet who won't cost anything but a very late pick.

2019 PROJECTION: 8-9 3.84 ERA 1.20 WHIP 137 K

Gio Gonzalez: With the Washington Nationals having decided to throw in the towel on their very disappointing 2018 season, they didn't waste much time finding a new home for aging veteran starter Gio Gonzalez in agreeing to send him to the Milwaukee Brewers. Past his prime now at the age of 33, Gonzalez showed predictable statistical declines that included a 4.21 ERA and a 7.42 K/9 rate that went under 8.00 for the first time since 2010. Having never been able to conquer career-long control problems (and actually seeing his BB/9 come in at a horrid 4.21 last season), Gonzalez is your classic case of a guy who is on a clear path downward in terms of the numbers.

2019 PROJECTION: 11-11 4.16 ERA 1.30 WHIP 155 K

Jon Gray: Yeah this guy again. There may not be a bigger yearly tease in all of fantasy baseball than hard-throwing Colorado Rockies pitcher Jon Gray whose combination of extreme strikeout ability but massive inconsistency robs the hair of many of his fantasy baseball owners. Last season went right along with this trend as a simply horrendous first half (5.44 ERA) necessitated a demotion back to the minor leagues in the hope Gray could re-focus. As often happens in such a situation, Gray came back to the Rockies a different pitcher in July when he rocked a 1.66 ERA in 21.1 innings but then the wheels came off again the rest of way in posting marks of 4.01 in August and 7.20 in September/October. Having finished with a composite 5.12 ERA, 1.35 WHIP, and .263 BAA; Gray was simply brutal in almost all of phases. The one area he did succeed in was strikeouts as shown by an impressive 9.56 K/9 but that is not nearly enough of a reason to go back to the well here for 2019 fantasy baseball. As we always say, you can't keep chasing dormant potential forever and that is especially true for a pitcher who calls Coors Field home.

2019 PROJECTION: 7-12 4.46 ERA 1.32 WHIP 173 K

Chase Anderson: Virtually anyone with a clue about fantasy baseball was not buying into the fluky 2.74 ERA put forth by Milwaukee Brewers starter

Chase Anderson in 2017 given the sizable BABIP luck (.265) that helped him post such a swell mark in the first place and that was shown by another drop to the last few rounds in average spring drafts last spring. Thus, it was no surprise when Anderson went out last season and saw that ERA shoot way up to 3.93 which was customarily where the veteran belonged in terms of his true ability. While Anderson is certainly a guy that can help in a spot start or especially in deeper leagues, he is overall a boring pitcher whose 7.29 K/9 rate adds to the unappealing nature of his stuff. Again, Anderson is not without value in some deeper fantasy baseball leagues but you should try to look for some more upside when rounding out your rotation.

2019 PROJECTION: 10-7 4.23 ERA 1.23 WHIP 137 K

Reynaldo Lopez: While Lucas Giolito got the majority of attention coming over to the White Sox in the Adam Eaton trade a few winters ago, it is looking like secondary pitching piece Reynaldo Lopez will turn out to be the better return for Chicago in the deal. As Giolito struggled mightily once again in 2018, Lopez served as a rare bright spot for the White Sox in their rebuilding season as he put forth a 3.91 ERA, 1.27 WHIP, and 151 strikeouts in 188.2 IP. Even though the numbers were barely of the SP 5 variety in terms of fantasy baseball, Lopez at least made himself part of the discussion throughout the season on that end which is nothing to scoff at since he was just 24. Of course a very lucky .260 BABIP helped more than a little in terms of Lopez securing his fluky 3.91 ERA (FIP of 4.64 and XIP of 5.22) and a 3.58 BB/9 was also pretty terrible. With Lopez additionally unable to generate much in the way of K's (7.20) to offset the expected BABIP regression in 2019, it is probably a good idea to avoid the righty in all but AL-only leagues.

2019 PROJECTION: 8-13 4.27 ERA 1.29 WHIP 157 K

Clay Buchholz: Count longtime veteran starter Clay Buchholz as another member of the pitching "reinvention" club as the 2014-17 punching bag turned in what can only be described as a surprisingly very good 98.1 innings with the Arizona Diamondbacks last season. Things didn't start off so hot in 2018 for Buchholz however as he was forced to accept a minor league deal with Kansas City as a last resort effort to hang around in the majors and even that failed as he got his release on May 1st after the rebuilding Royals decided they had no use for him. It was when Buchholz signed a minor league pact with the Arizona Diamondbacks soon after his Royals release that the statistical planets aligned for the righty as he shockingly pitched to a splendid 2.01 ERA, 1.04 WHIP, and a .217 BAA. Buchholz pitched so well and so in control (2.01 BB/9) that is hard to even believe this was the same pitcher who almost nobody wanted to even look at prior to the start of the 2018 season. Having previously lost his strikeout ability (pathetic K/9 rates under 7.00 in three of his previous four MLB campaigns), Buchholz made it a point to rely more on his off-speed stuff and pitch to contact at a higher rate than ever before with Arizona. Things obviously worked out for the better as Buchholz actually became a big mid-season add in fantasy baseball leagues given his string of dominant outings during the summer before the fun ended in mid-September due to a strained elbow. Now it does need to be noted that Buchholz' .255 BABIP was well into the lucky range but even his FIP (3.40) and XIP (4.00) ERA's were very good to decent enough respectively. We worry more about Buchholz' very small margin for error going forward due to the fact his average fastball velocity sank to a career-worst 90.7 last season despite all his positive results. Thus, it is imperative Buchholz continue down his pitching-to-contact path and that old home run troubles don't resurface. Finally, considering his age (35 this August) and increased propensity for getting injured, Buchholz should only be graded as an SP 5 for fantasy baseball purposes in 2019. While it was a fun story last season, we suggest you not go out of your way hoping for an encore.

2019 PROJECTION: 9-7 3.97 ERA 1.22 WHIP 143 K

Marco Gonzales: It is not the best look when the pitching powerful St. Louis Cardinals organization gives up on you but lefty Margo Gonzales found new life with the Seattle Mariners in 2018 when he registered a 4.00 ERA, 1.22 WHIP, and won 13 games for a team that was in contention throughout the season. While none of Gonzales' numbers jump off the page, there were some impressive things at work here such as a terrific 1.73 BB/9 which is a crucial skill to have for any pitcher operating in the American League. Gonzales also should have had an ERA under his actual 4.00 as he dealt with an unlucky .319 BABIP. Despite all these positives, Gonzales' raw stuff is that of just an SP 4/5 as his average fastball velocity was just 90.8 and he has also dealt with some injury woes since turning pro. In line for another batch of wins with solid enough ratios, Gonzales is not a bad way to round out your mixed league rotation.

2019 PROJECTION: 14-11 3.95 ERA 1.23 WHIP 135 K

Lance Lynn: After missing all of the 2016 season due to undergoing Tommy John surgery, righthanded starter Lance Lynn returned with decent results for the St. Louis Cardinals a year later as he registered a 3.43 ERA and won 11 games. Despite the tidy surface ERA, we spoke last spring about how Lynn's 2017 was full of red flags that made his outlook for that coming season's fantasy baseball campaign quite shaky. Specifically speaking, Lynn's post-Tommy John K rate and velocity both declined and his insanely lucky .244 BABIP showed FIP (4.82) and XFIP (4.75) ERA's that were more indicative of how he really was pitching. Fast forward a season later and our concerns about Lynn came completely true as he was hit hard almost throughout in a year split between the Cardinals and New York Yankees. No matter which team he pitched for, Lynn was terrible as his 4.77 ERA went right in line with the advanced marks from 2017. Making matters worse was Lynn's always shaky control got worse as his BB/9 rate soared to 4.37 which did more than overshadow the one positive he had in an increased K/9 of 9.25. Even though Lynn will be just 32 in May, he looks like the case of a guy who came back as a worse pitcher after Tommy John than before and so he is locked into SP 5 status for 2019 fantasy baseball.

2019 PROJECTION: 10-11 4.39 ERA 1.38 WHIP 157 K

Danny Duffy: At one time a prized power pitching prospect while ascending the minor league ladder of the Kansas City Royals, the current version of starter Danny Duffy looks to be that of just an SP4/5 both in real life and in fantasy baseball. Having been somewhat rushed to the major leagues in 2011 at the age of 22, Duffy fought through some ups and downs along the way with the Royals until seemingly realizing his vast potential by logging a 3.51 ERA and striking out 188 batters (9.42 K/9) in 2016. That performance looks to be nothing but an outlier now as constant injury trouble the last two seasons caused Duffy's average fastball velocity to drop from 95.5 in that 2016 campaign down to just 93.8 a year ago. With Duffy possessing less swing-and-miss ability, his ratios predictably went in the wrong direction and things became downright scary for large portions of 2017 as he finished with a composite 4.88 ERA, 1.49 WHIP, and 8.19 K/9. Putting the icing on the cake of what was a brutal year, Duffy missed almost all of September after suffering a left shoulder impingement as the injury trend continued unabated. While Duffy will still be only 30 for the 2019 season, he clearly is a shell of his former power pitching self. Also, after showing terrible control last season (4.06 BB/9) and a home run rate that went above 1.30 for the second year in a row (1.34), there is simply way too many negatives to ignore here for us to even recommend using the guy as an SP 5.

2019 PROJECTION: 10-10 4.28 ERA 1.33 WHIP 145 K

Ervin Santana: Proof positive that a pitcher needs five fully healthy fingers to take the mound, it was a beyond frustrating season filled with injuries to the middle digit of veteran aging starter Ervin Santana in 2018. The trouble began last February when Santana underwent a capsular release procedure on his middle finger that kept him out until July 25. Then 5 starts and 24.2 horrendous innings pitched (8.03 ERA) later, Santana went right back to the DL with an irritated nerve in the same finger that ultimately kept him out the remainder of the season. Obviously, it was a completely lost season for

Santana but keep in mind he engineered ERA's of 3.38 and 3.28 the two seasons prior which speak to him still being effective when healthy. At the same time, Santana turned 36 this past December which means the 2018 negatives could just be a sign of more trouble to come. Perhaps sensing this, the Twins declined their 2019 option which adds some uncertainty to Santana's current status.

2019 PROJECTION: 9-8 4.15 ERA 1.24 WHIP 138 K

Tyler Glasnow: Seemingly having run out of patience with the never-ending control problems of pitching prospect Tyler Glasnow, the Pittsburgh Pirates finally threw in the towel on the righty by trading him to the Tampa Bay Rays in late July. While he is still just 25, Glasnow serves an annual source of frustration to the fantasy baseball community due to the fact his very potent strikeout ability is offset by some of the worst control in all of baseball. 2018 was no different as Glasnow's 10.96 K/9 was phenomenal but the brutal 4.27 BB/9 and 4.27 ERA were clear negatives. What is interesting here though is the fact the Rays have never met a reclamation project they didn't feel they could save and given their high success rate in such transactions, Glasnow has to remain at least on the monitoring radar early on in 2019. Now we are certainly not saying he will go down this route or anywhere near it but last year at this time we were talking about how terrible Rays All-Star Blake Snell's control was and look how that turned out. Given the intriguing strikeout ability and remaining young age, Glasnow should not be given up on just yet.

2019 PROJECTION: 9-10 4.17 ERA 1.28 WHIP 156 K

Jaime Barria: With injuries ravaging the Los Angeles Angels rotation for large stretches of the 2018 season, the team was forced to promote 22-year-old pitching prospect Jaime Barria perhaps a tad earlier then they would have liked to help fill the void. All in all, Barria held his own however as he logged a 3.41 ERA, 1.27 WHIP, and .242 BAA in 129.1 debut innings. Despite the useful surface numbers, Barria's advanced metrics were not pretty as his reputation for being a pitch-to-contact guy in the minors followed him up to the Angels as he posted an ugly 6.82 K/9. We don't need to remind you that a lack of strikeout ability in the DH league is a potential problem and Barria's 3.41 ERA was fluky as well given the lucky .271 BABIP that helped him get there. We weren't fans of Barria when he was called up given the lack of strikeout punch and that won't change as he looks to cement a firm rotation spot for 2019 given the advanced statistical red flags.

2019 PROJECTION: 10-6 4.32 ERA 1.29 WHIP 134 K

Carlos Rodon: Well off the fantasy baseball radar during drafts last spring as he was expected to miss the first 2-3 months while recovering from shoulder surgery the previous September, Chicago White Sox hard-throwing lefty Carlos Rodon's eventual June return did nothing to change the inconsistency tag that always dogged him previously. Historically lauded for a big-time fastball that elicited a high number of strikeouts, it was quite disturbing to see Rodon record just a paltry 6.71 K/9 as his average fastball velocity dipped down to 93. While Rodon's 4.18 surface ERA was not terrible, his annually brutal control remained (4.10 BB/9) and a 1.12 HR/9 was nothing to write home about either. Given the never-ending negatives from Rodon's 2018 performance, one has to wonder if the shoulder surgery has sapped some bite out of his stuff and made him somehow even less trustworthy. Count us among the chorus that is tired of waiting for the potential that may never come to fruition for Rodon and so we suggest looking for a fresher SP 5 upside pitcher in his place.
2019 PROJECTION: 6-12 4.22 ERA 1.33 WHIP 153 K

Tanner Roark: Pretty much nothing went right for the Washington Nationals in a lost 2018 season that ended up with the team unloading a slew of players and perhaps ushering in a new era depending on what happens in free agency. Contributing to the malaise was starting pitcher Tanner Roark who posted a second straight shaky season in registering an ugly 4.34 ERA, 1.28 WHIP, and a record of 9-15. Already Roark's 2.83 ERA in 2016 looks like it belongs in the outlier bin as he has now gone above 4.00 in that category in three of the last four seasons. Making matters worse was Roark's mediocre 7.29 K/9 which was down from 8.24 the year prior. While we like Roark's durability, all of those starts are not helpful from a fantasy baseball perspective when they come with such shaky numbers. With even the potential for wins in question as the Nats' immediate outlook appears quite uncertain, Roark pretty much has nothing going for him in terms of current draft appeal.
2019 PROJECTION: 10-12 4.24 ERA 1.27 WHIP 155 K

Caleb Smith: Despite the fact the Miami Marlins look as pathetic as ever in terms of their current roster, they discovered they have something to work with when it comes to lefty starter Caleb Smith. Originally just a 14th round draft pick of the New York Yankees back in 2013, the team thought so little of Smith that they traded him and first baseman Garrett Cooper to the Marlins for only international bonus pool money last winter. Well, the Marlins certainly got one up on the Yankees as Smith quickly showed some very intriguing strikeout ability once he got his feet wet with the team early in 2018. While Smith did struggle with rough control during his first four outings last season, he soon found his groove to where the swing-and-miss rate began to jump off the page. It got to the point that through his initial 77.1 innings, Smith was rocking a potent 10.24 K/9 and he began to see his ownership grow by the day. Unfortunately, Smith's 2018 potential impact was stopped in its tracks when he suffered a Grade 3 lat strain that required season-ending surgery in late June. Expected to be 100 percent for 2019 spring training, Smith is worth pursuing as a speculative SP 5 given the strikeout ability but keep in mind he is still far from a finished product. Despite all the attention his strikeouts netted last season, Smith's control needs a ton of work (3.84 BB/9) and his 1.16 HR/9 was also a red flag number. Add in the fact that wins will be tough to come by on the Marlins and this cements Smith's SP 5 status in stone.

2019 PROJECTION: 8-10 4.23 ERA 1.30 WHIP 165 K

Matt Boyd: With previous season ERA's of 7.53, 4.53, and 5.27 his first three years in the majors, Detroit Tigers starter Matt Boyd had no business being drafted anywhere last spring. It was with this backdrop that made Boyd's early season performance so surprisingly good as he came out to register ERA's of 2.74 in March/April and then followed that up with another terrific 3.18 mark in May. Just when maybe some gullible souls in the fantasy baseball community began weighing to add Boyd to their rosters, the lefty remembered that he really does stink as he got bombed in each of the last four months of the season in compiling a composite 4.39 ERA and 1.16 WHIP. While the WHIP was actually pretty decent and the ERA not as bad as his earlier career numbers in that category, it does need to be said that Boyd went over 5.00 in the latter in two of the last four months of 2019. Adding to the trouble was Boyd's VERY lucky .258 BABIP which when adjusted, came out to FIP (4.44) and XFIP (4.73) ERA's which were more indicative of his career norms. With a truly putrid HR/9 rate of 1.43 adding to the nasty outlook here, Boyd should really not be on a fantasy baseball roster this season.

2019 PROJECTION: 7-12 4.48 ERA 1.32 WHIP 144 K

Kyle Gibson: Long a favorite punching bag of these pages, veteran righty Kirk Gibson actually figured out how to have a decent season in 2018 as he put forth a career-best 3.62 ERA for the Minnesota Twins; while also setting another personal best in K/9 at 8.19. After years of getting his head beaten in by opposing hitters, maybe the law of averages worked in Gibson's favor last season but either way, we still suggest avoiding the righty if possible this spring. Even though the ERA was helpful last season, Gibson had a bit of a lucky .285 BABIP and his control was brutal as shown by a nasty 3.62 BB/9. Thus, it is easy to keep in mind that Gibson posted 5.07 ERA's both in 2016 and 2017 before the uptick a year ago but the overall trends here are quite negative. In the end, Gibson qualifies as nothing but a 2018 tease who will likely come slamming back down to earth in a very ugly way this season and that makes it an easy call to avoid him almost entirely.

2019 PROJECTION: 8-11 4.39 ERA 1.32 WHIP 167 K

John Gant: While just originally a 2011 21st round draft pick, St. Louis Cardinals righty John Gant had a very good season both at Triple-A (1.65 ERA in 49 IP) and at the major league level (3.47 ERA in another 114 frames) a year ago. With that said, the Cardinals are already the third MLB organization for Gant who turned 26 last August and that speaks to a view of him as just a moderate prospect at best. Also while Gant's 3.47 surface ERA was impressive, the underlying numbers don't paint a pretty picture to say the least. First of all, Gant's .253 BABIP was very lucky and when his ERA was adjusted for that sizable bit of fortune, it came out to both shoddy numbers in FIP (4.07) and XFIP (4.66). Even beyond the luck factor, Gant's control was terrible as a 4.50 BB/9 showed and his mediocre 7.50 K/9 was just average. Even though Gant did enough good work last season to put himself in solid contention for a rotation spot to begin 2019, he ultimately profiles as barely an SP 5 option.

2019 PROJECTION: 7-4 4.19 ERA 1.32 WHIP 143 K

Andrew Suarez: After dominating his first four starts in the minor leagues to begin the 2018 season, the San Francisco Giants decided to take a look at their 2015 second round pick Andrew Suarez. The lefty starter never left once he put on a Giants uniform as he pitched to a 4.49 ERA, 1.30 WHIP, and punched out 130 batters in 160.1 innings. Despite the solid debut for a pitcher making his first go-round in the majors, Suarez' numbers were far from being fantasy baseball-friendly given his soft-tossing tendencies (7.30 K/9) and giving up 23 home runs while operating in a pitching-leaning ballpark was not so hot either.   Even though there is still some ceiling left for Suarez to tap into, there is no path for him to be a consistent fantasy baseball contributor.

2019 PROJECTION: 8-11 4.39 ERA 1.29 WHIP 138 K

Jake Odorizzi: At one time a semi-useful SP 5 who could eat innings and post around a mid-3.00 ERA, the last two seasons have not been overly impressive for veteran starter Jake Odorizzi. With his ERA going above the 4.00 mark in each of those campaigns (4.14 and 4.49 respectively), Odorizzi has also seen his average fastball velocity dip for the third straight year last season (down to just 91.4). That has made Odorizzi more hittable than ever and when you combine this with a walk rate that has gone above 3.80 the last two seasons, we are looking at a guy who doesn't even carry SP 5 value anymore.

2019 PROJECTION: 10-14 4.20 ERA 1.29 WHIP 146 K

THE REST

Sonny Gray: By the time you read this, veteran starter Sonny Gray could already be traded far away from the New York Yankees and the AL East after what could only be described as an abomination of a 2018 campaign. Gray's struggles were certainly no shock to this peanut stand as we had the righty featured in our BUSTS section of these pages last spring and that was due to his fly ball tendencies being a horrible match for both the division and Yankee Stadium. Predictably, Gray struggled so badly that the Yanks sent him to the bullpen during the summer and kept him there pretty much through the end of the season, save for a few spot starts. Already Gray's 3.55 ERA comeback in 2017 has been forgotten and the bigger picture here is that the guy has put up two of the worst pitching performances in the majors two of the last three seasons. If he were to end up with an NL club this winter perhaps we would have some renewed interest since he actually did pitch well on the road (3.17 ERA, 1.15 WHIP) but until a trade happens, feel free to ignore Gray outright.

Mike Fiers: Like Freddy Krueger and Jason Voorhees, veteran starter Mike Fiers seemingly comes back from the fantasy baseball dead during the second half once every three years or so. An ordinary pitcher on talent alone who struggles to stay even in the high-80's with his fastball, Fiers has engineered some truly sparkling second-half performances out of the clear blue sky during his time with the Milwaukee Brewers and Houston Astros and in 2018 he added the Oakland A's to this mix as well. Riding a 6-2 second half with a sparkling 3.34 ERA and 1.11 WHIP, Fiers was a smart add for those who were looking to clinch their league titles. Now 33 and going into free agency, Fiers will likely be looking at a one or two year deal at most but his fantasy baseball outlook is actually quite murky if you dug into last season's numbers. While he once again showed tip-top control (1.94 BB/9), Fiers' .269 BABIP was in the lucky range and when adjusted, came out to shaky FIP (4.75) and XFIP (4.51) marks. Add in a brutal 1.67 HR/9 rate and Fiers is more likely to do a total face-plant next season than even yielding SP 5 value.

Wade LeBlanc: Useful veteran journeyman starter Wade LeBlanc finally found some MLB stability in 2018 as a nice start to the year with the Seattle Mariners earned him a one-year contract extension for 2019. Helping to secure that commitment was LeBlanc's 3.72 and 1.18 WHIP for the Mariners in 162 frames but some perspective is needed here when discussing his immediate fantasy baseball outlook. The first issue is the fact LeBlanc is nothing but a career soft-tosser whose below-average 7.22 K/9 a year ago is as good as can be expected for his prospective owners. Secondly, a lucky .273 BABIP throws into serious doubt LeBlanc's 3.72 ERA and even more so when you gaze at the adjusted FIP (4.28) and XFIP (4.77) marks. Add in ongoing struggles on the road for the aging veteran and it is obvious this is barely even an AL-only story.

Mike Montgomery: Having served as a valuable swingman for the Chicago Cubs the last two-plus seasons, veteran arm Mike Montgomery is now on a streak of three straight years where he has posted an ERA under 4.00. Despite having some well below-average strikeout numbers (K/9 rates of 6.89 and 6.24 the last two seasons), Montgomery makes it work through an extreme groundball-heavy approach which limits home runs. Still only 29 once the 2019 fantasy baseball season gets underway, Montgomery could certainly catch SP 5 value once again but ideally, you want some more K potential/better upside from that spot.

Zach Eflin: As the Philadelphia Phillies hovered around playoff contention for most of the 2018 season, they received a nice boost from a rotation made up of some young arms. Among this group was righty prospect Zach Eflin who undertook a career-high 128 innings which resulted in a 4.36 ERA, 1.30 WHIP, and an 8.65 K/9 rate which was enough to get him into streaming status in terms of fantasy baseball last season. As far as the strengths of Eflin are concerned, he possesses solid control (2.60 BB/9) which is always a plus in a bandbox ballpark like in Philly and his average 95.2 fastball suggest some more K's could be arriving soon. What is not so good are the home runs (1.13 HR/9) which need to be remedied a bit so Eflin can get his ERA under 4.00. Given the present rate of numbers Eflin is mostly in the SP 5 range for 2019.

Junior Guerra: Any fantasy baseball veteran knew all too well that Milwaukee Brewers aging starter Junior Guerra was pitching way over his head during the first half of the 2018 season as a .284 BABIP helped push the ERA all the way down to 3.23 during that span. Alas, things turned exceptionally nasty in the second half as his BABIP swung the other way to .368 and so the 6.02 ERA was no shock at all. Now we are certainly not blaming the swings of Guerra's BABIP for his overall performance last season but instead will remind you the guy is simply not a good pitcher by any stretch of the imagination. All you need to do is look at his annually poor control (3.51 BB/9) and propensity to give up home runs (1.21 HR/9) to see that there is only barely SP 5 value here and even that can be debated. Since he will also be 34 by the time the 2019 season begins, Guerra is a major "avoid" guy for upcoming drafts.

Jimmy Nelson: Given the seriousness of the torn labrum and rotator cuff strain surgery in September of 2017, it was really no shock Milwaukee Brewers starter Jimmy Nelson failed to make it back to pitch last season. Nelson was slated to throw in the Arizona Fall League in order to get some work in before spring training but his return to the majors in 2019 is one big mystery in terms of what the stuff will look like. The real shame of it all is that Nelson was having a very nice 2017 before the surgery; recording a career-best 10.21 K/9 and 3.49 ERA. Unfortunately, there is no telling if Nelson will still possessing that kind of strikeout ability given the history of shoulder surgeries stealing fastball velocity. Given that concern and a few others as well, it is best to avoid this speculative stock until we see Nelson in action again.

Vince Velasquez: Once again the Philadelphia Phillies tried to force hard-throwing but seriously flawed pitcher Vince Velasquez into being a member of the starting rotation but the results were horrendous. First, there was the 4.85 ERA which was only mildly better than the 5.13 Velasquez posted the year prior. Then there was the ongoing brutal control as Velasquez' BB/9 rate of 3.62 was hideous. Add in a 1.34 WHIP and there was little to say that was positive from Velasquez last season as we once again are of the strong opinion he is a bullpen guy and actually could be a decent closer if ever given the chance. The reason we believe Velasquez is destined to eventually be a reliever is that he doesn't have a third pitch as a starter and that his fastball is actually quite good (average velocity of 94.6 and a K/9 of 9.88 last season). Until the Phillies finally make this sensible decision, Velasquez will be useless for fantasy baseball purposes.

Dan Straily: Long a solid and somewhat underrated SP 5 in yearly fantasy baseball mixed leagues, journeyman starter Dan Straily produced a typical season for him in 2018 that included a 4.12 ERA, 7.28 K/9, and a .233 BAA. Having turned only 30 this past December; Straily will likely have to play the one-year contract deal again with some MLB organization but he has enough skill to possibly hold down SP 5 value again in deeper leagues.

Alex Reyes: After missing all of the 2017 season amid very high sleeper appeal due to Tommy John elbow surgery, St. Louis Cardinals top pitching prospect Alex Reyes only managed 4 scoreless innings with the team last season before suffering a season-ending lat tear. Lauded for some crazy velocity and strikeout rates while coming up the minor league ladder, Reyes retains immense upside if he can just find some semblance of health. The Cards figure to try it again with the kid in spring training and monitoring his progress during that time is a must.

Tyson Ross: After undergoing the very serious thoracic outlet syndrome surgery back in 2016, there was little in the way of future expectations for veteran starter Tyson Ross due to the tendency of those coming back from the procedure having diminished stuff. After a brief but disastrous 49 inning stint with the Texas Rangers in 2017 adding validity to that concern, Ross fought back to have a nice season for the San Diego Padres a year ago. While Ross' 4.15 ERA and 1.30 WHIP were not overly positive, the fact he was able to come back and toss 149.2 innings for the team was a nice development. In addition, Ross re-discovered some lost K's from 2017 by going from a 6.61 K/9 that year to a better 7.34 mark last season. Still, Ross struggled again with control (3.73 BB/9) which has been a career-long negative and with the strikeout rate still well-below his pre-surgery standards, Ross is best left to the waiver wire.

Jeremy Hellickson: As boring a pitcher as there is in the fantasy baseball realm, journeyman starter Jeremy Hellickson was actually pretty decent last season as he logged a 3.45 ERA and 1.07 WHIP in 91.1 innings for the Washington Nationals. Those surface numbers were quite fluky though as Hellickson benefitted greatly from a lucky .252 BABIP that when adjusted resulted in FIP (4.22) and XFIP (4.27) ERA's which both went above 4.00. Then when you look at the brutal 6.41 K/9 Hellickson had last season, you can see there is really no reason to bother here in any fantasy baseball capacity this season.

Derek Holland: You got to give some credit to the determination of veteran starter Derek Holland who continues to get back up after some hellacious beatings in most of his MLB seasons and he was rewarded for that effort in 2018 by posting an underrated 3.57 ERA, 1.29 WHIP, and collecting 169 strikeouts in 171.1 IP. Now well past the part of his career where there was solid upside hype, Holland has settled into being an MLB journeyman who seems just as capable of producing a helpful line of numbers like a year ago or who can also get simply blown to smithereens such as the 4.95 and 6.20 ERA's from 2016-17. This doesn't make Holland very trustworthy when it comes to rounding out your fantasy baseball rotation and so given that as a backdrop, the lefty should probably be passed over again this spring.

Julio Urias: Lauded as one of the very best pitching prospects in all of baseball, Los Angeles Dodgers farmhand Julio Urias met a huge roadblock in his development when forced to undergo serious anterior capsule surgery on his shoulder in July of 2017. Given the very long rehab process, Urias only made it back to the Dodgers in late September where he tossed 4 scoreless innings in relief while striking out 7 batters. The crackling fastball that made Urias such a prominent prospect in the first place appeared to still be there and the movement on his pitches checked out as well. This was certainly an encouraging sign to take into the winter for Urias and those interested in his services for 2019 fantasy baseball but spring training will likely give us a better read on his immediate upside. Still just 22 and with an extremely bright future ahead of him, Urias looks like a major late-round sleeper who many others may not be paying much attention to just yet.

Adalberto Mejia: With the Minnesota Twins rotation being ravaged by injuries during the course of the 2018 season, it allowed the team to take another look at pitching prospect Adalberto Mejia who was not overly impressive in 2017 when the lefty registered a 4.50 ERA in 98 innings. A nice start at Triple-A (3.32 ERA, 8.81 K/9) made the Twins feel better about going back to the well with Mejia but not much was able to be gleaned about the kid due to the fact he only tossed 22.1 innings before going down for the season in early August with elbow nerve irritation. Just 25 when 2019 gets underway, Mejia is not an overly exciting prospect due to the fact he doesn't miss many bats and the control is shoddy. That means Mejia can safely be looked over in almost all leagues to begin the new season.

Framber Valdez: Given some injuries afflicting Lance McCullers and Charlie Morton during the second half of the 2018 season, the Houston Astros were forced to promote hard-throwing but wild pitching prospect Framber Valdez during the heat of a pennant race to help fill in some innings. While Valdez lived up to his pronounced control issues (5.45 BB/9), he was actually quite good in logging a 2.08 ERA and 8.57 K/9 in 34.2 innings. Despite the solid but small sample size line of work, Valdez is not likely going to have a spot in the Houston rotation to start the season if all the incumbents are healthy. Unless injuries in spring training open up a spot, he can be ignored during spring drafts.

Sean Reid-Foley: Even though his small 33.1 inning debut with the Toronto Blue Jays didn't go over well (5.13 ERA, 5.67 BB/9, 1.62 HR/9), righty pitching prospect Sean-Reid Foley should have the inside track to a rotation spot for 2019 on the strength of some major strikeout potential. With Reid-Foley hinting at such skill by punching out 42 batters in his 33.1 innings with the team last season, the radars of the fantasy baseball community are pinging a bit. As with most young hard-throwing pitchers, however, there will be struggles with control and poor pitch efficiency that will slow down the process towards optimum efficiency like we anticipate happening with Reid-Foley this season. Given the fact Reid-Foley will likely need 2019 to work out those kinks, he should really be just for the AL-only crowd.

Eric Lauer: Still in rebuild during the course of the 2018 season, the San Diego Padres took a look at a number of their pitching prospects to see who could make the grade as future rotation members. While he didn't have the instant success of fellow pitching farmhand Joey Lucchesi, lefty Eric Lauer perhaps did enough to make a claim on a rotation spot to begin the 2019 season. Despite a rough start in his rookie debut last season, Lauer got better as the year went on to end the season on a more positive note (first half/second half ERA 's of 4.87/3.15). As former 2015 first-round pick, Lauer has been an above-average strikeout guy during his minor league days but there are also current red flags such as high walk (3.70 BB/9) and home run (1.21 HR/9) rates that need to be remedied if we are even going to considering the kid for NL-only formats.

Jose Urena: Serving as a rare bright spot in the muck that was the Miami Marlins the last two seasons, righty starter Jose Urena showed that he can at least be a part of the eventual solution for the team's rebuild. While Urena's stuff is far from top-shelf, the guy makes the most of a limited arsenal as his 3.98 ERA last season almost mirrored another solid 3.82 mark the year prior. With that said, Urena is barely an SP 5 option in mixed fantasy baseball leagues due to the fact his K/9 rates (6.72 last season) are annually below-average and by a decent margin at that. Urena has also had some generous BABIP luck the last two seasons which have resulted in FIP and XFIP rates that have gone well over 4.00 (and even 5.00) in both campaigns. As a result, Urena should just be left to the NL-only crowd.

Alex Cobb: Despite the high rate of success for a pitcher maintaining their ability (and sometimes even improving) coming off Tommy John elbow surgery, there are some cases where the opposite takes place like what we have seen from Baltimore Orioles starter Alex Cobb. Prior to his own Tommy John procedure, Cobb was one of the best young pitchers in the major leagues while making his way with the Tampa Bay Rays as he recorded back-to-back years in 2013-14 with an ERA under 3.00 and a K/9 above 8.00. Then fate interrupted the fun as Cobb missed all of 2015 due to a torn UCL in his elbow and when he finally made his way back the following season, there was a noticeable difference both in the quality of stuff and the on-the-mound results. While Cobb's 3.66 ERA in 2017 with the Rays was still quite good, a major red flag revealed itself in the form of a drastically reduced K/9 rate that sank all the way down to a horrid 6.42. Knowing that having such an utter lack of swing-and-miss ability in the AL East would be deadly, the Rays showed no interest in bringing back Cobb when he reached free agency the following winter. Most other clubs had the same reservations as Cobb didn't sign with the Orioles until spring training was underway and we soon saw why through some truly putrid performances during the first half of the season (6.41 ERA, .310 BAA). Perhaps the lack of a full spring training hurt Cobb during that time as he pitched so much better in the second half (2.56, .229) but the bottom line 4.90 ERA was still beyond ghastly as there are only a handful of starters in a major league rotation today we would tell you to avoid more. Once again Cobb didn't strike anyone out last season (6.03 K/9) which continues to make him as bad a matchup with the AL East as you can get and with the Orioles likely remaining one of the worst teams in the majors for 2019, there won't be many chances for wins either. So unless you are in a league where the title is awarded to those who finish in last place, Cobb should be avoided everywhere during the draft.

Robbie Erlin: Now with five partial seasons of MLB experience pitching in the San Diego Padres rotation under his belt, it is easy to see that lefty starter Robby Erlin is the definition of mediocre. Never having posted an ERA under 4.00 in any of those seasons speaks to the limitations of Erlin and his annual mid-7.00 K/9 is nothing to write home about either. Only if you are in a very deep NL-only league would you even have a modicum of interest in the guy but even there you should try and do better.

Nick Kingham: Longtime Pittsburgh Pirates minor league righty Nick Kingham looked like he finally caught his big break when he proceeded to throw a one-hitter in 7 shutout innings while striking out 9 in his MLB debut when summoned to the team in late April. Alas, that represented the high point for Kingham who was nothing but hit hard from that point onward (composite 5.21 ERA, 1.38 WHIP) as he rode the shuttle back and forth from the majors to the minors. Already 27 and with a history of poor control and just a moderate K/9 rate (his first start notwithstanding), Kingham is sitting as just NL-only material even if he takes a rotation spot this spring.

Drew Smyly: Now a full two seasons since he last pitched in the major leagues due to Tommy John elbow surgery, power-armed starter Drew Smyly will try to get his career back on track after the Chicago Cubs traded him to the Texas Rangers last October. Given how long he has been out, it is tough to remember that Smyly was once a decent sleeper pitcher who had a knack for picking up a high number of K's. While that is all well and good, the fact Smyly has missed so much time means he is nothing but a dart throw late-round pick in deep leagues and more so for AL-only formats as moving into such a potent offensive park like in Texas certainly doesn't help the overall outlook either.

Anthony DeScalfani: After opening some eyes by pitching to a 3.28 ERA in 123.1 innings for the Cincinnati Reds back in 2016, it appeared the team had something intriguing with young starter Anthony DeScalfani. Unfortunately, DeScalfani was unable to build on that performance as he missed all of 2017 with injury and then came back for 115 frames last season (while also again missing lengthy time) where the righty posted an ugly 4.93 ERA. While his 93.7 average fastball velocity is quite good (leading to an 8.45 K/9 a year ago), DeScalfani was a home run machine last season (1.88 HR/9) which is a major negative operating in Great American Ballpark. Turning 29 in April, 2019 marks a crucial year for DeScalfani to get himself back on track but the overall mediocre results of late and ongoing injury concerns make him just a guy to monitor early on in the season.

Edwin Jackson: It seems like Edwin Jackson has a goal to work for every team in the major leagues as the Oakland A's represented the 13th MLB organization he has pitched for but either way, the guy still showed effective stuff to get major league hitters out as a June promotion resulted in a 3.33 ERA for a team that eventually clinched a wild card. With just a .219 BAA and a 1.22 WHIP going along with the impressive ERA, Jackson became a savior both for the A's and those who took a "what the heck" stab at him down the stretch of the fantasy baseball season. As good as Jackson's surface numbers were, the underlying metrics were not very pretty as shown by an ugly 6.65 K/9, 3.62 BB/9, and a beyond lucky .240 BABIP that when adjusted resulted in some horrid FIP (4.65) and XFIP (4.88) ERA's. This tells you that Jackson's run with the A's last season became a statistical fluke and that he was a barely employed pitcher prior to that run for a reason. As a result, there is no need to bother here unless Jackson pops up somewhere again as he almost surely will do for someone this season.

Michael Lorenzon: For the second time in three partial seasons with the Cincinnati Reds, hard-throwing starter Michael Lorenzon put forth an ERA under 3.15 for the team. Last season that number came out to 3.11 in 81 frames for the Reds, mostly pitching out of the bullpen but also picking up 3 starts. Lorenzon has been told he will compete for a rotation spot in spring training and his average 95.7 fastball velocity will make him one to monitor at least in deep mixed league and for the NL-only crowd.

Danny Salazar: The perennial pitching tease that is Cleveland Indians hard-throwing righty Danny Salazar added another sorry chapter to his still-young career in 2018 as he failed to throw a single pitch that counted in missing the entire season due to unending shoulder trouble that ended up requiring surgery. Once a vaunted power pitching prospect who possessed immense strikeout ability, Salazar may not even be able to serve as a starter anymore given how his body can't seem to hold up to the rigors of being in a rotation. Check back in on Salazar during spring training in deeper leagues but otherwise, it is time to move on from here.

Tyler Anderson: The 2018 Colorado Rockies qualified for the postseason not on the strength of their hitting but on a surprisingly good rotation highlighted by German Marquez and Kyle Freeland. Unfortunately, former 2011 first-round pick Tyler Anderson didn't get in on the fun as his 4.55 ERA and 1.27 WHIP in 176 innings showed. Even though Anderson had a decent K/9 (8.39), both his control (3.02 BB/9) and especially his home run rate (1.53 HR/9) were brutal. The latter is obviously a major red flag given the fact Anderson calls Coors Field home and that combined with the ugly ratios make him a clear pitcher to avoid.

Steven Wright: Injuries, off-the-field trouble, and a brutal 8.25 ERA to begin the 2017 season sent Boston Red Sox knuckleballer Steven Wright to the fringes of the fantasy baseball world. With memories of his big 2016 campaign (3.33 ERA) already becoming an afterthought, Wright successfully fought his way back to the Red Sox last summer to pick up some innings both in the rotation and bullpen. Wright did quite well during that time as he recorded a 2.68 ERA in 53.2 innings and that could put himself back in play to secure a spot in the rotation to begin the 2019 season. Given the always fickle nature of knuckleballers and the lack of a lengthy track record of decent production, Wright should be avoided in almost all drafts this spring.

Dylan Bundy: Other than an initial flurry during the first two months of the 2017 season when it seemed like fading Baltimore Orioles pitching prospect Dylan Bundy was finally going to realize his once vast potential, it has been nothing but massive beatings since. In fact, it is almost comical how bad Bundy has pitched the last two seasons as a whole in logging ERA's of 4.24 and 5.45 and currently being stuck on a truly hideous Orioles team makes 2019 looks just as hopeless. Despite still only turning 26 this past November, there is very little we can state that is positive about Bundy other than maybe his very good 9.65 K/9 rate last season. Giving up home runs like he is a batting practice pitcher (2.15 HR/9) is certainly as big a red flag as you can get operating in the AL East and since there will also be little in the way of wins to come by this season, Bundy is a total toss-out this fantasy baseball season.

Trevor Richards: While it was far from pretty, the Miami Marlins will give righty pitching prospect Trevor Richards another look for 2019 as he comes off a season that was highlighted by striking out 130 batters in 126.1 IP (9.26 K/9). Of course, Richards' 4.42 ERA and 1.39 WHIP were quite ugly and the control was certainly nothing to write home about either (3.85 BB/9). Since we all love strikeouts in the fantasy baseball community, Richards will likely remain on the early season monitor list but anything more than that would be a reach.

Matt Harvey: The Dark Knight lives no more. That simple six-word phrase would actually qualify as a firm understatement when you take a closer look at how free agent pitcher Matt Harvey has become one of the worst starters in the game the last three seasons. With ERA's of 4.86, 6.70, and 4.94 during that span, it was abundantly clear that the thoracic outlet syndrome Harvey underwent prior to that horror show run has completely ruined his once ace-level stuff for good. You can see this effect primarily through Harvey's listless fastball which was consistently hitting 98 prior to the surgery but now struggles to maintain reaching 94. That has been a disaster for Harvey in the sense his fly ball tendencies are currently resulting in a boatload of additional home runs given up which have gone a long way towards blowing up the ratios. Add in a K/9 that was once a very impressive 10.62 back in 2012 dipping all the way down to just 7.61 last season and it is as clear as day that Harvey may not even be an SP 5 anymore. While it may be crazy to say, Harvey looks finished at the age of 30.

Marco Estrada: The end appears to be near for aging veteran starter Marco Estrada after logging unsightly ERA's of 4.98 and 5.64 the last two seasons; while a chronic back problem and other health ailments helped diminish his diminished stuff even further. Truth be told, we haven't suggested a play on Estrada ever since he departed the Milwaukee Brewers and now at the age of 35 and with a K/9 that sank to just 6.45 last season, that trend certainly won't change now.

Felix Hernandez: As tremendous a starter as Seattle Mariners former Cy Young winner Felix Hernandez was during the first ten years of a career that seemed on track for possible inclusion to the Hall of Fame, the last two seasons have been as unsightly as it gets as the numbers have completely gone into the toilet among a slew of health problems. Clearly, all the years of very heavy usage starting at a young age have sapped Hernandez of his pitching strength and this is shown in vivid terms through ERA's of 4.36 and 5.55 the last two seasons. Once a 240-K monster, Hernandez was down to just a 7.23 K/9 in 2018 and if not for having one more year left on his contract, would already be close to out of the majors. Ignore completely the name brand when it comes to 2019 fantasy baseball drafts and instead salute what a tremendous career Hernandez has had.

Ryan Borucki: As the Toronto Blue Jays waved the white flag early on in the 2018 season, a sizable number of the team's prospect began to make their way to the majors to show whether or not they should be considered a part of the team's future. This included lefty starter Ryan Borucki who acquitted himself quite well in pitching to a 3.87 ERA and picking up 4 wins in 97.2 innings last season. Despite the tidy debut, Borucki is not a name you want to store away for future use in fantasy baseball given the extreme lack of strikeouts/velocity here. Logging just a 6.17 K/9 with the Blue Jays bears this concern out and that number followed another ugly 6.78 mark at Triple-A prior to his promotion. Borucki's control is also not great (3.04 BB/9) which when combined with the lack of K's and having to operate in the AL East makes the kid radioactive for fantasy baseball purposes.

Jake Faria: The Tampa Bay Rays hit on only one of their 2 intriguing young starters last season; seeing Blake Snell turn into one of the best pitchers in the game and Jake Faria go down in flames. At no point during his 65 innings with the Rays last season was Faria ever helpful and no one could blame the team for giving him some additional minor league seasoning after witnessing the ghastly 5.40 ERA. Keep in mind though that Faria was pretty impressive in 2017 when he pitched to a 3.43 debut ERA and so the talent is there under the surface. Unfortunately, you can't chase potential when the pitcher operates in the AL East cauldron.

Matt Shoemaker: It has now been two full seasons since veteran starter Matt Shoemaker even showed a modicum of fantasy baseball appeal as he has come in with ERA's of 4.52 and 4.94 during that span. Whether the brutal comebacker that fractured Shoemaker's skull at the end of the 2016 season is to blame for the drastic fade of his last two campaigns is the cause of the horrible numbers is certainly up for debate but either way, the aging hurler should be avoided in drafts.

Daniel Megden: With ERA's of 3.14 and 4.05 the last two partial seasons with the Oakland A's, 26-year-old righty Daniel Megden has helped some of the AL-only clan in a pinch. Unfortunately, Megden has pretty much zero mixed league value given his unsightly K/9 rates (5.60 in 115.2 innings in 2018) and with home runs also a potential landmine, no actionable move is needed with the guy.

Drew Pomeranz: Anyone with a semblance of fantasy baseball wisdom could have told you that Drew Pomeranz was headed for extended trouble entering into 2018 as he was entering into his first full season operating in the AL East with the Boston Red Sox. Few could imagine just how ugly things would get though as Pomeranz somehow pitched to a 6.20 ERA in 74 innings before missing a major portion of the season with shoulder trouble. Despite showcasing some very intriguing strikeout potential in the past, Pomeranz needs to get himself back to the NL before we even consider looking in his direction again.

Antonio Senzatela: We shockingly reached a point during the 2018 fantasy baseball season where not one but TWO Colorado Rockies starters (Kyle Freeland and German Marquez) became front-of-the-rotation assets even with the ongoing challenges of Coors Field. Despite turning just 24 this past January, don't count on righty Antonio Senzatela joining that group moving forward given his soft-tossing approach that resulted in a terrible 6.87 K/9 and a shaky 4.38 ERA. With a nearly neutral .302 BABIP indicating Senzatela's ERA was pretty much where it should be, don't count on any sort of breakthrough in 2019 that will make him anything more than an SP 4/5 guy in NL-only leagues.

Jeff Samardzija: What a mess the San Francisco Giants have on their hands now with aging starter Jeff Samardzija as the fading righty was only able to log 44.2 nasty innings (6.25 ERA) before going down for the season with shoulder trouble. At one time serving as one of the more underrated starters in the game, Samardzija's move to a spacious ballpark in San Francisco has not stopped the decline train from picking up speed. With an average fastball velocity that continues to decrease and a home run rate that is beyond terrible now, Samardzija needs to be avoided everywhere this season.

Daniel Norris: While Detroit Tigers starter Daniel Norris picked up the biggest victory he possibly could a few years ago when he beat back cancer, his actual pitching numbers the last two seasons are tough to look at as the ERA's have come in at 5.31 and 5.68. Injuries have taken a huge chunk out of those campaigns for Norris but perhaps we can find some hope in the 10.35 K/9 rate he put up last season in 44.1 innings. Everything else, unfortunately, was a giant mess as both Norris' walks (3.86 BB/9) and home runs given up (1.62 HR/9) were absolutely terrible. Even though Norris will be just 26 this April, there is no way you can even think about making a play here to at least begin the 2019 season.

Jakob Junis: A big spring training performance followed by a nice start in March/April all of a sudden put Kansas City Royals starter Jakob Junis on the fantasy baseball radar but the righty quickly proved he could not keep up the good work. It was toward the end of April where we noted Junis was pitching way over his head in terms of receiving generous BABIP luck and when that number eventually began to move back toward the mean, things could get ugly considering there was a lack of strikeout ability here to offset that eventual development. Well, Junis went right along with that prediction as he pitched to ERA's over 7.00 both in June and July and was lucky to make it out of a start in New York alive after he accidentally broke the wrist of Yankees outfielder Aaron Judge with an errant pitch. Even though Junis came back to post very solid numbers the last two months of the season, his composite 4.42 ERA and 1.28 WHIP were nothing but mediocre as he should not be in play for anything but AL-only formats this spring.

Jerad Eickhoff: If you didn't know any better, you would think Philadelphia Phillies starter Jerad Eickhoff was out of baseball considering he tossed just 5.1 innings with the team in 2018 after never-ending shoulder trouble kept him glued to the DL throughout. Once a very promising prospect who recorded a 3.65 ERA in 197.1 innings for the Phils back in 2016, Eickhoff was hit very hard the following season (4.71) which then proceeded the washout a year ago. Having turned just 28 last summer, Eickhoff is still young enough to make a name for himself again in the fantasy baseball world but first he has to grab hold of a rotation spot this spring. Until that happens, there is no reason to even speculate here.

Joe Ross: Tommy John surgery came calling for Washington Nationals pitching prospect Joe Ross in 2017 and that giant bit of misfortune put the brakes on the 2011 first-rounders steady progress with the team that included early eye-opening ERA's of 3.64 and 3.43 from 2015-16. Having fought back to throw 16 September innings for the Nats at the end of last season (5.06 ERA), Ross will be in the mix for a rotation spot in spring training. Despite the very small sample size, Ross was consistently hitting 94 with his fastball in those 16 innings and that at least shows he has not lost that part of his arsenal due to the surgery. That being said, Ross is just a spring monitor candidate who should not be drafted given the rest of the post-surgery unknowns.

Jordan Zimmerman: After a 2017 campaign that was as ugly as it can get (6.08 ERA, .265 BAA), there was nowhere to go but down for fading Detroit Tigers starter Jordan Zimmerman. While his 4.52 ERA last season was a sizable improvement, it still was a nasty number that cemented Zimmerman's status as a guy who looks to be completely shot.

Andrew Cashner: Even typing a blurb on Baltimore Orioles pitcher Andrew Cashner elicits nothing but a yawn as the veteran was simply non-competitive last season in putting up a 5.29 ERA, 1.58 WHIP, and a ridiculous .289 BAA. By now it was obvious Cashner's 3.40 ERA the year prior was as big a fluke as you can get and currently stuck on a brutal team and having literally zero ability to collect strikeouts (5.82 K/9), the righty should not be owned anywhere for even a spot start this season.

Wade Miley: A revelation in his 80.2 innings for the Milwaukee Brewers during the second half of 2018, journeyman starter Wade Miley saved his preciously fledgling career by posting a 2.57 ERA and 1.21 WHIP before becoming a trusted arm in the postseason. A free agent as of this writing, Miley is still the guy who recorded ERA's of 5.37 and 5.61 the two seasons prior and so he should not be treated as anything but a streaming arm if needed.

Zach Davies: When the best thing you can say about a pitcher is he looks like a teenager, you know you got some major statistical problems on your hands. Such was the case for Milwaukee Brewers starter Zach Davies in 2018 as the 25-year-old's middling fastball got tattooed to an ugly 4.77 ERA and that made his laughable 6.68 K/9 rate stand out even more. Even if you are in an NL-only league, Davies is one of the worst starting pitchers out there.

Adam Wainwright: In case you didn't already realize that veteran St. Louis Cardinals pitcher Adam Wainwright is completely washed up, just take a gander at the ERA's of 5.11 and 4.66 the last two seasons to go with missing extremely long stretches of both campaigns with injuries. Heading into free agency at the age of 37 and with seemingly nothing left in the pitching tank, Wainwright is a complete non-story in fantasy baseball no matter where he signs this winter.

Nick Tropeano: The once-promising career of Los Angeles Angels starter Nick Tropeano has descended into what can only be described as injury hell due to the fact the righty's 2016 Tommy John surgery (which wiped out his entire 2017) was followed by serious shoulder trouble last season that could lead to procedure being done on the joint by the time you read this. Already Tropeano's early success with the Angels (ERA's of 3.82 and 3.56 in 2015/16 respectively) have been almost completely forgotten and if he is forced to undergo shoulder surgery, you can forget about seeing the guy again until sometime during the summer. Considering that Tropeano already had some pronounced control and home run problems before the injury hailstorm, there is really no reason to think about drafting the guy even in AL-only formats.

Wei-Yin Chen: Already starting to realize how much of a mistake it was to give starter Wei-Yin Chen a five-year deal worth $80 million prior to 2016, the Miami Marlins swallowed hard in giving the 33-year-old lefty 133.1 innings last season which predictably did not go so well. Looking nothing like the somewhat underrated hurler he was as recently as 2015 while with the Baltimore Orioles, Chen was hit hard to the tune of a 4.79 ERA, 1.34 WHIP, and he would give up a staggering 19 home runs. With an average fastball velocity of just 91.5, Chen is not fooling anyone these days as shown in the ridiculous 1.28 HR/9. Chen is also not helping offset the latter as walks plagued him a year ago as well (3.17 BB/9) which was a new struggle compared to solid earlier work in that category. The bottom line here is that Chen looks completely shot which obviously means he should deservedly be passed over in all drafts.

Ian Kennedy: If it wasn't for the two more years left on the ridiculous free agent contract the Kansas City Royals signed flawed starter Ian Kennedy to prior to the 2016 season, it is likely the righty would be barely hanging on in the majors. This is understandable since Kennedy has come in with unsightly ERA's of 5.38 and 4.66 the last two seasons and still gives up home runs like he is serving batting practice. Even Kennedy's past as a solid strikeout guy has gone by the wayside (7.90 K/9) which pretty much makes him useless at this stage of the game.

Cody Reed: After bombing in trial looks with the Cincinnati Reds both in 2016 (7.36) and 2017 (5.09); the team last season tried once again to see if they could unlock the potential from lefty starter Cody Reed who was once a 2013 second-round pick. While there were some ups and downs along the way, Reed overall was decent as shown by his 3.98 ERA and 8.79 K/9 in 43 innings. That performance should be enough to give Reed the inside track on a rotation spot for the team to begin the 2019 season but this also doesn't mean he is worth your time in a fantasy baseball sense. For one thing, Reed's control was not great (3.14 BB/9) and free passes have been an issue even when operating in the minors. In addition, an average 92.8 fastball velocity is not great by any means and could lead to trouble for Reed operating in a homer haven like Great American Ballpark. Overall, Reed looks like an NL-only play at most and even in that type of league he is a borderline option.

Heath Fillmeyer: The 2018 debut of Kansas City Royals righty pitching prospect Heath Fillmeyer was not overly impressive as the former 2014 fifth-round pick of the Oakland A's posted a 4.26 ERA and a terrible 6.23 K/9 in 82.1 innings. It is clear going back to his minor league days that Fillmeyer will be severely below average in terms of strikeouts which right away is a major disqualifying tendency for fantasy baseball purposes. Add in additional struggles with control and Fillmeyer should not be looked at one bit when it comes to 2019 fantasy baseball drafts even if the Royals do give him a rotation spot in spring training.

Chris Stratton: Seemingly on a never-ending shuttle back-and-forth between the minors and major leagues, San Francisco Giants starter Chris Stratton put down firmer roots with the team in 2018 when he tossed a career-high 143 innings. Unfortunately, those innings were not overly impressive as the incredibly inconsistent Stratton registered a terrible 4.85 ERA, 1.40 WHIP, and 6.99 K/9. Given how poorly he pitched, the older-than-you-think Stratton (having turned 28 last August) is no lock to begin 2019 in the Giants' rotation and he certainly shouldn't be owned in 99 percent of fantasy baseball leagues either.

Lucas Giolito: Boy does Chicago White Sox failed pitching prospect Lucas Giolito stink. It is becoming obvious now why the Washington Nationals were willing to unload the former 2012 first-round pick as he was right there as one of the worst starters in the game for long stretches of last season. With a stomach-churning 6.13 ERA, 1.48 WHIP, and 6.49 K/9, Giolito is as bad a place as any to look for potential fantasy baseball pitching this spring. You literally can't do worse.

Jason Vargas: Honestly if you are reading this blurb on New York Mets aging veteran starter Jason Vargas, you must be in the deepest NL-only league there is. After all, there would be no other use for Vargas who was in the running as the worst pitcher in baseball for large stretches of the 2018 season. Despite having a decent finish, Vargas still finished with a pathetic 5.77 ERA, 1.41 WHIP, and 1.76 HR/9 despite calling spacious Citi Field home. Stating the obvious, you can do better with almost any other starter this season.

Shohei Ohtani: At least on the pitching side of things, Los Angeles Angels 2018 rookie sensation Shohei Ohtani will "miss" the entire 2019 season due to undergoing Tommy John elbow surgery last September. Ohtani becomes the latest Tommy John statistic in terms of hard-throwing pitchers coming from Japan (Daisuke Matsuzaka, Yu Darvish, and Masahiro Tanaka eventually will need the procedure) but boy was he electric prior to the UCL being torn. Despite only pitching once since last June, Ohtani's overpowering stuff was as advertised as he struck out 63 batters in 51.2 innings and recorded an ERA of 3.31 and a WHIP of 1.16. With a fastball that pushed up to 100-mph and off-speed stuff that moved in ways even science couldn't explain, Ohtani was the real deal on the pitching side just as he was when swinging a bat. Unfortunately, we will only be getting the hitting version of Ohtani this season and so he can safely be crossed of off all of your pitching cheat sheets.

Dinelson Lamet: Add hard-throwing San Diego Padres pitching prospect Dinelson Lamet to the ever-growing list of Tommy John victims as the 26-year-old didn't even make it out of spring training before going under the knife. While Lamet carried some very intriguing strikeout potential prior to the surgery, he is unlikely to make it back before August of 2019 and maybe not even at all. That makes him more of a story for 2020 than anything we can work with now.

Michael Kopech: The unending Tommy John trend among the young and hard-throwing pitching fraternity saw no end in 2018; with top Chicago White Sox prospect Michael Kopech falling prey to the surgery in early September after the 6-3 righty made just four starts with the big-league club during his initial foray into the majors. Drawing comparisons to the New York Mets' Noah Syndergaard on the strength of his massive strikeout ability (12.11 K/9 at Triple-A last season prior to his White Sox promotion), all of that potential goes on hold until 2020 as Kopech won't be ready to even throw a baseball until very late next summer. What a shame.

Garrett Richards: Having originally been diagnosed with a partially torn UCL in his pitching elbow back in 2016, it was only a matter of time before Los Angeles Angels hard-throwing starter Garrett Richards succumbed to Tommy John surgery. While Richards was able to pitch pretty well since the tear was discovered (2.28 ERA in 27.2 IP in 2017, 3.66 in 76.1 a year ago), the elbow flared up again last summer which led to the decision for Tommy John. Since Richards didn't wind up going under the knife until late in the 2018 season, his chances for returning in 2019. As a result, there is no actionable move to make here in terms of 2019 drafts this spring.

Taijuan Walker: After swinging a buy-low trade with the Seattle Mariners to acquire fading pitching prospect Taijuan Walker prior to 2017, the Arizona Diamondbacks had to be very encouraged that they had something here as the hard-throwing righty pitched to a 3.49 ERA for the team in 28 starts. Alas, Walker became another Tommy John statistic as he lasted just 13.0 innings in 2018 before tearing the UCL in his elbow and missing the rest of the year. While the hype has quieted here after all of the early accolades Walker picked up when rising through the Seattle system, he is unlikely to play anything but a bit role in 2019 fantasy baseball due to the fact he won't return until late summer. Revisit only when there are indications Walker is, in fact, ready to make such a return and thus, ignore him in drafts.

Johnny Cueto: After bombing out to a 4.52 ERA in 2017 that served as one of the more "bust-worthy" campaigns that season in fantasy baseball, it certainly appeared as though San Francisco Giants veteran starter Johnny Cueto was embarking on a major redemption tour as he roared out of the gates this past spring with a 0.84 ERA in March/April. Alas, things only went down from there as Cueto suffered an ankle injury that required a DL stint in late April which was then followed by soreness in his elbow in early May that sent him to the shelf once again. While Cueto did make it back for a horrific 21 July innings when he was battered to the tune of a 6.86 ERA, a torn UCL was quickly discovered that ultimately led to season-ending Tommy John surgery. As a result of the procedure, Cueto may very well miss the entire 2019 season and even if he were to make it back in September, it would likely be for just a few cameo outings. Despite what has been a very solid career, Cueto's days as even an SP 3 might be finished.

Jordan Montgomery: Having opened up a bunch of eyes in the fantasy baseball community by coming in as an unheralded rookie to win 9 games and record a solid 3.88 ERA as a rookie in the New York Yankees rotation in 2017, the encore was nothing but devastation for Jordan Montgomery as he was forced to undergo season-ending Tommy John surgery after throwing just 27.1 innings last season. The fact that Montgomery had the procedure in early June makes it unlikely he will be able to come back any earlier than mid-August next season and so that makes Montgomery a non-entity for 2019 fantasy baseball.

Jharel Cotton: While he was barely under fantasy baseball consideration even in AL-only leagues entering into 2018 spring training, Oakland A's righty Jharel Cotton never was able to throw a pitch that counted in the regular season as a result of a torn UCL in his elbow leading to Tommy John surgery. Despite there being a chance Cotton makes it back to the majors sometime late this summer, his 5.58 ERA in 24 starts in 2017 show he is not someone worth going near with regards to possible fantasy baseball usage.

Lance McCullers: Houston Astros power starting pitcher Lance McCullers didn't even make through November at the start of this past winter due to undergoing Tommy John surgery and so he will not throw a single pitch that counts this season.

CLOSERS

Draft Strategy: You can't live with closers but you also can't live without them when it comes to constructing a fantasy baseball roster. No single position in the game causes more stress than those who operate in the ninth inning and that is due to the extreme volatility which results in never-ending status changes throughout the entire season. Often by the end of the year, up to half or more of the closers who began the season in the gig have surrendered it to someone else and this is why we strongly suggest using only mid-to-late round picks for addressing saves.

DRAFT STRATEGY: Right along the same lines as catchers, the closer fraternity in yearly fantasy baseball leagues are so extremely volatile that using an early round pick among those who make up this group is a very bad idea. Given that half or more of the opening day closers each season typically cede their closing gigs at some point during the year and that their impact really only influences one category in standard ROTO categories (saves), your best bet is to address this spot by looking for upside guys in the middle-to-late rounds.

Baltimore Orioles (Mychal Givens): With the Baltimore Orioles having traded All-Star closer Zach Britton to the New York Yankees at the July 31 deadline last summer, it left the ninth inning duties to be handled by hard-throwing but wild Mychal Givens. While Givens does possess the strikeout-heavy (9.27 K/9) ability which is a must to pitch in the ninth inning, there are not many closers who can tote around a gross 3.52 BB/9 and remain successful. Since the Orioles are looking at another ugly season ahead, Givens is unlikely to receive many save chances either. Given the brutal control and lack of any sort of closing track record, we don't feel confident Givens will be a viable long-term closing option this season.

New York Yankees (Aroldis Chapman): It was sort of a mixed-bag season for New York Yankees All-Star closer Aroldis Chapman in 2018; what with the Cuban fireballer dominating on the mound as usual but also having to deal with injuries for the second year in a row. In terms of the numbers, Chapman overpowered hitters as he set a career-best strikeout rate with a ridiculous 16.31 K/9 that had even Edwin Diaz jealous. Add in a 2.45 ERA, 1.05 WHIP, and insane .136 BAA and Chapman was arguably as good as ever which is saying something considering the tremendous seasons he has previously put forth. The problem here though is the injuries and last season it was Chapman missing a month with knee tendinitis. When you add in the fact Chapman also missed extended time in 2017 with arm trouble he blamed on Chicago Cubs manager Joe Maddon overusing him in the playoff the previous year, we can see a bit of a trend here. It really should not be a surprise though due to the fact throwing as hard as Chapman does can take a major toll on a body physically and he is no youngster anymore as he turns 31 in February. So while the performances on the mound remain supreme and keep Chapman in his rightful spot as arguably the best closer in baseball, the always sky-high draft price is looking more riskier than ever given the injury issue.

Boston Red Sox (OPEN): As of this writing, the Boston Red Sox had yet to re-sign free agent closer Craig Kimbrel and while the veteran had another very good 2018 campaign (2.74 ERA, 0.99 WHIP, and 13.86 K/9), the team likely has some reservations about continuing the relationship after seeing the righty struggle throughout the postseason. Already having put forth some truly monstrous closing seasons going back to his early years with the Atlanta Braves, Kimbrel's advanced metrics are almost all heading in the wrong direction which is concerning. For one thing, Kimbrel's control was brutal for the second time in three years (4.48 BB/9) and he gave up home runs at a career-worst 1.01 HR/9 rate. In addition, Kimbrel has had quite a few injury scares over the last few seasons which make him a health risk for someone who annually carries a high draft cost. So whether Kimbrel goes back to Boston or ends up in another locale, he still has the overpowering fastball to put forth very good closing numbers for at least one more season but the risk is something not to be overlooked. Now if Kimbrel were to depart, the Red Sox can turn to hard-throwing Matt Barnes (3.65 ERA, 14.01 K/9) who would instantly become a potential breakout closer. Also while he was pretty miserable in 2018, Tyler Thornburg has a history of posting closer-like numbers and could succeed if given the opportunity.

Tampa Bay Rays (Jose Alvarado): Since the Tampa Bay Rays are not expected to re-sign veteran reliever/closer Sergio Romo, the ninth inning gig will likely fall to the very intriguing Jose Alvarado who has the stuff to be up to the task of finishing games. Just 23-years-old, Alvarado had a nuclear 11.25 K/9 rate last season (80 strikeouts in 64 innings) and his extreme groundball rate resulted in just one home run given up. On the flip side, Alvarado's 4.08 BB/9 was horrendous and closers who walk a bunch of batters are always a threat to lose their job at any point. Ultimately though we think Alvarado will be able to cut into the walk rate a bit as he further develops his pitches and the overpowering arsenal brings a high level of upside. Finally, with the Rays historically playing a decent number of close games every season, the saves should be plentiful which makes Alvarado one of the better closer values for 2019.

Toronto Blue Jays (Ken Giles): Yeah this could get ugly. With the Toronto Blue Jays unloading troubled closer Roberto Osuna to the Houston Astros last summer, the arrival of hard-throwing but severely flawed reliever Ken Giles as the return package puts him in place to open the 2019 season as the team's stopper. By now it is common knowledge that Giles is about as hair-raising a closer as there is in all of baseball due to a penchant for giving up home runs and also having a well-earned reputation for lacking the mental strength to finish games. Posting a 4.65 ERA and an elevated for a closer .265 BAA put Giles in play as one of the worst closers in all of baseball last season and it doesn't engender much optimism for his chances to succeed in 2019. Perhaps some optimism can be found in Giles recording a very good 2.30 ERA just the year prior but that was a lot of blown saves ago. So while there should be plenty of strikeouts, there also will likely be just as many ulcers when owning Giles this season.

Kansas City Royals (Wily Peralta): When the Kansas City Royals handed the team's closer role over to longtime failed starting pitcher Wily Peralta midway through the 2018 season, no one with any sort of fantasy baseball clue believed it would be an arrangement which would last very long. While we won't go so far as to say Peralta was just the latest pitcher who couldn't make it in a major league rotation but who then excelled when placed in the bullpen, the whole experiment went pretty well as he went a perfect 14-for-14 in locking down saves and registered an overall ERA of 3.67. In addition, Peralta's mid-90's fastball played so much better as a reliever (career-best 96.9 average velocity) and that led to him posting another personal high in K/9 with a 9.17 mark. Now for the bad news. A lucky .279 BABIP helped Peralta's ERA go below where it probably should have been and when adjusted, came out to very shaky 4.73 FIP and 4.66 XFIP. Even more disturbing was Peralta's ghastly 6.03 BB/9 which was such a bad number that it was almost impossible to believe. Then when you add in an elevated 1.05 HR/9 that is not very closer-friendly, it becomes clear Peralta is likely on borrowed time if he begins the 2019 season finishing games for the Royals as anticipated. Save yourself the headaches and don't even bother.

Chicago White Sox (Nate Jones): Since the Chicago White Sox are still in the midst of a rebuild, there will not be a bunch of saves coming for prospective 2018 closer Nate Jones. Having missed virtually all of 2017 with injury, Jones continued to deal with rampant health trouble last season in compiling just 30 innings where he pitched reasonably well (3.00 ERA, 5 saves, 9.60 K/9). Unfortunately, Jones also put forth some major red flags primarily centered on hideous control (4.50 BB/9) and a propensity for giving up home runs (1.20 HR/9). While certainly a bit on the small sample size, Jones has to do a whole lot better if he wants to keep hold of the closer role for the duration of 2019. On that front, the White Sox do have an intriguing potential option in strikeout machine (79 K's in 51.1 innings) Jace Fry whose 1.11 WHIP was so much better than Jones' ugly 1.43. By the time you read this Jones could even have been traded by the White Sox which means Fry could easily be the guy to begin the season. Overall though, the White Sox are not presenting very trustworthy closer candidates for 2019 fantasy baseball and this whole situation looks to be one you should try to avoid.

Detroit Tigers (Shane Greene): The unspoken but obvious plan the Detroit Tigers had in 2018 with regards to keeping the very mediocre Shane Greene in the closer role for the duration of the season in order to try and draw trade interest leading up to the July 31 deadline completely fell apart given the fact the guy was completely abysmal in registering a 5.12 ERA, 1.37 WHIP, and yielding home runs at a ridiculous 1.71 HR/9 pace. As a result of that putrid performance, the Tigers had no choice but to hold onto Greene and now unbelievably they are likely going to begin 2019 with him in the closer role yet again. The problem is that the rest of the Tigers' pen pitched just as badly last season; with perhaps hard-throwing but inconsistent Joe Jimenez (4.31 ERA, 1.20 WHIP) having the best chance of unseating Greene. Last year in these pages we had Greene down in print as one of the worst closers in all of baseball who should be avoided like the plague and the same statement certainly applies once again this season.

Cleveland Indians (Brad Hand): After watching previously excellent incumbent closer Cody Allen struggle for large portions of the first half of the 2018 season, the Cleveland Indians perhaps made a very prudent long-term move when they acquired hard-throwing stopper Brad Hand from the San Diego Padres at the July 31 deadline. While the two essentially shared save chances the final two months of the season, it was Hand who had the much better overall performance as he recorded a 2.75 ERA, 1.11 WHIP, and struck out an insane 106 batters in 72 innings (13.25 K/9). Remember it was this publication that made a rare exception to our rule of not drafting closers early last spring in saying it was all right to spend a bit extra on Hand given the massive strikeout ability and overall top-notch numbers and he more than came through. As far as Allen is concerned, the previously top-tier closer (5 straight seasons with an ERA under 3.00 from 2013-17), was a shell of his former All-Star self in almost every way a year ago. A composite 4.70 ERA and 1.36 WHIP were almost hard to believe it was coming from Allen as he fought his control like never before (4.43 BB/9) and he is also now down 2.5 mph on his fastball velocity since 2014 which has caused the K rate to decline as well. With Allen having not been given a qualifying offer from the Indians early this past offseason, he will have to find saves somewhere else.

Minnesota Twins (Trevor Hildenberger/Taylor Rogers): With the Minnesota Twins quickly realizing early on in the 2018 season they were not going to able to reprise their shocking wild card-winning campaign from the year prior, the process of unloading veterans began in earnest as closer Fernando Rodney was ushered out the door to the Oakland A's. Despite being older than dirt, Rodney pitched shockingly well yet again as he logged a 3.09 ERA and locked down 25 saves in 31 chances before the trade. Meanwhile, the Twins don't have many appealing ninth-inning candidates to begin 2019 if last season's numbers have anything to do with it. Closer favorite Trevor Hildenberger was downright brutal (5.42 ERA, 1.38 WHIP, 8.63 K/9) last season and was even worse when given save duties once Rodney was traded away. Another possible option could be veteran setup man Addison Reed who has plenty of experience closing games but he too struggled with a nasty 4.50 ERA, 1.43 WHIP, and drastically reduced 7.07 K/9. One name to keep an eye on may be lefty Taylor Rogers who actually pitched very well in registering 2.63 ERA, 0.95 WHIP, and closer-like 9.88 K/9. On numbers alone, Rogers would be the pick but he has to overcome the discrimination of managers refusing to go with lefties in the ninth.

Los Angeles Angels (OPEN): Barring the team signing someone in free agency, it looks to be a wide-open competition for the Los Angeles Angels closing gig to begin the 2019 season. There was certainly a ton of volatility in the ninth inning throughout the year as multiple relievers took their turn trying to earn saves (Blake Parker, Hansel Robles, Jim Johnson, and Ty Buttrey) with varying degrees of success. In trying to break this group down, we can probably eliminate Johnson since he is a free agent unlikely to return and Robles was cast off by the New York Mets off all teams midway through 2018 due to his extreme knack for blowing up games through surrendered home runs. That leaves Parker and Buttrey who both put forth good but not great ERA's (3.26, 3.31 respectively) and each hurler has the ability to miss bats as well. We like Parker's chances better given his more pronounced MLB experience and for the fact, he possesses good control (2.14 BB/9) to go with the ability to pick up strikeouts but either guy would be one of the lower-tier stoppers.

Seattle Mariners (Edwin Diaz): Meet the top closer in the game folks. While there were some growing pains that the Seattle Mariners' Edwin Diaz had to fight through in 2017, the nuclear-armed dynamo was nothing short of spectacular last season in registering a 1.96 ERA, 0.79 WHIP, and locking down an insane 57 saves. The strikeout ability was simply absurd as

Diaz punched out 124 batters in 73.1 innings which was good for an eye-popping 15.22 K/9 which is a level that is rarely seen. With Diaz successfully cutting down on his walks (4.36 BB/9 in 2017, just 2.09 a year ago) and also possessing a tremendous 0.61 HR/9 rate, opposing hitters have almost no chance against the righty. While we never suggest paying top dollar for a closer no matter how good they are, Diaz clearly is the guy who should be off the board first among this group if you do choose to go that route.

Oakland A's (Blake Treinen): Perhaps the Washington Nationals threw in the towel too early on Blake Treinen when they quickly ripped the closer role from his grasp at the start of the 2017 season due to some early struggles and then shipped him off to the Oakland A's during the summer for a package highlighted by Sean Doolittle. While Doolittle has been solid for the Nats since the deal, Treinen has been insanely good which was fully shown in a Cy Young-caliber 2018 performance that was off the charts. Logging one of the best seasons ever for a reliever, Treinen's 0.78 ERA was the fifth-best since 1900 for a pitcher who logged at least 40 frames. Add in a 0.83 WHIP, a .157 BAA, and 100 K's in 80.1 IP (11.20 K/9) and Treinen was in the discussion with Edwin Diaz as the best closer in baseball. While there really is nowhere to go but down statistically for Treinen off such a dominant year, he is locked in as a top-tier closer for spring drafts.

Texas Rangers (Jose LeClerc): When we refer to our strong preference for not paying a high draft price for closers, the flip side to this strategy centers on looking for upside ninth inning pitchers who have the ability to take their performance to another level going forward. These potential value plays should have at the very least a high strikeout rate to further improve the odds of profitability and that brings us to the Texas Rangers' Jose LeClerc who is one of our favorite upside closers for 2019 fantasy baseball. Having opened up plenty of eyes while nailing down 12 saves with a dominant 1.56 ERA and 13.27 K/9, LeClerc still remains a bit off the fantasy baseball radar given the fact he didn't move into the ninth inning until late in the season when many were already onto their football drafts. While LeClerc doesn't always know where the overpowering fastball is going (3.90 BB/9), his ability to miss bats is near Edwin Diaz level which alone makes the guy very intriguing. Despite the yearly volatility of almost every reliever, on ability alone, LeClerc has a chance for some staying power.

Houston Astros (Roberto Osuna): Obviously the biggest talking point when it came to Houston Astros closer Roberto Osuna last season was the deserved 75-game suspension handed down from MLB due to a reported domestic violence incident. Given the tremendous amount of bad publicity

Osuna generated, the Toronto Blue Jays quickly shipped him off to the Houston Astros during the summer in showing a zero tolerance for such an offense. With all that said, Osuna managed another very good year when on the mound as he registered a 2.37 ERA and 0.90 WHIP; while also locking down 21 saves in 22 chances. What was interesting here is that Osuna's K/9 dropped dramatically from the year prior (11.67 in 2017, just 7.58 a year ago) but the average fastball velocity of 95.7 remained in his customary range which quiets any sort of alarm there. Since the Astros remain one of the best teams in baseball, there should be plentiful save opportunities once again for Osuna in 2019 and whether you like or hate him, the skill level places the guy into the top 10 in terms of closer rankings.

New York Mets (OPEN): One of the more unsettled ninth inning situations as of this writing is centered in New York with the Mets as a truly brutal 2018 campaign gave the team the impetus to trade away former All-Star closer Jeurys Familia to the Oakland A's last summer. Taking over in Familia's place was failed starter Robert Gsellman whose overall 4.28 ERA and below-average for a closer 7.88 K/9 show he is not set up to succeed long-term in the gig. It is unlikely the Mets will go to spring training with Gsellman in the closer role given the remaining high expectations with this rotation-dominant team and so a free agency move is likely here.

Philadelphia Phillies (Seranthony Dominguez): While manager Gabe Kapler made it a point to not say publicly who his locked-in closer was throughout the 2018 season, it was obvious rifle-armed youngster Seranthony Dominguez is the most deserving of the title going forward. Despite some control problems that almost all young power arms deal with (3.41 BB/9), Dominguez' extreme 98.4 average fastball was tailor-made for finishing games. Given such eye-opening velocity, it was no shock Dominguez punched out 74 batters in just 58 innings and it is that nuclear pitch which makes him a very good upside closer for 2019 fantasy baseball. This kid is going places.

Washington Nationals (Sean Doolittle): If it weren't for the annual injury woes, Washington Nationals closer Sean Doolittle would be considered on par with almost any other closer in baseball regarding skill-level alone. Few relievers are better in terms of strikeout rate (12.00 K/9 in 2018) and what really puts Doolittle on a separate tier from almost any other stopper is the fact he also has tip-top control (1.20 BB/9) and keeps the ball in the park (0.60 HR/9). Unfortunately, Doolittle has not pitched more than 51 innings in each of the last four seasons and that major injury risk is a big negative in terms of his prospective value for 2019.

Miami Marlins (Drew Steckenrider): The Miami Marlins wasted little time moving on from talented but vastly inconsistent closer Kyle Barraclough once the 2018 season was in the books; dumping him on the Washington Nationals before the World Series even got underway. Given how bad Barraclough bombed his closer audition, it was no surprise the Marlins didn't see a future for him in the ninth inning going forward. As a result of the trade, Drew Steckenrider figures to have the inside track to begin 2019 as the team's closer but he too struggled finishing games towards the end of last season once Barraclough was yanked from the role. While Steckenrider is capable of missing bats (10.30 K/9), he also struggled with control (3.76 BB/9) which is not what any manager really wants to see from their stopper. Also considering the Marlins will likely be one of the worst teams in the majors yet again this season, don't count on Steckenrider or whoever else is closing games to receive many save chances.

Atlanta Braves (Arodys Vizcaino): If you were to just look at the 2018 numbers for Atlanta Braves closer Arodys Vizcaino, you had to be impressed by the excellent 2.11 ERA, 1.17 WHIP, and .213 BAA. Unfortunately, those digits don't tell the whole story here as Vizcaino missed almost the entire second half of the year with persistent shoulder trouble which places a big red flag next to his name for 2019 fantasy baseball drafts. What is also noteworthy here was the very good performance of A.J. Minter who performed well as the closer when Vizcaino was out. So while Vizcaino will head to spring training with the inside track to begin the seasons as the Braves' closer, a case can be made that Minter should be the guy as well. This is one situation you want to keep a close watch on during the spring exhibition slate.

Cincinnati Reds (Raisel Iglesias): Consider it a major upset that the rebuilding Cincinnati Reds didn't find a trade partner for underrated closer Raisel Iglesias last summer as the postseason push began for those teams who were in contention. It was certainly a surprise no one came calling for a guy who recorded a 2.38 ERA, 1.07 WHIP, and minuscule .197 BAA while locking down 30 saves for the Reds last season but the righty could be on the move this time around as his current team is still 1-2 years away from contention at the very least. While we can worry about the trade possibilities at a later date, Iglesias is primed to be a top ten closer once again as long as he is picking up saves this season.

St. Louis Cardinals (Jordan Hicks): It seems like the St. Louis Cardinals are on a never-ending quest to find some semblance of stability in the ninth inning and 2018 was no different as they saw Trevor Rosenthal go down with a torn UCL in his elbow prior to the start of the year and then went through a slew of other options during the season such as Bud Norris, Jordan Hicks, and even starter Carlos Martinez. While Martinez did a tremendous job in the role during the second half of the year, the Cardinals plan to put the hard-throwing veteran back into the rotation for the start of 2019. This leaves Hicks as the best option at present time to serve as the team's closer and with a ridiculous average fastball velocity of 10.1.7 last season, the 22-year-old righty has the overpowering arsenal to get the job done. Of course, Hicks is far from a finished product which is no surprise given how young he is and the biggest potential roadblock to success is a nasty 5.21 BB/9 which could make the ninth inning appearances quite dicey for the kid. It also needs to be noted that for as hard as Hicks throws, he doesn't generate a high number of strikeouts as his K/9 last season was just a mediocre 8.11. This tells you Hicks' fastball is coming in straight and not generating a high number of swings and misses like we used to see from Kyle Farnsworth back in the day or more recently out of starter Nathan Eovaldi. So as you can see, Hicks should not be overvalued this spring based on the velocity and he is far from guaranteed to succeed which means based on some advanced metrics which means some caution should be taken when weighing an investment.

Pittsburgh Pirates (Felipe Vazquez): Anyone who witnessed how badly Pittsburgh Pirates closer Felipe Vazquez pitched during the first half of 2018 had to be absolutely shocked that the lefty managed to last the entire year in the role. This becomes even more of a surprise when you take into consideration Vazquez coming down with a scary bout of forearm pain during the height of the struggles. Credit goes to Vazquez for sticking it out though and he would ultimately rally to finish with a very good 2.70 ERA, 1.24 WHIP, and 11.44 K/9. Of course, Vazquez' performance was a sharp decline from his otherworldly 2017 campaign (1.67 ERA, 0.89 WHIP, 10.51 K/9) but the fact the guy ended on such a high note was a nice way to go into the 2019 drafting season. When digging into the numbers in terms of why Vazquez had so many issues early on, focusing on what was a very unlucky .331 BABIP and a bit of a rise in walk rate (3.09 BB/9) had a lot to do with it. That all seems to be in the rearview mirror though and so Vazquez is back to being in the top 12 or so closers for 2019 fantasy baseball. Just be cognizant of the fact the very capable Keone Kela remains in setup as a strong threat if Vazquez were to find extended struggles again this season.

Milwaukee Brewers (Jeremy Jeffress, Corey Knebel): The 2018 Milwaukee Brewers certainly had the market cornered when it came to high-end bullpen arms as they stormed to the NL Championship Series behind a very potent bullpen led by co-closers Jeremy Jeffress and Corey Knebel;

plus the overpowering Josh Hader who arguably was the most dominant reliever in all of baseball last season. The question now is which of the three will be handed the ninth inning to begin the 2019 season as all three are capable of being top options if given the chance. In trying to break this trio down, we eliminate Hader from contention due to manager Craig Counsell rightfully falling in love with the idea of deploying him as a multiple-inning dominator in setup. So that leaves Knebel and Jeffress who both have the high-strikeout ability to more than get the job done. What is interesting here is that Knebel had the gig all to his own to begin 2018 but then some severe struggles during the summer got him demoted back to the minor leagues. This opened the door for Jeffress to inherit the ninth as he was previously dominating in setup alongside Hader. While Jeffress finished the regular season strong in locking down saves, he then immediately began to struggle badly in the postseason which opened the door for Knebel to move back into the ninth inning. Got all that? So as you can see, there is uncertainty here about which way Counsell will lean and since the guy already is an outside the box thinker, it would not shock us in the least if he goes with a committee to finish games at least to begin the season. If we did have to make a pick, Knebel would be the choice given that he signed a sizable contract prior to 2018 to serve as the team's closer and also for the fact he finished last season strong which should allay some fears about the mid-year struggles.

Chicago Cubs (Brandon Morrow): When the Chicago Cubs and free agent reliever Brandon Morrow came to an agreement last winter with the idea of him serving as the team's closer for the 2018 season, those in the fantasy baseball community all had the same collective reaction in terms of anticipating overpowering pitching but also a constant battle with injuries. Having become the latest failed starter who transitioned into a tremendous power reliever, Morrow also carried a well-earned reputation for being one of the most injury-prone pitchers in all of baseball which became reinforced yet again last season. When it came to the on-the-mound results, few were better than Morrow when it came to the closer fraternity as he didn't give up a single earned run in April and was virtually unhittable for large stretches of the first half as he held a composite ERA of just 1.47, a WHIP of 1.08, and struck out 31 batters in 30.2 IP. Unfortunately, Morrow's 22nd save on July 17th would prove to be the final time he would appear in a game last season as a bout of what was first identified as biceps soreness sent him to the DL. While the Cubs and Morrow spoke optimistically about an eventual return, it was later discovered that there was a deep bone bruise on his pitching elbow and eventually a series of setbacks while attempting to rehab the injury led the team to the veteran down for good in the middle of September. Signed through 2019 (with an option for 2020), Morrow is set to open up the new season once again as the Cubs' closer but the same theme holds true in terms of him being a guy you simply can't ever depend on staying healthy. In fact, any investment in Morrow comes with the internal hope that his almost guaranteed DL stints will be of the shorter variety (like what those who also invest in Washington Nationals starter Stephen Strasburg deal with on a yearly basis) but the fact he turned 34 last July likely means this is a pipe dream. Again while the numbers should be dominant on the rare occasions Morrow is healthy, owning the guy is a roller coaster ride that is guaranteed to make you sick.

Arizona Diamondbacks (OPEN): It may have taken five-and-a-half months but the Arizona Diamondbacks finally realized what we already knew in terms of Brad Boxberger not being a very good closer. Registering a 4.39 ERA and 1.43 WHIP, Boxberger was one of the worst closers in the game and he certainly was not deserving of the long leash the D-Backs gave him. By the end of the season, the team had opened up a committee that also included Japanese import Yoshihisha Hirano and youngster Archie Bradley which throws this setup into chaos as we move towards spring training. In terms of Hirano and Bradley, both guys pitched much better than Boxberger (respective ERA's of 2.44/3.64) and so we have to figure the two of them will battle it out in the exhibition season for the right to be the closer to begin the year. This one could go either way so get ready to adjust your cheat sheets based on how the spring tea leaves are reading.

Colorado Rockies (Wade Davis): With the Colorado Rockies aiming to put together a high-level bullpen in order to shorten games to address annual rotation problems due to the Coors Field effect, bringing in closer Wade Davis on a three-year deal worth $52 million seemed to be their big get in order to put this plan in place. While Davis was deservedly considered one of the best relievers in all of baseball in annually posting some truly minuscule ratios, some troubling advanced metrics began popping up such as leaking velocity, a rising walk rate, and some health scares along the way. All seemed well during the first half of 2018 however as Davis was picking up saves almost on a daily basis and he would log ERA's of 2.38 and 2.31 the first two months. Then the proverbial wheels began to come off as Davis embarked on a fourth-month skid that had fantasy baseball save vultures circling overhead with requests that Adam Ottavino take over. While Davis held onto the gig and finished a franchise-record 43 saves, the 4.13 ERA showed that it was far from a smooth sailing to get there. Digging into the advanced metric world, what quickly jumps out was Davis' K/9 going from 12.12 in 2017 all the way down to 10.74 a year ago. This was quite the drop and it sort of makes sense when you consider Davis' average fastball velocity of 94.4 was his worst since 2013 (his last season as a starter). Clearly there is some erosion going on here which is not a major news item anyway since we already noted Davis has had some health trouble in recent years. With the control remaining abysmal (3.58 BB/9) and home runs going out at a very scary rate (1.10 HR/9) considering the ballpark, Davis is looking as shaky as ever in terms of his fantasy baseball standing. Be very careful how you proceed with the veteran this spring.

San Francisco Giants (Will Smith): While we have Will Smith down as our predictive closer for the San Francisco Giants to begin the 2018 season, there are also a few other options who could easily be tabbed for the assignment as well. Given the massive amount of injuries which impacted the Giants' pen last season, Smith was joined by the team's previous stopper Mark Melancon and top setup man Hunter Strickland in earning saves at some point. It was Smith who was the most successful however and the fact he finished the year in the ninth inning is a feather in his cap going into spring training. With regards to the numbers, Smith was fantastic as he logged a 2.55 ERA, 0.98 WHIP, and a tremendous 12.06 K/9. Smith's performance was not totally unexpected as he was once looked at as a closer candidate during some very good seasons previously with the Milwaukee Brewers but some serious injuries derailed that path. Since the numbers clearly work in the ninth inning, Smith only may have to deal with the notion of his left-handedness being more valuable in a setup capacity. If Smith does, in fact, move back to working in setup, then you have to believe Melancon will get another look since he was originally signed prior to 2017 to serve as the team's closer. Unfortunately, the aging Melancon has dealt with quite a few injuries over the last two seasons and those health woes have taken somewhat of a bite out his stuff (declining velocity and K/9 rates). Melancon still managed a solid 3.23 ERA but the 1.59 WHIP and 7.15 K/9 were major red flags. So as of this writing, Smith and Melancon should be ranked in that order in terms of prospective save chances; with the former having some very intriguing upside.

San Diego Padres (Kirby Yates): After the San Diego Padres dealt All-Star Brad Hand to the Cleveland Indians during the summer, the closing baton on the team was passed to top setup man Kirby Yates who was already in the midst of his best MLB season. Despite the added pressure of closing games, Yates was terrific as he finished the year with a 2.14 ERA, 0.92 WHIP, and a 12.86 K/9. A late bloomer who didn't find much MLB traction until 2017, Yates now appears to be a very good closing value to begin the 2019 season. We always suggest looking for high-K guys who are a bit off the radar when panning for upside in the closing world and Yates certainly fits the mold on that front. With that said, the lack of a track record closing games does add some risk when it comes to investing in Yates but the numbers do suggest he stands just as good a chance of being a success.

Los Angeles Dodgers (Kenley Jansen): It was a season to forget for Los Angeles Dodgers closer Kenley Jansen in 2018 as a shockingly brutal start to the year (5.59 ERA in March/April) transitioned into another stint on the DL during the summer due to heart trouble that has plagued him for years. Starting with the numbers, Jansen's composite 3.01 ERA and 0.99 WHIP were both career-highs and even more disturbing was the massive decline in strikeout rate (K/9 of 14.36 in 2017, just 10.30 last season) which was brought on by a fastball velocity which dropped for the third season in a row. Also directly related to the loss of fastball potency was Jansen's HR/9 rate soaring to 1.63 which is a truly horrendous mark. Things don't get much better on the health front either as Jansen is scheduled for a second heart procedure over the winter which further adds to the risk here. So while Jansen remains firmly in his prime at the age of 31, all of a sudden he looks like someone who should be avoided since there are so many potential issues in play.